READ
AMEI

Current Directions in ABNORMAL PSYCHOLOGY

EDITED BY
Thomas F. Oltmanns and Robert E. Emery

PEARSON
Prentice Hall

Upper Saddle River, New Jersey 07458

PEARSON
Prentice
Hall

Upper Saddle River, New Jersey 07458

10 9 8 7 6 5 4

ISBN 0-13-189579-6

Printed in the United States of America

Contents

General and Theoretical Issues

Etiology, Treatment, and Classification

Articles from *Current Directions in Psychological Science* are perfect original source supplements for Abnormal Psychology—accessible, current, and theoretically rich overviews written by leading experts in the field. The supplementary readings are especially useful for the first section of the course, which deals with broad conceptual issues including etiology, treatment, and psychological assessment. These topics are basic to abnormal psychology—and are revisited within the context of specific disorders throughout the course, but at first encounter students can find the topics to be difficult, abstract, and perhaps even seemingly irrelevant to the topic at hand, abnormal behavior. The readings we have selected from *Current Directions* go a long way toward engaging students in the relevance of the course material by exploring "hot topics" in more depth while complementing the broader message of conceptual material covered in the text.

In *Psychology and Neuroscience: Making Peace*, Gregory Miller and Jennifer Keller thoughtfully address one of the basic misunderstandings in psychology: reductionism and the lingering dualism in thinking about mind (psychology) and body (biology). They strongly reinforce the message that psychological experiences cannot be reduced to biological, for example by critiquing the common misconception that depression is now known to be nothing more than a "chemical imbalance" in the brain (p. 214). These scholars argue for viewing biology and psychology not as competing explanations but in terms of systems theory, that is, as explanations offered at different levels of analysis. Their thoughtful consideration of various misunderstandings of neuroscience as somehow being more "basic" than psychology will help students to grasp the problems with a reductionist view of abnormal behavior, an inaccurate position that unfortunately often is embraced by the popular media.

In the next article, Frans de Waal, a noted primate researcher who has published a number of superb, popular books on primate behavior, discusses one of the hottest of hot topics: evolutionary psychology. Skeptics should note that his article, *Evolutionary Psychology: The Wheat and the Chaff*, is more of a critique of simplistic evolutionary explanations than a polemic about the value of the evolutionary approach. The value of an evolutionary perspective is a given to de Waal, as is a systems conceptualization, but his article challenges students with incisive questions about specific areas where weak evolutionary explanations have been offered, for example, the purported adaptive value of rape.

Eric Turkheimer is another friendly critic of biological theorizing. Like de Waal, in *Three Laws of Behavior Genetics and What They Mean*, Turkheimer assumes that major genetic influences on normal and abnormal behavior are a given. In fact, his first law of behavior genetics is that all human behavioral traits are heritable. In Turkheimer's view, the question for the genetic side of the gene-environment debate is no longer whether genes affect behavior but how—and he suggests that current behavior genetic explanations offer little guidance about how genes affect complex social behavior. In addition, this article raises the very important issue of shared and nonshared environmental influences on normal and abnormal behavior, and the difficulty in specifying causes if the environment affects different people in unique ways.

The much-debated issue of whether behavior is situation specific or consistent across time and situations is discussed by one of the leading theorists in the field, Walter Mischel and his colleagues Yuichi Shoda and Rodolfo Mendoza-Denton. In their article, *Situation-Behavior Profiles as a Locus of Consistency in Personality*, these authors take students through a brief and very clear history of the debate. They argue that the debate has been misguided in various respects and present new data suggesting that consistency in behavior may be found in how some individuals respond to similar situations.

The final two articles in this first section deal with treatment, a topic that usually is more accessible to students and of considerable interest to them. Avraham Kluger and Angelo DeNisi review the positive—and negative—effects of feedback interventions, treatments where information is provided on performance in order to enhance it. In their article, *Feedback Interventions: Toward the Understanding of a Double-Edged Sword*, these authors note that feedback is almost as likely to produce negative as positive results. They explain this pattern in terms of the (mis)allocation of attention, and suggest clear goal setting is the solution to producing consistently positive gains. Finally, C. Barr Taylor and Kristine Luce provide a highly accessible overview of various attempts to use the computer as an assessment and treatment tool. Students surely will be fascinated by the innovations these authors highlight in *Computer- and Internet-Based Psychotherapy Interventions*, and students hopefully both will be cautioned and challenged by the scientists' call for more research on the effectiveness of these technologically-based treatments.

Psychology and Neuroscience: Making Peace

Gregory A. Miller[1] and Jennifer Keller

Department of Psychology, University of Illinois at Urbana-Champaign, Champaign, Illinois

Abstract

There has been no historically stable consensus about the relationship between psychological and biological concepts and data. A naively reductionist view of this relationship is prevalent in psychology, medicine, and basic and clinical neuroscience. This view undermines the ability of psychology and related sciences to achieve their individual and combined potential. A nondualistic, nonreductionist, noninteractive perspective is recommended, with psychological and biological concepts both having central, distinct roles.

Keywords

psychology; biology; neuroscience; psychopathology

With the Decade of the Brain just ended, it is useful to consider the impact that it has had on psychological research and what should come next. Impressive progress occurred on many fronts, including methodologies used to understand the brain events associated with psychological functions. However, much controversy remains about where biological phenomena fit into psychological science and vice versa. This controversy is especially pronounced in research on psychopathology, a field in which ambitious claims on behalf of narrowly conceived psychological or biological factors often arise, but this fundamental issue applies to the full range of psychological research. Unfortunately, the Decade of the Brain has fostered a naively reductionist view that sets biology and psychology at odds and often casts psychological events as unimportant epiphenomena. We and other researchers have been developing a proposal that rejects this view and provides a different perspective on the relationship between biology and psychology.

A FAILURE OF REDUCTIONISM

A term defined in one domain is characterized as *reduced* to terms in another domain (called the reduction science) when all meaning in the former is captured in the latter. The reduced term thus becomes unnecessary. If, for example, the meaning of the (traditionally psychological) term "fear" is entirely representable in language about a brain region called the amygdala, one does not need the (psychological) term "fear," or one can redefine "fear" to refer merely to a particular biological phenomenon.

Impressive progress in the characterization of neural circuits typically active in (psychologically defined) fear does not justify dismissing the concept or altering the meaning of the term. The phenomena that "fear" typically refers to include a functional state (a way of being or being prepared to act), a cognitive processing bias, and a variety of judgments and associations all of which are conceived psychologically (Miller & Kozak, 1993). Because "fear" means more than a given type of neural activity, the concept of fear is not reducible to neural activity. Researchers are learning a great deal about the biology of fear—and the psychology of fear—from studies of the amygdala (e.g., Lang, Davis, & Öhman, in press), but this does not mean that fear *is* activity in the amygdala. That is simply not the meaning of the term. "Fear" is not reducible to biology.

This logical fact is widely misunderstood as evidenced in phrases such as "underlying brain dysfunction" or "neurochemical basis of psychopathology." Most remarkably, major portions of the federal research establishment have recently adopted a distinctly nonmental notion of mental health, referring to "the biobehavioral factors which may underly [sic] mood states" (National Institute of Mental Health, 1999). Similarly, a plan to reorganize grant review committees reflects "the context of the biological question that is being investigated" (National Institutes of Health, 1999, p. 2). Mental health researchers motivated by psychological or sociological questions apparently should take their applications elsewhere.

More subtly problematic than such naive reductionism are terms, such as "biobehavioral marker" or "neurocognitive measure," that appear to cross the boundary between psychological and biological domains. It is not at all apparent what meaning the "bio" or "neuro" prefix adds in these terms, as typically the data referred to are behavioral. Under the political pressures of the Decade of the Brain, psychologists were tempted to repackage their phenomena to sound biological, but the relationship of psychology and biology cannot be addressed by confusing them.

WHOSE WORK IS MORE FUNDAMENTAL?

Such phrases often appear in contexts that assume that biological phenomena are somehow more fundamental than psychological phenomena. Statements that psychological events are nothing more than brain events are clearly logical errors (see the extensive analysis by Marr, 1982). More cautious statements, such as that psychological events "reflect" or "arise from" brain events, are at best incomplete in what they convey about the relationship between psychology and biology. It is not a property of biological data that they "underlie" psychological data. A given theory may explicitly propose such a relationship, but it must be treated as a proposal, not as a fact about the data. Biological data provide valuable information that may not be obtainable with self-report or overt behavioral measures, but biological information is not inherently more fundamental, more accurate, more representative, or even more objective.

The converse problem also arises—psychology allegedly "underlying" or being more fundamental than biology. There is a long tradition of ignoring biological phenomena in clinical psychology. As Zuckerman (1999) noted, "One thing that both behavioral and post-Freudian psychoanalytic theories had in common was the conviction that learning and life experiences alone could account for all disorders" (p. 413). In those traditions, it is psychology that "underlies" biology, not the converse. Biology is seen as merely the implementation of psychology, and psychology is where the intellectually interesting action is. Cognitive theory can thus evolve without the discipline of biological plausibility. As suggested at the midpoint of the Decade of the Brain (Miller, 1995), such a view would justify a Decade of Cognition.

Such a one-sided emphasis would once again be misguided. Anderson and Scott (1999) expressed concern that "the majority of research in the health sciences occurs within a single level of analysis, closely tied to specific disciplines" (p. 5), with most psychologists studying phenomena only in terms of behavior. We advocate not that every study employ both psychological and biological methods, but that researchers not ignore or dismiss relevant literatures, particularly in the conceptualization of their research.

Psychological and biological approaches offer distinct types of data of potentially equal relevance for understanding psychological phenomena. For example, we use magnetoencephalography (MEG) recordings of the magnetic fields generated by neural activity to identify multiple areas of brain tissue that are generating what is typically measured electrically at the scalp (via electroencephalography, or EEG) as the response of the brain associated with cognitive tasks (Cañive, Edgar, Miller, & Weisend, 1999). One of the most firmly established biological findings in schizophrenia is a smaller than normal brain response called the P300 component (Ford, 1999), and there is considerable consensus on the functional significance of P300 in the psychological domain. There is, however, no consensus on what neural generators produce the electrical activity or on what distinct functions those generators serve. Neural sources are often difficult to identify with confidence from EEG alone, whereas for biophysical reasons MEG (which shows brain function) coupled with structural magnetic resonance data (which show brain anatomy) promises localization as good as any other available noninvasive method. If researchers understand the distinct functional significance of various neural generators of P300, and if only some generators are compromised in schizophrenia, this will be informative about the nature of cognitive deficits in schizophrenia. Conversely, what researchers know about cognitive deficits will be informative about the function of the different generators.

MEG and EEG do not "underlie" and are not the "basis" of (the psychological phenomena that define) the functions or mental operations invoked in tasks associated with the P300 response. Neural generators implement functions, but functions do not have locations (Fodor, 1968). For example, a working memory deficit in schizophrenia could not be located in a specific brain region. The psychological and the neuromagnetic are not simply different "levels" of analysis, except in a very loose (and unhelpful) metaphorical sense. Neither underlies the other, neither is more fundamental, and neither explains away the other. There are simply two domains of data, and each can help to explicate the other because of the relationships theories propose.

Psychophysiological research provides many other examples in which the notion of "underlying" is unhelpful. Rather than attributing mood changes to activity in specific brain regions, why not attribute changes in brain activity to changes in mood? In light of EEG (Deldin, Keller, Gergen, & Miller, 2000) or behavioral (Keller et al., 2000) data on regional brain activity in depression, are people depressed because of low activity in left frontal areas of the brain, or do they have low activity in these areas because they are depressed? Under the present view, such a question, trying to establish causal relations between psychology and biology, is misguided. These are not empirical issues but logical and theoretical issues. They turn on the kind of relationship that psychological and biological concepts are proposed to have.

CLINICAL IMPLICATIONS

In psychopathology, one of the most unfortunate consequences of the naive competition between psychology and biology is the assumption that dysfunctions conceptualized biologically require biological interventions and that those conceptualized psychologically require psychological interventions. The best way to alter one system may be a direct intervention in another system. Even, for example, if the chemistry of catecholamines (chemicals used for communication to nerve, muscle, and other cells) were the best place to intervene in schizophrenia, it does not follow that a direct biological intervention in that system would be optimal. A variety of experiences that people construe as psychosocial prompt their adrenal glands to flood them with catecholamines. There are psychological interventions associated with this chemistry that can work more effectively or with fewer side effects than medications aimed directly at the chemistry.

Unfortunately, the assumption that disorders construed biologically warrant exclusively biological interventions influences not only theories of psychopathology but also available treatments. For example, major depression is increasingly viewed as a "chemical imbalance." If such (psychological) disorders are assumed to "be" biological, then medical insurers are more likely to fund only biological treatments. Yet Thase et al. (1997) found that medication and psychotherapy were equally effective in treating moderately depressed patients and that the combination of these treatments was more effective than either alone in treating more severely depressed patients. Hollon (1995) discussed how negative life events may alter biological factors that increase risk for depression. Meany (1998) explained how the psychological environment can affect gene activity. The indefensible conceptualization of depression solely as a biological disorder prompts inappropriately narrow (biological) interventions. Thus, treatment as well as theory is hampered by naive reductionism.

WHAT TO DO?

"Underlying" (implying one is more fundamental than the other) is not a satisfactory way to characterize the relationship between biological and psychological concepts. We recommend characterizing the biological as "implementing" the psychology—that is, we see cognition and emotion as implemented in neural systems. Fodor (1968) distinguished between *contingent* and *necessary* identity in the relationship between psychological and biological phenomena. A person in any given psychological state is momentarily in some biological state as well: There is a *contingent* identity between the psychological and the biological at that moment. The psychological phenomenon implemented in a given neural circuit is not the same as, is not accounted for by, and is not reducible to that circuit.

There is an indefinite set of potential neural implementations of a given psychological phenomenon. Conversely, a given neural circuit might implement different psychological functions at different times or in different individuals. Thus, there is no *necessary* identity between psychological states and brain states. Distinct psychological and biological theories are needed to explain their respective domains, and additional theoretical work is needed to relate them.

Nor is it viable (though it is common) to say that psychological and biological phenomena "interact." Such a claim begs the question of how they interact and even what it means to interact. The concept of the experience of "red" does not "interact" with the concept of photon-driven chemical changes in the retina and their neural sequelae. One may propose that those neural sequelae implement the perceptual experience of "red," but "red" *means* not the neural sequelae, but something psychological—a perception.

Biology and psychology often are set up as competitors for public mind-share, research funding, and scientific legitimacy. We are not arguing for a psychological explanation of cognition and emotion *instead of* a biological explanation. Rather, we are arguing against framing biology and psychology in a way that forces a choice between those kinds of explanations. The hyperbiological bias ascendant at the end of the 20th century was no wiser and no more fruitful than the hyperpsychological bias of the behaviorist movement earlier in the 20th century. Scientists can avoid turf battles by approaching the relationship between the psychological and the biological as fundamentally theoretical, not empirical. Working out the biology will not make psychology obsolete, any more than behaviorism rendered biology obsolete. Scientists can avoid dualism by avoiding interactionism (having two distinct domains in a position to interact implies separate realities, hence dualism). Psychological and biological domains can be viewed as logically distinct but not physically distinct, and hence neither dualistic nor interacting. Psychological and biological concepts are not merely different terms for the same phenomena (and thus not reducible in either direction), and psychological and biological explanations are not explanations of the same things. If one views brain tissue as implementing psychological functions, the expertise of cognitive science is needed to characterize those functions, and the expertise of neuroscience is needed to study their implementation. Each of those disciplines will benefit greatly from the other, but neither encompasses, reduces, or underlies the other.

Fundamentally psychological concepts require fundamentally psychological explanations. Stories about biological phenomena can richly inform, but not supplant, those explanations. Yet when psychological events unfold, they are implemented in biology, and those implementations are extremely important to study as well. For example, rather than merely pursuing, in quite separate literatures, anomalies in either expressed emotion or biochemistry, research on schizophrenia should investigate biological mechanisms involved in expressed-emotion phenomena. Similarly, the largely separate literatures on biological and psychosocial mechanisms in emotion should give way to conceptual and methodological collaboration. Research in the next few decades will need not only the improving spatial resolution of newer brain-imaging technologies and the high temporal resolution of established brain-imaging technologies, but also the advancing cognitive resolution of the best psychological science.

Recommended Reading

Anderson, N.B., & Scott, P.A. (1999). (See References)

Cacioppo, J.T., & Berntson, G.G. (1992). Social psychological contributions to the Decade of the Brain. *American Psychologist,* 47, 1019–1028.

Kosslyn, S.M., & Koenig, O. (1992). *Wet mind: The new cognitive neuroscience.* New York: Free Press.

Miller, G.A. (1996). Presidential address: How we think about cognition, emotion, and biology in psychopathology. *Psychophysiology,* 33, 615–628.

Ross, C.A., & Pam, A. (1995). *Pseudoscience in biological psychiatry: Blaming the body.* New York: Wiley.

Acknowledgments—The authors' work has been supported in part by National Institute of Mental Health Grants R0I MH39628, F31 MH11758, and T32 MH19554; by the Department of Psychiatry of Provena Covenant Medical Center; and by the Research Board, the Beckman Institute, and the Departments of Psychology and Psychiatry of the University of Illinois at Urbana-Champaign. The authors appreciate the comments of Howard Berenbaum, Patricia Deldin, Wendy Heller, Karen Rudolph, Judith Ford, Michael Kozak, Sumie Okazaki, and Robert Simons on an earlier draft.

Note

1. Address correspondence to Gregory A. Miller, Departments of Psychology and Psychiatry, University of Illinois, 603 E. Daniel St., Champaign, IL 61820; e-mail: gamiller@uiuc.edu.

References

Anderson, N.B., & Scott, P.A. (1999). Making the case for psychophysiology during the era of molecular biology. *Psychophysiology,* 36, 1–14.

Cañive, J.M., Edgar, J.C., Miller, G.A., & Weisend, M.P. (1999, April). *MEG recordings of M300 in controls and schizophrenics.* Paper presented at the biennial meeting of the International Congress on Schizophrenia Research, Santa Fe, NM.

Deldin, P.J., Keller, J., Gergen, J.A., & Miller, G.A. (2000). Right-posterior N200 anomaly in depression. *Journal of Abnormal Psychology, 109,* 116–121.

Fodor, J.A. (1968). *Psychological explanation.* New York: Random House.

Ford, J.M. (1999). Schizophrenia: The broken P300 and beyond. *Psychophysiology,* 36, 667–682.

Hollon, S.D. (1995). Depression and the behavioral high-risk paradigm. In G.A. Miller (Ed.), *The behavioral high-risk paradigm in psychopathology* (pp. 289–302). New York: Springer-Verlag.

Keller, J., Nitschke, J.B., Bhargava, T., Deldin, P.J., Gergen, J.A., Miller, G.A., & Heller, W. (2000). Neuropsychological differentiation of depression and anxiety. *Journal of Abnormal Psychology, 109,* 3–10.

Lang, P.J., Davis, M., & Öhman, A. (in press). Fear and anxiety: Animal models and human cognitive psychophysiology. *Journal of Affective Disorders.*

Marr, D. (1982). *Vision: A computational investigation into the human representation and processing of visual information.* New York: Freeman.

Meany, M.J. (1998, September). *Variations in maternal care and the development of individual differences in neural systems mediating behavioral and endocrine responses to stress.* Address presented at the annual meeting of the Society for Psychophysiological Research, Denver, CO.

Miller, G.A. (1995, October). *How we think about cognition, emotion, and biology in psychopathology.* Presidential address presented at the annual meeting of the Society for Psychophysiological Research, Toronto, Ontario, Canada.

Miller, G.A., & Kozak, M.J. (1993). A philosophy for the study of emotion: Three-systems theory. In N. Birbaumer & A. Öhman (Eds.), *The structure of emotion: Physiological, cognitive and clinical aspects* (pp. 31–47). Seattle, WA: Hogrefe & Huber.

National Institute of Mental Health. (1999, February 12). [Announcement of NIMH workshop, "Emotion and mood"]. Unpublished e-mail.

National Institutes of Health. (1999, February). *Peer review notes.* Washington, DC: Author.

Thase, M.E. Greenhouse, J.B., Frank, E. Reynold, C.F., Pilkonis, P.A., Hurley, K. Grochocinski, V., & Kupfer, D.J. (1997). Treatment of major depression with psychotherapy or psychotherapy-pharmacotherapy combinations. *Archives of General Psychiatry,* 54, 1009–1015.

Zuckerman, M. (1999). *Vulnerability to psychopathology: A biosocial model.* Washington, DC: American Psychological Association.

Evolutionary Psychology: The Wheat and the Chaff

Frans B.M. de Waal[1]
Yerkes Primate Research Center, Emory University, Atlanta, Georgia

Abstract

Evolutionary approaches are on the rise in the social sciences and have the potential to bring an all-encompassing conceptual framework to the study of human behavior. Together with neuroscience, which is digging the grave of mind-body dualism, evolutionary psychology is bound to undermine the still reigning human-animal dualism. If a Darwinian reshaping of the social sciences seems inevitable, even desirable, this should not be looked at as a hostile takeover. The underlying theme of this essay is that it is time for psychologists to join the Darwinian revolution, yet the essay also critically reviews current evolutionary psychology. It questions the loose application of adaptationist thinking and the fragmentation of the genome, behavior, and the brain. From biology we learn that not every species-typical trait is necessarily advantageous, and from neuroscience we learn that not every psychological ability or tendency necessarily needs to have its own specialized brain circuitry. But even if the concept of adaptation is hard to apply, psychologists would do well to start looking at human behavior in the light of evolution.

Keywords

evolution; adaptation; modularity; biology

Few topics are as hotly debated within psychology today as evolutionary psychology. It is not that the issues are new—some go back to William James and the heyday of social Darwinism—but evolutionary ideas about human behavior are being forwarded with new force, backed by innovative concepts derived from the study of animal behavior, at a time when the once-popular environmental and cultural explanations are increasingly recognized as inadequate.

The stated goal of evolutionary psychology is to provide an evolutionary account of human behavior. By hypothesizing about the selection pressures that have shaped behavior in the past, evolutionary psychologists expect to arrive at testable hypotheses about present behavior. Because evolutionary psychology does not focus on genetic explanations at the exclusion of other explanations, it is not genetically deterministic, even though it obviously emphasizes genetic evolution more than psychologists have been used to. Whereas its objectives are broad and laudable enough, evolutionary psychology is unfortunately better known for a few narrow theories about why women fall for rich guys, why stepfathers are not to be trusted, and how rape is only natural. Moreover, in the promotion of these ideas, theoretical convictions have often been more conspicuous than data. Nonetheless, there is no way around an evolutionary approach to human behavior. Although I take a critical approach to evolutionary psychology in this essay, my arguments should not be taken to mean that it has no future. On the contrary, I see evolutionary psychology as an inevitable, even desirable development plagued by serious growing pains that need to be addressed for its own good.

Looking at the social sciences as a relative outsider, I see thousands of ideas that are barely interconnected (Staats, 1991). One could argue that they do not need to interconnect, yet this amounts to an admission that every area within the discipline is free to come up with its own explanations. This approach results in a serious lack of mooring to the thinking in psychology, a lack of an overarching scheme within which everything must make sense.

A younger generation of psychologists, anthropologists, and even economists and political scientists is gaining enthusiasm for a Darwinian framework, which has the potential to tie together the forest of hypotheses about human behavior now out there. My hope is that this generation will turn evolutionary psychology into a serious and rigorous science by being critical of its premises without abandoning the core idea that important aspects of human behavior have been naturally selected. In the end, evolutionary theory may serve as the umbrella idea so desperately needed in the social sciences (Wilson, 1998).

Even though psychology is at the forefront in moving closer to the life sciences, it has not yet freed itself from certain aspects of Western philosophy, which ultimately came out of the Christian tradition. Psychology is still burdened with ancient dualisms, such as those between body and mind, human and animal, and nature and culture. It will have to rid itself of these dualisms before it can fully integrate with the life sciences and their non-Christian, Aristotelian foundation. Whereas we can safely leave it to cognitive neuroscience to do away with any lingering mind-body dualism, and to students of animal culture to bridge the nature-culture gap, psychology will also need to get over its pervasive human-animal dualism.

DARWINISM 101

But before evolutionary psychology can be successful, social scientists will need training in evolutionary theory. Many of the problems surrounding evolutionary psychology have nothing to do with whether human behavior has been subject to evolution by natural selection—which to me is a given—but rather concern how broad or narrow a view of evolution one embraces. Many followers of evolutionary psychology overlook some of the simplest truths coming out of evolutionary theory.

Dobzhansky (1973) wrote an article with the now-famous title "Nothing in Biology Makes Sense Except in the Light of Evolution." This obviously means that leaving evolution out of basic science education constitutes a fatal deficiency. Because of continuing resistance to evolutionary theory, however, this deficiency unfortunately characterizes large parts of the U.S. public school system. After such an education, the young social scientist goes to the university, where the curriculum, with few exceptions, also neglects evolutionary theory. As a result, the way evolutionary theory is applied to human behavior is often riddled with curious errors. The most basic one is taking the existence of a trait to mean that it must be good for something, thus ignoring the warning of Williams (1966), a contemporary evolutionary biologist, that "adaptation is a special and onerous concept that should be used only when it is really necessary" (pp. 4–5).

An example straight out of the evolutionary psychology—literature and I could offer hundreds more—is found right in the opening sentence of a recent article. It states: "Both male facial hair and male pattern baldness are genetically based, suggesting that they contributed to fitness" (Muscarella & Cunningham, 1996, p. 99). Later in the same article, we learn that male pattern baldness may signal social maturity, described as a friendly kind of dominance based on wisdom. Is this supposed to explain why we have an entire industry that removes hair from men's heads? Obviously, every man wants to look mature and wise!

The first common mistake in evolutionary explanations, then, is to think that if something is genetically influenced it must serve a purpose. Alzheimer's disease and cystic fibrosis have a genetic basis, as do many other diseases, but no one would argue that they contribute to fitness. In addition, many characteristics are by-products of others, and all that matters from an evolutionary perspective is that the entire set of traits serves survival and reproduction. Many individual traits are imperfectly designed or positively costly. A human example is our back: Our species is not fully suited for an upright posture, hence many of us suffer back problems, such as hernias, slipped disks, and neck pain. Walking upright must have had great benefits for these costs to be tolerable, even though there exists no universally accepted theory of why we walk upright.

It is no wonder that biologists often refer to the evolutionary process as "tinkering." Ballast often remains visible in the end-product. Ironically, then, the natural world is rampant with flawed designs that reflect the trouble evolution has had turning one form into another, such as a quadruped into a biped.

RAPE AS ADAPTATION

The lesson from the foregoing is that one cannot atomize the organism. One cannot single out a trait for an adaptive story, as is often done in evolutionary psychology. Rather, one needs to (a) consider the entire set of traits and (b) trace the organism's phylogeny, that is, the ancestral forms that produced it.

In moving this observation to human behavior, it is impossible to ignore the evolutionary psychology book that has raised most eyebrows. In *A Natural History of Rape,* Thornhill and Palmer (2000) postulated that rape is an adaptation; that is, rape may have been favored by natural selection because it furthered male reproduction. The authors extrapolated straight from Thornhill's insect studies, which showed that there are indeed species with male anatomical features that seem designed to force females into sexual contact. But these are flies, and in humans rape is part of a far larger picture. Rape occurs at the interface of sex and power, two rich and complex areas of human behavior that are obviously interconnected. It is hard to see how any serious treatment of rape can rip it from this larger context, explaining it as an isolated behavior, as Thornhill and Palmer tried to do.

To be called an adaptation, rape would need to have its own genetic basis separate from the genetic bases of other sexual tendencies, as well as personality characteristics, such as impulsivity or aggressivity. Rape would also need to offer special reproductive advantages, and have been favored by selection for this very reason. These are heavy requirements that raise a number of pressing questions. Do we know if rapists are genetically unique? What are the advantages of rape, if any, in terms of reproduction? Are there costs associated with rape? In relation to the latter question, imagine a small ancestral community in which a man raped the wives and daughters of other men. I do not think this man would have had good survival chances. And why do men sometimes rape partners who are perfectly willing to engage in consensual sex? Declaring rape an adaptation raises a multitude of questions, questions that Thornhill and Palmer have failed to answer.

A major problem with the strategy of singling out rape for evolutionary explanation is that the behavior is shown by only a small minority. The same criticism applies to Daly and Wilson's (1988) well-known work on infanticide by stepparents. They explained this category of infanticide as arising from a lack of shared genes with adoptive offspring. I would argue that in seeking to understand rare behavior we should never ignore the norm. If child abuse by stepfathers is evolutionarily explained, why do so many more stepfathers lovingly care for their children than abuse them? And if rape is such an advantageous reproductive strategy, why are there so many *more* men who do not rape than who do? I have called this the dilemma of the rarely exercised option: A Darwinian account of an atypical behavioral choice is incomplete without at least an equally good account of the typical choice (de Waal, 2000).

THE MODULE EXPLOSION

Followers of evolutionary psychology often talk about a gene for this or a brain module for that, seeking to dissect the whole to explain each part separately. If this cannot be done with the components of a watch spread out on the table, it most certainly cannot be done with the genome, the organism, and its behavior. As for the brain, the current trend to divide brain function into modules reminds me of early ethology, when there was no limit to the number of instincts one could propose: from self-preservation to aggression, and from sex to motherhood. In the 1950s, each species-typical tendency had its own instinct, and Konrad Lorenz's *Instinktlehre* (German for "instinct doctrine") even included a "parliament" of instincts to indicate how all components together influence decisions. These ideas applied mainly to nonhuman species, but human instincts have been proposed many times as well, most energetically by self-declared evolutionary psychologist McDougall (1908). Similarly, proponents of evolutionary psychology have compared the brain to a Swiss army knife to which evolution has one by one added modules for everything from face recognition, to tool use, preference for kin over nonkin, child care, friendship, detection of cheaters, and theory of mind[2] (Tooby & Cosmides, 1992).

One problem with this approach—apart from the fact that brain modules at any specific task level have yet to be demonstrated—is that this would make for an incredibly unwieldy brain, much like a computer to which a new chip would need to be added each time we install another program: one chip for word processing, one for games, one for spreadsheets, and so on. Instead, a computer is a multipurpose device that allows each application to draw on its full potential.

This is not to imply that the brain is a *tabula rasa*. It seems prepared to acquire certain skills more easily than others, and to be waiting for certain kinds of information. The studies by Tooby and Cosmides (1992) do indeed suggest such preparation, as do many animal studies, going back to the early work on imprinting, according to which ducks and geese are preprogrammed to pick up information about their species in the first days of life. What makes this happen is unclear, however, and the various labels now in use to indicate genetic influences on behavior—from biogrammar, to biological algorithm, brain module, epigenetic rule, and learning predisposition—are really not much better at solving the mystery than the good-old instinct concept. The term module, in particular, carries the connotation of a brain part that is self-contained, encapsulated, and localized, rendering the idea unpalatable to neuroscientists (Panksepp & Panksepp, 2000). Quite possibly, our preparedness for particular sets of stimuli or problems (e.g., the facility with which we recognize faces; Gauthier & Tarr, 1997) boils down to learned stimulus relevance rather than specialized brain circuitry.

Williams (1966) was right to warn that adaptation is an onerous concept that should be applied parsimoniously. What evolutionary psychology needs to develop is a taste for multilevel thinking in which attention freely shifts between immediate (proximate) explanations of behavior, which are the traditional domain of psychology, and evolutionary (ultimate) explanations. In other words, it needs to address both the "how" questions of how things work and the "why" questions of why evolution favored a particular behavior—to put a little less evolution and a little more psychology into its explanations.

CONCLUSION

Current problems with evolutionary psychology may be serious, but they are not insurmountable. Evolutionary psychology is bound to overcome them. I dare predict that 50 years from now every psychology department will have Darwin's bearded portrait on the wall. Evolutionary approaches have the potential to introduce a conceptual framework that will accommodate or replace the current proliferation of disconnected theories in the study of human behavior.

Even though evolutionary psychology, like the rest of psychology, oftentimes acts as if the human species is a world apart, it cannot help but undermine its own anthropocentrism given the source of the theories that it is so eagerly adopting. They derive from scientists, such as Darwin, who first of all were naturalists. If evolutionary psychology embraces Edward Wilson it cannot help but get covered in ants, and if it embraces William Hamilton it cannot overlook the beetles and parasites that fascinated this brilliant biologist. With regard to animals closer to us, the parallels are even more striking. Chimpanzees, for example, engage in political alliances when jockeying for power, show empathy toward others in distress, establish an economy of services and favors, and reconcile with opponents after a fight by means of a kiss and embrace (Fig. 1; de Waal, 1982/1998, 1996). Because evolutionary explanations require close attention to phylogeny, and given that primatologists are used to behavioral complexity not unlike that of our own species, evolutionary psychology and primatology make natural partners.

The questions asked by evolutionary psychology may strike some readers as simplistic, yet they are here to stay. Questions about why we choose particular

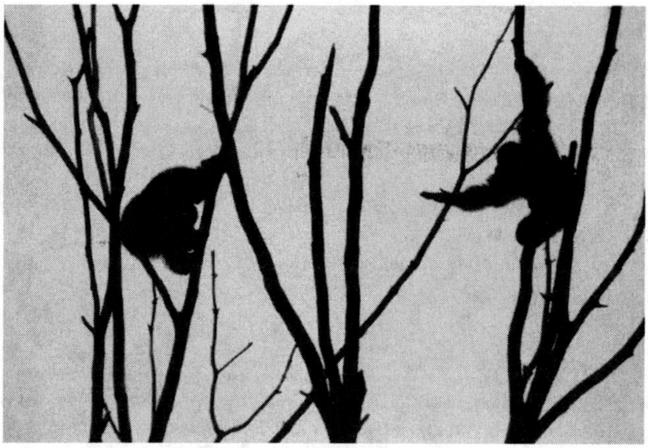

Fig. 1. Example of chimpanzees' use of eye contact and hand gestures to invite a reconciliation. This photograph shows the situation 10 min after a protracted, noisy conflict between two adult males at the Arnhem Zoo in the Netherlands. The challenged male (left) fled into the tree, but 10 min later his opponent stretched out a hand. Within seconds, the two males had a physical reunion and climbed down together to groom each other on the ground. Photograph by the author.

mates, avoid incest, and favor kin, and what modes of cooperation we engage in, for example, are not the traditional questions of psychology, yet they emerge naturally from an evolutionary perspective. These basic questions are central to any evolutionary approach. Psychologists who do not like the simplicity of the answers currently coming out of evolutionary psychology should make an effort to improve them, to broaden its intellectual horizon, because all of psychology would stand to gain from a more enlightened evolutionary psychology.

Recommended Reading

de Waal, F.B.M. (1999). The end of nature versus nurture. *Scientific American, 281*, 94–99.

de Waal, F.B.M. (2001). *The ape and the sushi master: Cultural reflections by a primatologist.* New York: Basic Books.

Mayr, E. (2001). *What evolution is.* New York: Basic Books.

Zimmer, C. (2001). *Evolution: The triumph of an idea.* New York: Harper Collins.

Acknowledgments—I thank Allison Berger and Virginia Holt for providing the transcript of my 2001 Focus on Science Plenary Address, which was presented at the annual meeting of the American Psychological Association in San Francisco and was on the topic of this essay. I am also grateful to Mauricio Papini and Scott Lilienfeld for comments on previous versions of the manuscript.

Notes

1. Address correspondence to Frans B.M. de Waal, Living Links, Yerkes Primate Research Center, Emory University, 954 N. Gatewood Rd., Atlanta, GA 30322.

2. Theory of mind means that one understands the mental states of others (a capacity that may be limited to humans and apes).

References

Daly, M., & Wilson, M. (1988). *Homicide*. Hawthorne, NY: Aldine de Gruyter.

de Waal, F.B.M. (1996). *Good natured: The origins of right and wrong in humans and other animals*. Cambridge, MA: Harvard University Press.

de Waal, F.B.M. (1998). *Chimpanzee politics*. Baltimore: Johns Hopkins University Press. (Original work published 1982)

de Waal, F.B.M. (2000, April 2). Survival of the rapist [Review of the book *A natural history of rape: Biological bases of sexual coercion*]. *New York Times Book Review*, pp. 24–25.

Dobzhansky, T. (1973). Nothing in biology makes sense except in the light of evolution. *American Biology Teacher, 35*, 125–129.

Gauthier, I., & Tarr, M.J. (1997). Becoming a "Greeable" expert: Exploring mechanisms for face recognition. *Vision Research, 37*, 1673–1682.

McDougall, W. (1908). *An introduction to social psychology*. New York: Putnam.

Mscarella, F., & Cunningham, M.R. (1996). The evolutionary significance and social perception of male pattern baldness and facial hair. *Ethology & Sociobiology, 17*, 99–117.

Panksepp, J., & Panksepp, J.B. (2000). The seven sins of evolutionary psychology. *Evolution and Cognition, 6*, 108–131.

Staats, A.W. (1991). Unified positivism and unification psychology: Fad or new field? *American Psychologist, 46*, 899–912.

Thornhill, R., & Palmer, C.T. (2000). *A natural history of rape: Biological bases of sexual coercion*. Cambridge, MA: MIT Press.

Tooby, J., & Cosmides, L. (1992). The psychological foundations of culture. In J. Barkow, L. Cosmides, & J. Tooby (Eds.), *The adapted mind: Evolutionary psychology and the generation of culture* (pp. 19–136). New York: Oxford University Press.

Williams, G. (1966). *Adaptation and natural selection*. Princeton, NJ: Princeton University Press.

Wilson, E.O. (1998). *Consilience: The unity of knowledge*. New York: Knopf.

Three Laws of Behavior Genetics and What They Mean

Eric Turkheimer[1]

Department of Psychology, University of Virginia, Charlottesville, Virginia

Abstract

Behavior genetics has demonstrated that genetic variance is an important component of variation for all behavioral outcomes, but variation among families is not. These results have led some critics of behavior genetics to conclude that heritability is so ubiquitous as to have few consequences for scientific understanding of development, while some behavior genetic partisans have concluded that family environment is not an important cause of developmental outcomes. Both views are incorrect. Genotype is in fact a more systematic source of variability than environment, but for reasons that are methodological rather than substantive. Development is fundamentally nonlinear, interactive, and difficult to control experimentally. Twin studies offer a useful methodological shortcut, but do not show that genes are more fundamental than environments.

Keywords

genes; environment; development; behavior genetics

The nature-nurture debate is over. The bottom line is that everything is heritable, an outcome that has taken all sides of the nature-nurture debate by surprise. Irving Gottesman and I have suggested that the universal influence of genes on behavior be enshrined as the first law of behavior genetics (Turkheimer & Gottesman, 1991), and at the risk of naming laws that I can take no credit for discovering, it is worth stating the nearly unanimous results of behavior genetics in a more formal manner.

- *First Law.* All human behavioral traits are heritable.
- *Second Law.* The effect of being raised in the same family is smaller than the effect of genes.
- *Third Law.* A substantial portion of the variation in complex human behavioral traits is not accounted for by the effects of genes or families.

It is not my purpose in this brief article to defend these three laws against the many exceptions that might be claimed. The point is that now that the empirical facts are in and no longer a matter of serious controversy, it is time to turn attention to what the three laws mean, to the implications of the genetics of behavior for an understanding of complex human behavior and its development.

VARIANCE AND CAUSATION IN BEHAVIORAL DEVELOPMENT

If the first two laws are taken literally, they seem to herald a great victory for the nature side of the old debate: Genes matter, families do not. To understand why such views are at best an oversimplification of a complex reality, it is necessary to consider the newest wave of opposition that behavior genetics has generated. These new critics, whose most articulate spokesman is Gilbert Gottlieb (1991, 1992, 1995), claim that the goal of developmental psychology is to specify the actual developmental processes that lead to complex outcomes. In lower animals, whose breeding and environment can be brought under the control of the scientist, it is possible to document such developmental processes in exquisite detail. The critics draw an unfavorable comparison between these detailed animal studies and twin studies of behavior genetics, which produce only statistical conclusions about the relative importance of genes and environment in development.

The greatest virtue of the new (challenge is that it abandons the implausible environmentalist contention that important aspects of behavior will be without genetic influence. Gottlieb (1992) stated, "The present . . . viewpoint holds that genes are an inextricable component of any developmental system, and thus *genes are involved in all traits*" (p. 147). Unlike earlier critics who deplored the reductionism they attributed to behavior genetic theories of behavior, the developmental biologists take behavior genetics to task for not being mechanistic *enough*. Once vilified as the paragon of determinist accounts of human behavior, behavior genetics is now chastised for offering vague and inconclusive models of development (Gottlieb, 1995; Turkheimer, Goldsmith, & Gottesman, 1995), and judged by the standards of developmental psychobiology in lower animals, it is true enough that behavior genetic theories of complex human behavior seem woefully poorly specified. But ultimately the charge is unfair, because there is no equivalent in developmental psychobiology to the behavior genetic study of marital status or school performance. The great preponderance of the exquisite experimental science that goes into animal psychobiology is quite simply impossible to conduct in humans.

Human developmental social science is difficult—equally so for the genetically and environmentally inclined—because of the (methodologically vexing, humanistically pleasing) confluence of two conditions: (a) Behavior emerges out of complex, nonlinear developmental processes, and (b) ethical considerations prevent us from bringing most human developmental processes under effective experimental control. Figure 1 is a schematic illustration of the problem. Individual genes (Genes 1, 2, and 3) and their environments (which include other genes) interact to initiate a complex developmental process that determines adult personality. Most characteristic of this process is its interactivity: Subsequent environments to which the organism is exposed depend on its earlier states, and each new environment changes the developmental trajectory, which affects future expression of genes, and so forth. Everything is interactive, in the sense that no arrows proceed uninterrupted from cause to effect; any individual gene or environmental event produces an effect only by interacting with other genes and environments.

For the behavior geneticist, however, the quasi-experimental gift of genetically identical and nonidentical twins offers a remarkable, if deceptively simple, method to span this daunting interactive complexity. Thanks to the fact that identical twins are on average exactly twice as similar genetically as nonidentical twins, one can use straightforward statistical procedures to estimate the proportion of variability in complex outcomes that is associated with causally distant genes, all the while maintaining a state of near-perfect ignorance about the actual

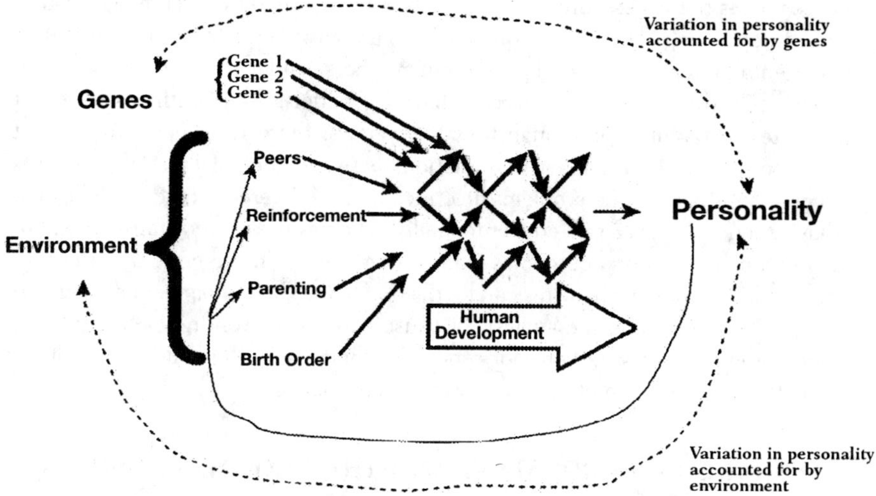

Fig. 1. Schematic diagram of contrasting roles of genes and environment in development of personality. One-headed arrows link causes to effects; two-headed arrows indicate correlations. Genes and environments are both causal inputs into an interactive developmental system (represented by the network of arrows in the center of the figure), but because people select and shape their own environments (as represented by lighter one-headed arrows from personality to environments), correlations across the developmental system (dotted two-headed arrows) are easier to detect for genes than for environments.

causal processes that connect genes to behavior. This methodological shortcut is not available to rivals of behavior genetics who seek to measure the effects of families on behavior. How similar was my rearing environment to that of my siblings? And how similar was it to the environment of my adopted sibling, if I have one, or to the environment of my biological sibling who was raised by someone else? The apparent victory of nature over nurture suggested by the first two laws is thus seen to be more methodological than substantive. In a world in which there were occasional occurrences of "identical environmental twins," whose experiences were exactly the same, moment by moment, and another variety who shared exactly (but randomly) 50% of their experiences, environmentalists could reproduce the precision of their rivals, and like the behavior geneticists could measure with great precision the total contribution of the environment while knowing almost nothing about the developmental processes that underlie it.

The old-fashioned nature-nurture debate was about whether or not genes influence complex behavioral outcomes, and that question has been decisively answered in the affirmative. The new question is how we can proceed from partitioning sources of variance to specifying concrete developmental processes (Turkheimer, 1998), and although critics like Gottlieb are correct that heritability per se has few implications for a scientific understanding of development, they have failed to emphasize two crucial points. First, heritability does have one certain consequence: It is no longer possible to interpret correlations among biologically related family members as prima facie evidence of sociocultural causal mechanisms. If the children of depressed mothers grow up to be depressed themselves, it does not necessarily demonstrate that being raised by a depressed mother is itself depressing. The children might have grown up equally depressed if they had been adopted and raised by different mothers, under the influence of their biological mother's genes. For every behavior geneticist who continues to report moderate heritabilities as though they were news, there is an environmentalist who reports causally ambiguous correlations between genetically related parents and children. Second, the problem the critics have uncovered extends well beyond behavior genetics: It is a rare environmentalist who has never used statistical methods to predict behavioral outcomes from earlier events, in the hope that the specific developmental mechanisms can be filled in later. The disconnect between the analysis of variance and the analysis of causes, to use Lewontin's (1974) phrase, is not a proprietary flaw in behavior genetic methodology; in fact, it is the bedrock methodological problem of contemporary social science.

NONSHARED ENVIRONMENT AND THE GLOOMY PROSPECT

Even after the effects of genes and the shared effects of families have been accounted for, around 50% of the differences among siblings is left unexplained. In recent years, scientists interested in the genetics of behavior have come to call this unexplained portion the "nonshared environment." Although according to the second law shared environment accounts for a small proportion of the variability in behavioral outcomes, according to the third law, nonshared environment usually accounts for a substantial portion. So perhaps the appropriate conclusion is not so much that the family environment does not matter for development, but rather that the part of the family environment that is shared by siblings does not matter. What does matter is the individual environments of children, their peers, and the aspects of their parenting that they do not share. Plomin and Daniels (1987) reviewed evidence of the predominance of nonshared environmental variance and posed a seminal question: Why are children in the same family so different? They proposed that siblings are different because nonshared environmental events are more potent causes of developmental outcomes than the shared environmental variables, like socioeconomic status, that have formed the traditional basis of sociocultural developmental psychology.

Plomin and Daniels's explanation involves a subtle conceptual shift, best described in terms of a distinction between the objective and effective environment (Goldsmith, 1993; Turkheimer & Waldron, 2000). What qualifies an environmental event as nonshared? There are two possibilities. The first is objective: An event is nonshared if it is experienced by only one sibling in a family, regardless of the consequences it produces. The other possibility is effective: An environmental event is nonshared if it makes siblings different rather than similar, regardless of whether it was experienced by one or both of them. Plomin and Daniels's proposal, then, is that the nonshared environment as an effectively defined variance component can be explained by objectively nonshared environmental events. The question, "Why are children in the same family so different?" is answered, "Because measurable differences in their environments make them that way."

This proposal has been enormously influential, spawning an entire area of empirical inquiry into the consequences of measured environmental differences among siblings. Ironically, that same literature has quite decisively demonstrated that the conjecture is false. A review of 43 studies that measured differences in the environments of siblings and related them to differences in the siblings' developmental outcomes (Turkheimer & Waldron, 2000) has shown that although upwards of 50% of the variance in behavioral outcomes is accounted for by the effectively defined variance component called nonshared environment, the median percentage accounted for by objectively defined nonshared events is less than 2%. What could be going on?

Plomin and Daniels (1987) almost identified the answer to this question, but dismissed it as too pessimistic:

> One gloomy prospect is that the salient environment might be unsystematic, idiosyncratic, or serendipitous events such as accidents, illnesses, or other traumas . . . . Such capricious events, however, are likely to prove a dead end for research. More interesting heuristically are possible systematic sources of differences between families. (p. 8)

The gloomy prospect is true. Nonshared environmental variability predominates not because of the systematic effects of environmental events that are not shared among siblings, but rather because of the unsystematic effects of all environmental events, compounded by the equally unsystematic processes that expose us to environmental events in the first place (Turkheimer & Gottesman, 1996).

A model of nonshared variability based on the gloomy prospect is radically different from the Plomin model based on systematic consequences of environmental differences among siblings. Most important, the two models suggest very different prospects for a genetically informed developmental psychology. Again and again, Plomin and his colleagues have emphasized that the importance of nonshared environment implies that it is time to abandon shared environmental variables as possible explanations of developmental outcomes. And although modern environmentalists might not miss coarse measures like socioeconomic status, it is quite another thing to give up on the causal efficaciousness of normal families, as Scarr (1992), Rowe (1994), and Harris (1998) have urged. If, however, nonshared environmental variability in outcome is the result of the unsystematic consequences of both shared and nonshared environmental events, the field faces formidable methodological problems—Plomin and Daniels's gloomy prospect—but need not conclude that aspects of families children share with siblings are of no causal importance.

CONCLUSION: ANTICIPATING THE GENOME PROJECT

It is now possible for behavior genetics to move beyond statistical analyses of differences between identical and nonidentical twins and identify individual genes that are related to behavioral outcomes. What should we expect from this endeavor? Behavior geneticists anticipate vindication: At long last, statistical variance components will be rooted in the actual causal consequences of actual genes. Critics of behavior genetics expect the opposite, pointing to the repeated failures to replicate associations between genes and behavior as evidence of the shaky theoretical underpinnings of which they have so long complained.

There is an interesting parallel between the search for individual genes that influence behavior and the failed attempt to specify the nonshared environment in terms of measured environmental variables. In each case, investigators began with statistically reliable but causally vague sources of variance, and set out to discover the actual causal processes that produced them. The quest for the nonshared environment, as we have seen, got stuck in the gloomy prospect. Although individual environmental events influence outcomes in the most general sense, they do not do so in a systematic way. One can detect their effects only by accumulating them statistically, using twins or adoptees.

If the underlying causal structure of human development is highly complex, as illustrated in Figure 1, the relatively simple statistical procedures employed by developmental psychologists, geneticists, and environmentalists alike are being badly misapplied. But misapplied statistical procedures still produce what appear to be results. Small relations would still be found between predictors and outcomes, but the underlying complex causal processes would cause the apparent results to be small, and to change unpredictably from one experiment to the next. So individual investigators would obtain "results," which would then fail to replicate and accumulate into a coherent theory because the simple statistical model did not fit the complex developmental process to which it was being applied. Much social science conducted in the shadow of the gloomy prospect has exactly this flavor (e.g., Meehl, 1978).

The gloomy prospect looms larger for the genome project than is generally acknowledged. The question is not whether there are correlations to be found between individual genes and complex behavior—of course there are—but instead whether there are domains of genetic causation in which the gloomy prospect does not prevail, allowing the little bits of correlational evidence to cohere into replicable and cumulative genetic models of development. My own prediction is that such domains will prove rare indeed, and that the likelihood of discovering them will be inversely related to the complexity of the behavior under study.

Finally, it must be remembered that the gloomy prospect is gloomy only from the point of view of the working social scientist. Although frustrated developmental psychologists may be tempted to favor methodologically tractable heuristics over chaotic psychological reality, it is a devil's choice: In the long run, the gloomy prospect always wins, and no one would want to live in a world where it did not. Psychology is at least one good paradigm shift away from an empirical answer to the gloomy prospect, but the philosophical response is becoming clear: The additive effect of genes may constitute what is predictable about human development, but what is predictable about human development is also what is least interesting about it. The gloomy prospect isn't.

Recommended Reading

Gottlieb, G. (1992). (See References)
Lewontin, R.C. (1974). (See References)
Meehl, P.E. (1978). (See References)
Plomin, R., & Daniels, D. (1987). (See References)

Note

1. Address correspondence to Eric Turkheimer, Department of Psychology, 102 Gilmer Hall, P.O. Box 400400, University of Virginia, Charlottesville, VA 22904-4400; e-mail: turkheimer@virginia.edu.

References

Goldsmith, H. (1993). Nature-nurture issues in the behavioral genetic context: Overcoming barriers to communication. In R. Plomin & G. McClearn (Eds.), *Nature, nurture and psychology* (pp. 325–339). Washington, DC: American Psychological Association.

Gottlieb, G. (1991). Experiential canalization of behavioral development: Theory. *Developmental Psychology, 27*, 4–13.

Gottlieb, G. (1992). *Individual development and evolution.* New York: Oxford University Press.

Gottlieb, G. (1995). Some conceptual deficiencies in "developmental" behavior genetics. *Human Development*, 38, 131–141.

Harris, J.R. (1998). *The nurture assumption: Why children turn out the way they do.* New York: Free Press.

Lewontin, R.C. (1974). The analysis of variance and the analysis of causes. *American Journal of Human Genetics, 26*, 400–411.

Meehl, P.E. (1978) Theoretical risks and tabular asterisks: Sir Karl, Sir Ronald, and the slow progress of soft psychology. *Journal of Consulting and Clinical Psychology, 46*, 806–834.

Plomin, R., & Daniels, D. (1987). Why are children in the same family so different from one another? *Behavioral and Brain Sciences, 10*, 1–60.

Rowe, D.C. (1994). *The limits of family influence: Genes, experience, and behavior.* New York: Guilford Press.

Scarr, S. (1992). Developmental theories for the 1990s: Development and individual differences. *Child Development, 63*, 1–19.

Turkheimer, E. (1998). Heritability and biological explanation. *Psychological Review, 105*, 782–791.

Turkheimer, E., Goldsmith, H.H., & Gottesman, I.I. (1995). Commentary. *Human Development, 38*, 142–153.

Turkheimer, E., & Gottesman, I.I. (1991). Is $H^2 = 0$ a null hypothesis anymore? *Behavioral and Brain Sciences, 14*, 410–411.

Turkheimer, E., & Gottesman, I.I. (1996). Simulating the dynamics of genes and environment in development. *Development and Psychopathology, 8*, 667–677.

Turkheimer, E., & Waldron, M.C. (2000). Nonshared environment: A theoretical, methodological, and quantitative review. *Psychological Bulletin, 126*, 78–108.

Situation-Behavior Profiles as a Locus of Consistency in Personality

Walter Mischel,[1] Yuichi Shoda, and Rodolfo Mendoza-Denton

Psychology Department, Columbia University, New York, New York (W.M., R.M.-D.), and Psychology Department, University of Washington, Seattle, Washington (Y.S.)

Abstract

Traditional approaches have long considered situations as "noise" or "error" that obscures the consistency of personality and its invariance. Therefore, it has been customary to average the individual's behavior on any given dimension (e.g., conscientiousness) across different situations. Contradicting this assumption and practice, recent studies have demonstrated that by incorporating the situation into the search for consistency, a new locus of stability is found. Namely, people are characterized not only by stable individual differences in their overall levels of behavior, but also by distinctive and stable patterns of situation-behavior relations (e.g., she does *X* when *A* but *Y* when *B*). These *if . . . then . . . profiles* constitute behavioral "signatures" that provide potential windows into the individual's underlying dynamics. Processing models that can account for such signatures provide a new route for studying personality types in terms of their shared dynamics and characteristic defining profiles.

Keywords

personality; consistency; interactionism; *if . . . then . . .* profiles

Traditionally, personality psychology has been devoted to understanding the dispositional characteristics of the person that remain invariant across contexts and situations. Further, it has been assumed that the manifestations of invariance in personality should be seen in consistent differences between individuals in their behavior across many different situations. For example, a person who is high in conscientiousness should be more conscientious than most people in many different kinds of situations (at home, at school, with a boss, with friends). The data over the course of a century, however, made it increasingly evident that the individual's behavior on any dimension varies considerably across different types of situations, thus greatly limiting the ability to make situation-specific predictions and raising deep questions about the nature and locus of consistency in personality (Mischel, 1968; Mischel & Peake, 1982).

By the 1970s, the discrepancy between the data and the field's fundamental assumptions precipitated a paradigm crisis (Bem & Allen, 1974). The crux of this crisis was captured in the so-called personality paradox: How can our intuitions about the stability of personality be reconciled with the evidence for its variability across situations? A long-term research program was launched to try to resolve this paradox (Mischel & Peake, 1982; Mischel & Shoda, 1995). This program was motivated by the proposition that the variability of behavior across situations, at least partly, may be a meaningful expression of the enduring but dynamic personality system itself and its stable underlying organization. The findings that emerged have led to a reconceptualization of the nature and locus of personality invariance, reconciling the variability of behavior on the one hand with the stability of the personality structure on the other.

EVIDENCE FOR THE CONTEXTUALIZED *IF . . . THEN . . .* EXPRESSION OF PERSONALITY INVARIANCE

Figure 1 shows behavioral data that are typical of those found for any two individuals in a given domain of behavior across many different situations. In traditional conceptions, the variability in an individual's behavior across situations (the ups and downs along the *y*-axis) is seen as unwanted, uninformative variance reflecting either situational influences or measurement error. In dealing with this variability, the most widely accepted approach has been to aggregate the individual's behavior on a given dimension across many situations to arrive at the person's "true score." The average summary score that results allows one to ask whether individuals are different in their overall level of a disposition, and is useful for many purposes—yet it may conceal potentially valuable information about where and when individuals differ in their unique patterns of behavior. If these patterns of situation-behavior relations are indeed stable and meaningful, rather than just measurement error, they may be thought of as *if . . . then . . .* (if situation *A*, then the person does *X*, but if situation *B*, then the person does *Y*) "signatures" that contain clues about the underlying personality system that produces them.

In a study testing for the stability and meaningfulness of such situation-behavior profiles, the behavior of children was observed *in vivo* over the course of a summer within a residential camp setting (Shoda, Mischel, & Wright, 1994). The data collection yielded an extensive archival database that allowed systematic analyses of coherence in behavior as it unfolded across naturalistic situations and over many occasions, under unusually well-controlled research conditions that ensured the reliability and density of measurement.

In selecting situations for the analysis, it was important to move beyond the nominal situations specific to any given setting (such as the woodworking room, dining hall, or playground) that would necessarily be of limited generalizability and usefulness outside the specific setting. Rather, the relevant psychological features of situations—the "active ingredients" that exert a significant impact on the behavior of the person and that cut across nominal settings—were iden-

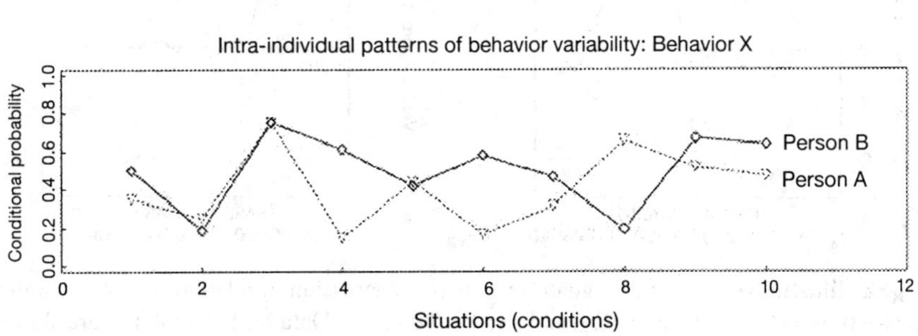

Fig. 1. Typical individual differences in the conditional probability of a type of behavior in different situations. Reprinted by permission from Mischel and Shoda (1995, Fig. 1, p. 247).

tified. Within this camp setting, five types of psychological situations that could be objectively recorded emerged: three negative situations ("teased, provoked, or threatened by peer," "warned by adult," and "punished by adult") and two positive situations ("praised by adult" and "approached socially by peer"). The children's social behavior (e.g., verbal aggression, withdrawal, friendly behavior, prosocial behavior) was unobtrusively observed and recorded as it occurred in relation to each of the selected interpersonal situations, with an average of 167 hr of observation per child over the course of the 6-week camp.

With this unusually extensive data archive, it was possible to assess the stability of the hypothesized situation-behavior relationships for each person. Figure 2 shows illustrative profiles for two children's verbally aggressive behavior across the five types of situations. The frequencies of behavior were first standardized, so that the remaining intraindividual variance in the profiles reflects behavior above and beyond what would be normally expected in the situation indicated—and is thus attributable to the individual's distinctive personal qualities. The two lines within each panel indicate the profiles based on two separate, nonoverlapping samples of situations.

As the figure shows, compared with the other children at the camp, Child 9 showed a distinctively higher level of verbal aggression when warned by adults, but a lower-than-average level when approached positively by a peer. In contrast, Child 28 displayed higher levels of verbal aggression in comparison with others when approached positively by a peer, not when warned by an adult. In contrast to the prediction that intraindividual variability in behavior across situations reflects noise and should thus have an average stability of zero, the results provided strong evidence that participants' *if . . . then . . .* profiles were both distinctive and stable.

THE PERSONALITY PARADOX RECONSIDERED

Further analyses tested the hypothesis that individuals' self-perceptions of consistency are related to the stability of their situation-behavior profiles (Mischel

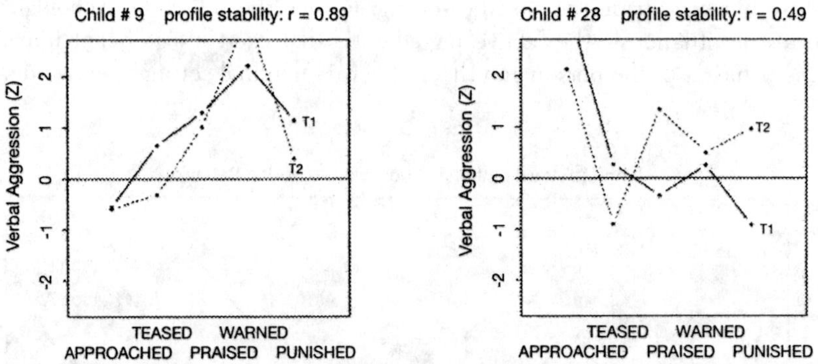

Fig. 2. Illustrative *if . . . then* signatures of verbal aggression in relation to five situations in two time samples, T1 and T2 (solid and dotted lines). Data for two children are shown in standardized scores (Z) relative to the normative levels of verbal aggression in each situation. The profile stability coefficients for the children are shown above the graphs. Reprinted by permission from Mischel and Shoda (1995, Fig. 2, p. 249).

& Shoda, 1995). These analyses utilized data from a field study in which college students were repeatedly observed on campus in various situations relevant to their conscientiousness in the college setting (Mischel & Peake, 1982). The results revealed that students who perceived themselves as consistent did not show greater overall cross-situational consistency than those who did not. However, the average correlation for situation-behavior profile stability was near .5 for individuals who perceived themselves as consistent, whereas it was trivial for those who viewed themselves as inconsistent. It is the stability in the situation-behavior profile and not the cross-situational consistency of behavior that seems to be related to the perception of consistency.

The intuition of consistency, then, seems to be neither paradoxical nor illusory. It is in fact based on a different type of behavioral consistency than has been sought for so many years. Cross-situational variability seems to be an essential expression of the enduring but dynamic personality system itself and its stable underlying organization. Given such findings, the need arose for a conception of personality that could generate—and allow one to predict and understand—not only the overall average differences between people, but also their stable and unique patterns of intraindividual variability.

TOWARD A DYNAMIC CONCEPTION OF PERSONALITY

To address this need, psychologists are beginning to reconceptualize personality not as a mere collection of attributes, but as a coherent organization of mental-emotional representations interacting within a network of relationships and constraints (e.g., Hinton, McClelland, & Rumelhart, 1986). This type of model, familiar in cognitive science, provides a framework for conceptualizing an organized personality processing system that is sensitive to different features of situations and can respond discriminatively to them in characteristic and stable ways.

Cognitive-affective personality system (CAPS) theory (Mischel & Shoda, 1995) represents one instantiation of how such a processing system might function. Within this framework, the stable units of personality consist of mental representations whose activation or inhibition leads to the behaviors displayed. At a molar level of analysis, these mental representations, or cognitive-affective units (CAUs), include the individual's construals, goals, expectations, beliefs, and affects, as well as self-regulatory standards, competencies, plans, and strategies. Each individual is characterized by a relatively stable activation network among the units within the system, reflecting the culture and subculture (Mendoza-Denton, Shoda, Ayduk, & Mischel, 1999), as well as the individual's social learning history, genetic endowment, and biological history (e.g., temperament).

Individual differences in this model arise not only from differences in the chronic accessibility of CAUs, but also from the distinctive organization of interrelationships among them within each person. As the individual moves across situations that contain different psychological features, different mediating units and their characteristic interrelationships become activated. When the *ifs* posed by the situation change, so do the *thens* generated by the personality system, but the *if . . . then . . .* relationships remain the same, reflecting the stable organization of CAUs distinctive for that individual. Computer simulations drawing from such a conceptualization of personality have demonstrated that the CAPS model can account for both interindividual differences in mean levels of behavior and stable intraindividual variability of behavior across psychological situations (Mischel & Shoda, 1995).

FROM IDOGRAPHIC TO NOMOTHETIC ASSESSMENT OF PROCESSING DISPOSITIONS

In CAPS theory, a personality type consists of people who share a common organization of relations among mediating units in the processing of certain situational features—a common network of interrelated CAUS. The kinds of assessment tools needed to study such personality types can range from situation-specific questionnaires (e.g., Chiu, Hong, Mischel, & Shoda, 1995) to rigorously monitored daily diary studies (e.g., Ayduk, Downey, Testa, Yen, & Shoda, 1999), to experimental studies of the impact of various situational triggers on the individual's behavior (e.g., Shoda & Tiernan, in press). Such assessments can be undertaken through either a top-down or a bottom-up approach. In top-down approaches, the researcher begins with a theory of the internal processing dynamics that may characterize a type, and then hypothesizes the distinctive *if . . . then . . .* profile for that type, as well as the psychological triggers that define the profile (e.g., Downey & Feldman, 1996; Morf & Rhodewalt, 2001). Bottom-up approaches, by contrast, take advantage of recent advances in statistical techniques to extract person classes, behavior classes, and situation classes from people's responses to standardized inventories (Vansteelandt & Van Mechelen, 1998).

Such research programs are steps toward building a personality typology that takes account of both the situation and the characteristic organization of the underlying system that distinguishes each type. The CAPS model provides a framework for outlining the particular networks that distinctively characterize different individuals and personality types. From such an approach to typologies, psychologists may be able ultimately to meet a central goal in personality assessment articulated years ago (Mischel, 1968): to make specific predictions about how certain subtypes of individuals are likely to think, feel, and behave in certain kinds of situations.

Recommended Reading

Cervone, D., & Shoda, Y. (1999). *The coherence of personality: Social-cognitive bases of consistency, variability, and organization.* New York: Guilford.

Mischel, W., & Shoda, Y. (1995). (See References)

Shoda, Y., & Mischel, W. (1998). Personality as a stable cognitive-affective activation network: Characteristic patterns of behavior variation emerge from a stable personality structure. In S. Read & L.C. Miller (Eds.), *Connectionist models of social reasoning and social behavior* (pp. 175–208). Mahwah, NJ: Erlbaum.

Shoda, Y., Mischel, W., & Wright, J.C. (1994). (See References)

Acknowledgments—Preparation of this article was supported by National Institute of Mental Health Grant MH39349.

Note

1. Address correspondence to Walter Mischel, Department of Psychology, Columbia University, 406 Schermerhorn Hall, 1190 Amsterdam Ave., Mail Code 5501, New York, NY 10027; e-mail: wm@psych.columbia.edu.

References

Ayduk, O., Downey, G., Testa, A., Yen, Y., & Shoda, Y. (1999). Does rejection elicit hostility in rejection-sensitive women? *Social Cognition, 17*, 245–271.

Bem, D.J., & Allen, A. (1974). On predicting some of the people some of the time: The search for cross-situational consistencies in behavior. *Psychological Review, 81*, 506–520.

Chiu, C., Hong, Y., Mischel, W., & Shoda, Y. (1995). Discriminative facility in social competence: Conditional versus dispositional encoding and monitoring-blunting of information. *Social Cognition, 13*, 49–70.

Downey, G., & Feldman, S. (1996). Implications of rejection sensitivity for intimate relationships. *Journal of Personality and Social Psychology, 70*, 1327–1343.

Hinton, G.E., McClelland, J.I., & Rumelhart, D.E. (1986). Distributed representations. In D.E. Rumelhart & J.L. McClelland (Eds.), *Parallel distributed processing: Explorations in the microstructures of cognition, Vol. I: Foundations* (pp. 77–109). Cambridge, MA: MIT Press/ Bradford Books.

Mendoza-Denton, R., Shoda, Y., Ayduk, O., & Mischel, W. (1999). Applying cognitive-affective processing system theory to cultural differences in social behavior. In W.L. Lonner, D.L. Dinnel, D.K. Forgays, & S.A. Hayes (Eds.), *Merging past, present, and future in cross-cultural psychology: Selected proceedings from the 14th International Congress of the International Association for Cross-Cultural Psychology* (pp. 205–217). Lisse, Netherlands: Swets & Zeitlinger.

Mischel, W. (1968). *Personality and assessment.* New York: Wiley.

Mischel, W., & Peake, P.K. (1982). Beyond deja vu in the search for cross-situational consistency. *Psychological Review, 89*, 730–755.

Mischel, W., & Shoda, Y. (1995). A cognitive-affective system theory of personality: Reconceptualizing situations, dispositions, dynamics, and invariance in personality structure. *Psychological Review, 102*, 246–268.

Morf, C., & Rhodewalt, F. (2001). Unraveling the paradoxes of narcissism: A dynamic self-regulatory processing model. *Psychological Inquiry, 12*, 177–196.

Shoda, Y., Mischel, W., & Wright, J.C. (1994). Intraindividual stability in the organization and patterning of behavior: Incorporating psychological situations into the idiographic analysis of personality. *Journal of Personality and Social Psychology, 65*, 1023–1035.

Shoda, Y., & Tiernan, S. (in press). Searching for order within a person's stream of thoughts, feelings, and behaviors over time and across situations. In D. Cervone & W. Mischel (Eds.), *Advances in personality science* (Vol. 1). New York: Guilford.

Vansteelandt, K., & Van Mechelen, I. (1998). Individual differences in situation-behavior profiles: A triple typology model. *Journal of Personality and Social Psychology, 75*, 751–765.

Feedback Interventions: Toward the Understanding of a Double-Edged Sword

Avraham N. Kluger and Angelo DeNisi[1]

School of Business Administration, The Hebrew University of Jerusalem, Jerusalem, Israel (A.N.K.), and Department of Management, Texas A&M University, College Station, Texas (A.D.)

Feedback intervention (FI), that is, providing people with some information regarding their task performance, is one of the mostly widely applied psychological interventions. Yet there is a growing body of evidence that such interventions yield highly variable effects on performance (Ilgen, Fisher, & Taylor, 1979; Kluger & DeNisi, 1996; Latham & Locke, 1991; Salmoni, Schmidt, & Walter, 1984). Indeed, in a meta-analysis, we found that although FIs improve performance on average, they reduce performance in more than one third of the cases (Kluger & DeNisi, 1996; see Fig. 1). The latter fact is contrary to the common belief that FIs most often improve performance. Furthermore, we (Kluger & DeNisi, 1996) found no evidence that information about failure (negative FIs) and information about success (positive FIs) have differential effects, on average, on performance. In summary, the data suggest that, at least under certain circumstances, FIs can impair performance and that the processes through which FIs affect performance require more than simple explanations.

Although FIs are widely used (e.g., performance appraisals, grades, teaching evaluations), little is known about how they work. As a result, psychologists do not understand when and why FIs might have negative rather than positive (or no) effects on performance. In the present article, we offer an initial explanation of the effects produced by FIs, drawing upon three theoretical constructs that have been developed in connection with control theory: the regulation of feedback-standard discrepancies, locus of attention, and task complexity. These theoretical constructs pertain mostly to the motivational processes induced by FI. The learning processes induced by FI are beyond the scope of this review.[2] We begin by tracing the development of the assumption that FIs are always highly effective interventions (for a more thorough review, see Kluger & DeNisi, 1996).

BRIEF HISTORICAL REVIEW

Two figures probably contributed the most to the belief that FIs almost always improve performance: Thorndike and Ammons. Thorndike (1913) provided the initial theoretical arguments for the effectiveness of feedback with his law of effect. This theoretical perspective equated a positive FI with reinforcement and a negative FI with punishment (Thorndike, 1927). Both a positive FI and a negative FI should improve performance because one reinforces the correct behavior and the other punishes the incorrect behavior.

Although several reports were empirically consistent with these predictions (e.g., Thorndike, 1927), the law of effect was never sufficiently detailed to account for the inconsistent findings. For example, Thorndike (1913, p. 286) noted that school grades can impede learning, but he suggested that their normative nature (comparison with others) and their low level of specificity attenuate their effectiveness as FIs. The effect of norms cannot be explained by the law of effect, even though the effects of norms are consistent with empirically supported theories linking normative FI with ego involvement ("how well am I doing relative to other people?") versus task involvement ("how can I improve my performance?") (cf. Butler, 1987).

Furthermore, the specificity feature of the law of effect, which suggests that as the FI becomes more specific, its effect on performance becomes more positive, is inconsistent with some data. To salvage the specificity argument, some researchers suggested that moderate levels of specificity have the most positive effects on performance (e.g., Salmoni et al., 1984). Yet this revised argument, too, has not received consistent support. In conclusion, the law of effect generated a sizable empirical literature (cf. the review and criticism by Annett, 1969) because it has the advantage of parsimony, but it appears to be too broad to explain the empirical complexities associated with FI.

Ammons's contribution to the belief that FIs are almost always effective stems from his authoritative article on the effectiveness of feedback (Ammons, 1956). This highly cited review summarized the results of 50 years of literature regarding knowledge of performance (KP), also referred to as knowledge of results (KR). (These old terms refer to a form of FI.) Ammons offered two broad statements: KP increases learning, and KP increases motivation. However, his work suffered from three drawbacks. First, he did not explore evidence inconsistent with his generalizations. An example of the partial support for his conclusion regarding learning can be found in his report of Pressey's work on the self-scoring device. The self-scoring device was a mechanical device—used in the pre-computer days—that allowed students to see the correctness of their answers to multiple-choice exams. That is, the self-scoring device provided a type of KP (or FI). Ammons (1956) duly noted Pressey's (1950) conclusion that the immediate self-scoring device improves learning in most cases, but ignored Pressey's report that this device decreased learning in some others (e.g., learning of Russian vocabulary). Second, some of Ammons's conclusions were based on little evidence. For example, the support for his conclusion regarding the effects of KP on motivation was questionable, at best. Specifically, he admitted that the support for the effects of KP on motivation "has been collected informally" and is "inferred" from other findings (p. 285). He suggested that the fact that people often like to receive feedback is evidence for the positive effect of KP on performance. That is, he confused the motivation to hear the feedback with the motivation to improve performance. Finally, Ammons's review of the literature was not comprehensive. He did not even refer to some troubling studies that were inconsistent with his major conclusions (for sources dating back to 1906, see Kluger & DeNisi, 1996).

After Ammons's review, empirical inconsistencies continued to accumulate. But although a few scholars carefully noted these inconsistencies (e.g., Ilgen et al., 1979), the view that has dominated thinking about FIs during the second half of the 20th century is well typified by the following statement: "The positive effect of FB [feedback] on performance has become one of the most accepted principles in psychology" (Pritchard, Jones, Roth, Stuebing, & Ekeberg, 1988, p. 338).

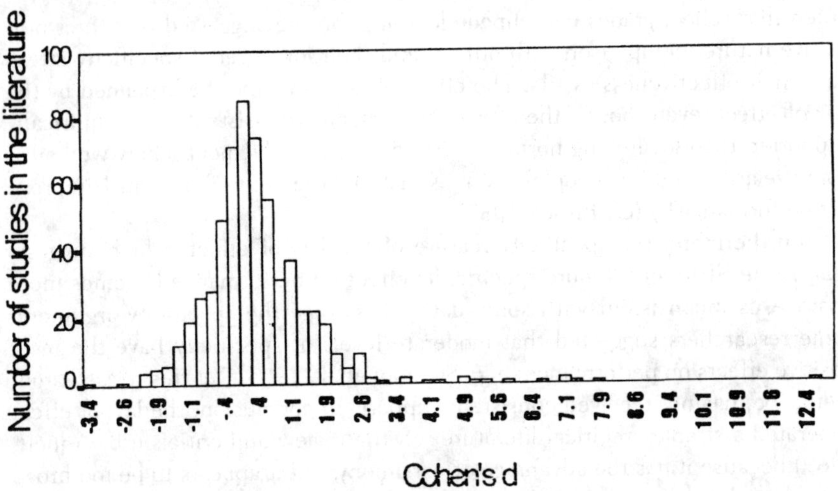

Fig. 1. Distribution of 607 comparisons of performance levels of people who received feedback intervention and people who did not receive feedback intervention. The performance differences are expressed in standard deviation units (*d* values); positive values indicate that the feedback intervention improved performance, and negative values indicate that the feedback intervention debilitated performance.

This brief historical review illustrates that the effects of FI on performance have never been consistent or simple. Moreover, it underscores the fact that there is really very little theory concerning how FI might affect performance. As a result, to understand the effects of FI on performance, researchers need to develop theoretical propositions about the processes that mediate between the FI stimulus and performance. We hope that the theoretical considerations we discuss here will begin to generate research aimed at understanding these processes better.

Our theoretical suggestions are based on control theory (Carver & Scheier, 1981), but also depend heavily on feedback intervention theory (FIT; Kluger & DeNisi, 1996). FIT has three basic arguments that are relevant here: (a) behavior is regulated by comparisons of feedback with goals or standards (and identification of gaps between the two); (b) attention is limited, and only those feedback-standard gaps that receive attention actively participate in behavior regulation; and (c) FIs change the locus of attention and therefore affect behavior.

DISCREPANCIES

Both control theory and FIT claim that behavior is regulated through the control of discrepancies or errors in the system. When a self-regulating system detects discrepancies or errors, the system is motivated to reduce or lower the perceived discrepancies. Even among competing cognitive theories, the detection and evaluation of feedback-standard (or feedback-goal) discrepancies is considered a fundamental source for motivational processes.

However, most cognitive treatments of the process of discrepancy reduction are indifferent to the valence (positive vs. negative) of the discrepancy. That is, these views suggest that effects are symmetrical, and that both a positive discrepancy and a negative discrepancy yield a self-regulatory action that is a function of the absolute magnitude of the discrepancy. Similarly, behaviorism (Thorndike, 1927) has symmetrical predictions, in that rewards and punishment can produce learning equally.

Other theorists have argued, however, that the reaction to positive and negative events is vastly different (cf. Taylor, 1991). That is, they contend that the direction of the feedback-standard discrepancy has major consequences, that reinforcement and punishment have different and asymmetric effects on behavior (Taylor, 1991).

Yet, despite these disagreements, the theories that emphasize symmetry actually recognize asymmetry, and vice versa (for more details, see Kluger, in press). Thus, both theoretical approaches may be correct. People may possess parallel systems that in concert support survival; one operates with symmetric rules and the other with asymmetric rules. These systems may contain both affective and cognitive subsystems. Indeed, the more positive is the direction of the feedback-standard discrepancy (overshooting vs. undershooting the standard), the higher is the resultant pleasantness (the most salient dimension of affect; Kluger, Lewinsohn, & Aiello, 1994) and the amount of nontask (other) thoughts (Kluger, in press). These effects are asymmetrical about the standard. In contrast, the larger the absolute size of the feedback-standard discrepancy (regardless of direction), the higher the resultant arousal (the second dimension of affect; Kluger et al., 1994) and the amount of task-related thoughts (Kluger, in press). These effects are symmetrical about the standard.

Thus, we can offer an initial explanation for the perplexing finding that the valence of feedback does not have a simple moderating effect on FI effectiveness. We suggest that it does not have a simple effect because it activates two response systems, one that responds to valence symmetrically and one that responds asymmetrically. The coexistence of two types of responses to FIs hints that these processes may have different effects on performance (e.g., pleasantness may enhance creativity, but arousal may debilitate it). Understanding the role of these systems in mediating the effects of FIs on performance awaits more theoretical development and empirical investigation.

LOCUS OF ATTENTION

The second relevant theoretical construct is locus of attention. We assume that FIs are interventions with high potential to change locus of attention and that knowing where attention is directed provides a better position to predict FIs' effects on performance. That is, after receiving feedback, an individual is very likely to be thinking about something different from what he or she was thinking about before receiving the intervention. Attention can be directed to the self, to the task at hand, or even to the details of the task at hand. We predicted that when FIs cause attention to be directed to the self, the risk that FIs will debilitate, rather than enhance, performance increases (Kluger & DeNisi, 1996).

Our reasoning was that attention to the self can attenuate the effects of FIs because it depletes cognitive resources necessary for task performance (Kanfer & Ackerman, 1989) and produces affective reactions that may interfere with task performance. Therefore, we hypothesized that FIs that contain cues that direct attention to the self, or that are given in a self-threatening environment, will produce weak or even negative effects on performance. Indeed, both FIs that contain praise and FIs that contain destructive criticism (which are likely to direct attention to the self) yield lower performance effects than FIs that do not contain cues to the self (Kluger & DeNisi, 1996). Moreover, we have shown that other cues that are likely to direct attention to the self are correlated with attenuated effects of FIs on performance (e.g., verbal FIs vs. computerized FIs).

Attention is sometimes directed to the self via normative cues, that is, cues that make the individual compare himself or herself to other people (as percentile scores do). Evidence showing that FIs that direct attention to the self via normative cues are largely ineffective is found in education research. For example, traditional teacher evaluation forms appear to have little effectiveness for developing college professors (Marsh & Roche, 1997). When these forms are used, professors usually receive information on their standing relative to their peers. In contrast, developmental efforts that rate the individual on various performance dimensions that highlight his or her weaknesses and strengths appear to be more effective (Marsh & Roche, 1997). Similarly, in one study, grades increased ego involvement, but did not affect performance relative to a control condition with no FI, whereas task-focused FI (specific comments) increased task involvement and consequently performance (Butler, 1987).

Although attention to the self can debilitate the effectiveness of FIs, this need not always be the case. There are two factors—one cognitive and one motivational—that may determine whether an FI that directs attention to the self has an enhanced effect: the type of task being performed (discussed in the next section) and the types of self-goals activated by the FI. Self-goals may be better understood in light of Higgins's classification of the self into actual, ideal, and ought self (e.g., Higgins, 1997). The actual self is what a person believes he or she is, the ideal self is what a person believes he or she wishes to be, and the ought self is what a person believes he or she should be. According to Higgins, people can pay attention, among other things, to discrepancies between the actual and the ideal self or to discrepancies between the actual and the ought self. Attention to discrepancies from the ideal self focuses people on promotion goals (possible gains), and leads people to try to attain their ideals (which in our view can never be reached if defined broadly as wishes and dreams). In contrast, attention to discrepancies from the ought self focuses people on prevention goals (possible losses), and leads people to try to meet socially prescribed task standards. Consequently, the reaction to FIs that direct attention to the self will depend largely on the aspect of the self that becomes salient.

Specifically, when attention is focused on the ought self, people will compare the feedback to their ought standard, that is, their perceived obligation. The result of the comparison will push performance toward the standard: Feedback about superior performance will be followed by performance decline, and feedback about inferior performance will be followed by performance improvement. In other words, people receiving positive feedback reduce performance, and people receiving negative feedback improve performance. Such effects are well known, and have been observed both in laboratory experiments (Podsakoff

& Farh, 1989) and in field studies of reactions to performance appraisals (e.g., Reilly, Smither, & Vasilopoulos, 1996).

In contrast to FIs that direct attention to discrepancies from the ought standard, FIs that direct attention to discrepancies from the ideal standard are likely to yield feedback with negative valence only. We hypothesize such an effect because we assume that ideals, as opposed to obligations, can never be achieved. (Our definition of ideals refers to wishes and dreams and is more inclusive than Higgins's definition of ideals as aspirations that can be achieved.) In fact, we obtained data consistent with our argument that ideals cannot be achieved. Specifically, in a small-scale experiment ($N = 21$), we asked students to mark an endpoint on a line reflecting the size of either their actual-ideal discrepancy or their actual-ought discrepancy. The length of the actual-ideal discrepancy line was 42 mm (35%) longer than the actual-ought discrepancy line, $t(19) = 1.91$ $p < .05$, one-tailed. If an FI directs people's attention to a comparison of the actual and ideal selves, they are likely to assess the gap as negative, and they will be motivated to increase activities that will narrow the perceived actual-ideal discrepancies (albeit only as long as the gap is perceived to be bridgeable). We suspect that FIs focusing on the ideal self are common in various developmental training programs (e.g., the Center for Creative Leadership; Guthrie & Kelly-Radford, in press).

An interesting applied question is how organizations can make their employees frame their jobs as part of their ideals and not as part of their obligations. A partial answer to this question may lie in the leadership literature that contrasts transformational (charismatic) leaders with transactional (more typical) leaders (e.g., Howell & Avolio, 1993). That is, charismatic leaders are thought to direct the attention of their followers to their ideals, whereas traditional leaders are thought to direct attention to the obligation of the follower to a contractual transaction with the leader. Therefore, future research should test whether various FI cues are interpreted when attention is directed to various self-loci and whether they, consequently, produce different motivational and performance outcomes.

TASK PROPERTIES

The final theoretical construct that should be taken into account in trying to understand how FIs affect performance is task properties. Analyses that we conducted (Kluger & DeNisi, 1996) indicated that the effectiveness of an FI depends on the type of task, yet we do not have a theory that successfully differentiates among task types. For example, we do not know what crucial features result in the different effects of FIs regarding tennis playing and FIs regarding managing a group of employees. Resorting to a simple classification, we can, however, consider task mastery (subjective difficulty) and task complexity (objective difficulty; e.g., remembering 5 cues vs. 15 cues). From the perspective of control theory, FIs that direct attention to the self on complex tasks deplete the resources needed for task performance and direct some of these resources to self-related goals (e.g., self-enhancement). In contrast, FIs that direct attention to the self on simple tasks may augment performance in a manner similar to social facilitation effects. (Social facilitation effects are the effects of the presence of other people on performance: Performance of subjectively simple tasks is facilitated, and performance of subjectively complex tasks is hindered.) Indeed, our analyses suggest that the effects of FIs grow more positive either as the task becomes more subjectively familiar or as it becomes more objectively simple. Ironically, then, people who probably need feedback the most benefit the least from typical FIs. These findings are consistent with findings regarding other motivational interventions whose performance benefits are attenuated or even reversed as task complexity increases (cf. Kanfer & Ackerman, 1989).

There are two new avenues to explore regarding how task properties moderate the effects of FIs on performance. First, a motivational intervention can have opposing effects on various components of task performance. Kairi (1996) measured both reaction time (time from stimulus onset to release of a finger from a waiting key) and movement time (time from finger release to hitting the target) in an "odd man out" task. Participants were asked, in each trial, to choose from among three lights the one that was the greatest distance from the other two. Kairi manipulated social facilitation by having an experimenter sit next to the participants in the experimental group and by letting participants in the control group perform alone in a room. The presence of the experimenter improved movement time, but slowed (insignificantly) reaction time. Perhaps the difficulty in finding performance effects of FIs is due, in part, to their opposing effects on different components of overall task performance.

The second avenue to be explored is based on the distinction between two cognitive systems. Many scholars recognize that some cognitions are governed by a rational or rule-based system, and others are governed by an association-based or experiential-based system (Sloman, 1996). The rational system may be more susceptible to resource depletion, and hence tasks that are largely dependent on this system may be more susceptible to negative effects on performance. This is another possibility that awaits empirical research.

PRACTICAL IMPLICATIONS

Our review suggests that FIs can be double-edged swords. Practitioners may ask what they can do to minimize the documented risks associated with FIs. One clear answer lies in using FIs only in combination with goal-setting intervention. Providing FIs that relate to previously established goals is likely to direct attention to the task at hand and not to the self. Indeed, both our meta-analysis and other reviews (Kluger & DeNisi, 1996) suggest that a goal-setting intervention augments FIs' effects on performance. Moreover, we have found that employees who wish to have more feedback than they are receiving often suffer from the absence of clear goals. Similarly, current models of effective training evaluation emphasize that building measures for evaluation requires a process of need analysis and goal setting. It seems that providing FIs without clear goals increases the risk that the recipient's goals will not be those intended by the FI provider. But, perhaps more critically, we also suggest that the practitioner interested in developing and implementing FIs take the time to test the effectiveness of these interventions rather than simply assuming that they will work.

Recommended Reading

Balzer, W.K., Doherty, M.E., & O'Connor, R., Jr. (1989). (See References)
Kluger, A.N., & DeNisi, A. (1996). (See References)
Salmoni, A.W., Schmidt, R.A., & Walter, C.B. (1984). (See References)

Acknowledgments—The work reported here was supported by a grant from the Israel Foundations Trustees and by a grant from the Recanati Fund of the School of Business Administration at the Hebrew University.

Notes

1. Address correspondence to Avraham N. Kluger, School of Business Administration, The Hebrew University–Mt. Scopus, Jerusalem 91905, Israel; e-mail: mskluger@pluto.mscc.huji.ac.il.

2. Detrimental FI effects on learning processes have been noted with respect to learning of judgment tasks (for a review, see Balzer, Doherty, & O'Connor, 1989), motor skills (Salmoni et al., 1984), and other tasks (Kluger & DeNisi, 1996).

References

Ammons, R.B. (1956). Effects of knowledge of performance: A survey and tentative theoretical formulation. *Journal of General Psychology, 54*, 279–299.

Annett, J. (1969). *Feedback and human behaviour.* Harmondsworth, England: Penguin.

Balzer, W.K., Doherty, M.E., & O'Connor, R., Jr. (1989). Effects of cognitive feedback on performance. *Psychological Bulletin, 106*, 410–433.

Butler, R. (1987). Task-involving and ego-involving properties of evaluation: Effects of different feedback conditions on motivational perceptions, interest, and performance. *Journal of Educational Psychology, 79*, 474–482.

Carver, C.S., & Scheier, M.F. (1981). *Attention and self regulation: A control theory of human behavior.* New York: Springer-Verlag.

Guthrie, V.A., & Kelly-Radford, L. (in press). Developing leaders with a feedback intensive program. In C.D. McCauley, R. Moxley, & E. Van Velsor (Eds.), *The Center for Creative Leadership handbook of leadership development.* San Francisco: Jossey-Bass.

Higgins, E.T. (1997). Beyond pleasure and pain. *American Psychologist, 52*, 1280–1300.

Howell, J.M., & Avolio, B.J. (1993). Transformational leadership, transactional leadership, locus of control, and support for innovation: Key predictors of consolidated-business-unit performance. *Journal of Applied Psychology, 78*, 891–902.

Ilgen, D.R., Fisher, C.D., & Taylor, M.S. (1979). Consequences of individual feedback on behavior in organizations. *Journal of Applied Psychology, 64*, 349–361.

Kairi, B. (1996). *The moderating effect of social facilitation on the relationship of response time and intelligence.* Unpublished master's thesis, The Hebrew University of Jerusalem, Jerusalem, Israel.

Karifer, R., & Ackerman, P.L. (1989). Motivation and cognitive abilities: An integration/aptitude-treatment interaction approach to skill acquisition. *Journal of Applied Psychology, 74*, 657–690.

Kluger, A.N. (in press). Feedback-expectation discrepancy, arousal and locus of cognition. In M. Erez, U. Kleinbeck, & H. Thierry (Eds.), *Work motivation in the context of a globalizing economy.* Mahwah, NJ: Erlbaum.

Kluger, A.N., & DeNisi, A. (1996). The effects of feedback interventions on performance: Historical review, a meta-analysis and a preliminary feedback intervention theory. *Psychological Bulletin, 119*, 254–284.

Kluger, A.N., Lewinsohn, S., & Aiello, J. (1994). The influence of feedback on mood: Linear effects on pleasantness and curvilinear effects on arousal. *Organizational Behavior and Human Decision Processes, 60*, 276–299.

Latham, G.P., & Locke, E.A. (1991). Self-regulation through goal setting. *Organizational Behavior and Human Decision Processes, 50*, 212–247.

Marsh, H.W., & Roche, L.A. (1997). Making students' evaluations of teaching effectiveness effective: The critical issues of validity, bias, and utility. *American Psychologist, 52*, 1187–1197.

Podsakoff, P.M., & Farh, J.H. (1989). Effects of feedback sign and credibility on goal setting and task performance. *Organizational Behavior and Human Decision Processes, 44*, 45–67.

Pressey, S.L. (1950). Development and appraisal of devices providing immediate automatic scoring of objective tests and concomitant self-instruction. *Journal of Psychology, 29*, 417–447.

Pritchard, R.D., Jones, S.D., Roth, P.L., Stuebing, K.K., & Ekeberg, S.E. (1988). Effects of group feedback, goal setting, and incentives on organizational productivity [Monograph]. *Journal of Applied Psychology, 73*, 337–358.

Reilly, R.R., Smither, J.W., & Vasilopoulos, N.L. (1996). A longitudinal study of upward feedback. *Personnel Psychology, 49*, 599–612.

Salmoni, A.W., Schmidt, R.A., & Walter, C.B. (1984). Knowledge of results and motor learning: A review and critical reappraisal. *Psychological Bulletin, 95*, 355–386.

Sloman, S.A. (1996). The empirical case for two systems of reasoning. *Psychological Bulletin, 119*, 3–22.

Taylor, S.E. (1991). Asymmetrical effects of positive and negative events: The mobilization-minimization hypothesis. *Psychological Bulletin, 110*, 67–85.

Thorndike, E.L. (1913). *Educational psychology: Vol. 1. The original nature of man.* New York: Teachers College, Columbia University.

Thorndike, E.L. (1927). The law of effect. *American Journal of Psychology, 39*, 212–222.

Computer- and Internet-Based Psychotherapy Interventions

C. Barr Taylor[1] and Kristine H. Luce

Department of Psychiatry, Stanford University Medical Center, Stanford, California

Abstract

Computers and Internet-based programs have great potential to make psychological assessment and treatment more cost-effective. Computer-assisted therapy appears to be as effective as face-to-face treatment for treating anxiety disorders and depression. Internet support groups also may be effective and have advantages over face-to-face therapy. However, research on approach remains meager.

Keywords

computer applications; Internet applications; psychotherapy and technology

In recent years, the increasing number of users of computer and Internet technology has greatly expanded the potential of computer- and Internet-based therapy programs. Computer- and Internet-assisted assessment methods and therapy programs have the potential to increase the cost-effectiveness of standardized psychotherapeutic treatments by reducing contact time with the therapist, increasing clients' participation in therapeutic activities outside the standard clinical hour, and streamlining input and processing of clients' data related to their participation in therapeutic activities. Unfortunately, the scientific study of these programs has seriously lagged behind their purported potential, and these interventions pose important ethical and professional questions.

COMPUTER-BASED PROGRAMS

Information

A number of studies have demonstrated that computers can provide information effectively and economically. An analysis of a large number of studies of computer-assisted instruction (CAI) found that CAI is consistently effective in improving knowledge (Fletcher-Flinn & Gravatt, 1995). Surprisingly, few studies evaluating the use of CAI for providing information related to mental health or psychotherapy have been conducted.

Assessment

Traditional paper-based self-report instruments are easily adapted to the computer format and offer a number of advantages that include ensuring data completeness and standardization. Research has found that computer-administered assessment instruments work as well as other kinds of self-report instruments and as well as therapist-administered ones. Clients may feet less embarrassed about reporting sensitive or potentially stigmatizing information (e.g., about sexual behavior or illegal drug use) during a computer-assisted assessment than during a face-to-face assessment, allowing for more accurate estimates of mental health behaviors. Studies show that more symptoms, including suicidal thoughts, are reported during computer-assisted interviews than face-to-face interviews. Overall, the evidence suggests that computers can make assessments more efficient, more accurate, and less expensive. Yet computer-based assessment interviews do not allow for clinical intuition and nuance, assessment of behavior, and nonverbal emotional expression, nor do they foster a therapeutic alliance between client and therapist as information is collected.

Recently, handheld computers or personal digital assistants (PDAs) have been used to collect real-time, naturalistic data on a variety of variables. For example, clients can record their thoughts, behaviors, mood, and other variables at the same time and when directed to do so by an alarm or through instructions from the program. The assessment of events as they occur avoids retrospective recall biases. PDAs can be programmed to beep to cue a response and also to check data to determine, for instance, if responses are in the right range. The data are easily downloaded into computer databases for further analysis. PDAs with interactive transmission capabilities further expand the potential for real-time data collection. Although PDAs have been demonstrated to be useful for research, they have not been incorporated into clinical practice.

Computer-Assisted Psychotherapy

Much research on computer-based programs has focused on anxiety disorders (Newman, Consoli, & Taylor, 1997). Researchers have developed computer programs that direct participants through exercises in relaxation and restfulness; changes in breathing frequency, regularity, and pattern; gradual and progressive exposure to aspects of the situation, sensation, or objects they are afraid of; and changes in thinking patterns. Although the majority of studies report symptom reduction, most are uncontrolled trials or case studies and have additional methodological weaknesses (e.g., small sample sizes, no follow-up to assess whether treatment gains are maintained, focus on individuals who do not have clinical diagnoses).

Computer programs have been developed to reduce symptoms of simple phobias, panic disorder, obsessive-compulsive disorder (OCD), generalized anxiety disorder, and social phobia. In a multicenter, international treatment trial (Kenardy et al., 2002), study participants who received a primary diagnosis of panic disorder were randomly assigned to one of four groups: (a) a group that received 12 sessions of therapist-delivered cognitive behavior therapy (CBT), (b) a group that received 6 sessions of therapist-delivered CBT augmented by use of a handheld computer, (c) a group that received 6 sessions of therapist-delivered CBT augmented with a manual, or (d) a control group that was assigned to a wait list. Assessments at the end of treatment and 6 months later showed that the 12-session CBT and the 6-session CBT with the computer were equally effective. The results suggested that use of a handheld computer can reduce therapist contact time without compromising outcomes and may speed the rate of improvement.

An interactive computer program was developed to help clients with OCD, which is considered one type of anxiety disorder. The computer provided three weekly 45-min sessions of therapy involving vicarious exposure to their obsessive thoughts and response prevention (a technique by which clients with OCD are taught and encouraged not to engage in their customary rituals when they have an urge to do so). Compared with a control group, the clients who received the intervention had significantly greater improvement in symptoms. In a follow-up study with clients diagnosed with OCD, computer-guided telephone behavior therapy was effective; however, clinician-guided behavior therapy was even more effective. Thus, computer-guided behavior therapy can be a helpful first step in treating patients with OCD, particularly when clinician-guided behavior therapy is unavailable. Computers have also been used to help treat individuals with other anxiety disorders, including social phobia and generalized anxiety disorder, a condition characterized by excessive worry and constant anxiety without specific fears or avoidances.

CBT also has been adapted for the computer-delivered treatment of depressive disorders. Selmi, Klein, Greist, Sorrell, and Erdman (1990) conducted the only randomized, controlled treatment trial comparing computer- and therapist-administered CBT for depression. Participants who met the study's criteria for major, minor, or intermittent depressive disorder were randomly assigned to computer-administered CBT, therapist-administered CBT, or a wait-list control. Compared with the control group, both treatment groups reported significant improvements on depression indices. The treatment groups did not differ from each other, and treatment gains were maintained at a 2-month follow-up.

Little information exists on the use of computer-assisted therapy for treating patients with complicated anxiety disorders or other mental health problems. Thus, further study is needed.

THE INTERNET

Internet-based programs have several advantages over stand-alone computer-delivered programs. The Internet makes health care information and programs accessible to individuals who may have economic, transportation, or other restrictions that limit access to face-to-face services. The Internet is constantly available and accessible from a variety of locations. Because text and other information on the Internet can be presented in a variety of formats, languages, and styles, and at various educational levels, it is possible to tailor messages to the learning preferences and strengths of the user. The Internet can facilitate the collection, coordination, dissemination, and interpretation of data. These features allow for interactivity among the various individuals (e.g., physicians, clients, family members, caregivers) who may participate in a comprehensive treatment plan. As guidelines, information, and other aspects of programs change, it is possible to rapidly update information on Web pages. The medium also allows for personalization of information. Users may select features and information most relevant to them, and, conversely, programs can automatically determine a user's needs and strengths and display content accordingly.

Information

Patients widely search the Internet for mental health information. For example, the National Institute of Mental Health (NIMH) public information Web site receives more than 7 million "hits" each month. However, the mental health information on commercial Web sites is often inaccurate, misleading, or related to commercial interests. Sites sponsored by nonprofit organizations provide better and more balanced information, but search engines often list for-profit sites before they generate nonprofit sites. Furthermore, education Web sites rarely follow solid pedagogical principles.

Screening and Assessment

Many mental health Web sites have implemented screening programs that assess individuals for signs or symptoms of various psychiatric disorders. These programs generally recommend that participants who score above a predetermined cutoff contact a mental health provider for further assessment. The NIMH and many other professional organizations provide high-quality, easily accessible information combined with screening instruments. Houston and colleagues (2001) evaluated the use of a Web site that offered a computerized version of the Center for Epidemiological Studies' depression scale (CES-D; Ogles, France, Lunnen, Bell, & Goldfarb, 1998). The scale was completed 24,479 times during the 8-month study period. Fifty-eight percent of participants screened positive for depression, and fewer than half of those had previously been treated for depression. The Internet can incorporate interactive screening, which already has been extensively developed for desktop computers. Screening can then be linked to strategies that are designed to increase the likelihood that a participant will accept a referral and initiate further assessment or treatment.

On-Line Support Groups

Because Internet-delivered group interventions can be accessed constantly from any location that has Internet access, they offer distinct advantages over their face-to-face counterparts. Face-to-face support groups often are difficult to schedule, meet at limited times and locations, and must accommodate inconsistent attendance patterns because of variations in participants' health status and schedules. On-line groups have the potential to help rural residents and individuals who are chronically ill or physically or psychiatrically disabled increase their access to psychological interventions.

A wide array of social support groups is available to consumers in synchronous (i.e., participants online at the same time) or asynchronous formats. The Pew Internet and American Life Project (www.pewinternet.org) estimated that 28% of Internet users have attended an on-line support group for a medical condition or personal problem on at least one occasion. After a morning television show featured Edward M. Kennedy, Jr., promoting free on-line support groups sponsored by the Wellness Community (www.wellness-community.org), the organization received more than 440,000 inquiries during the following week! The majority of published studies on Internet-based support groups suggest that the groups are beneficial; however, scientific understanding of how and when is limited. Studies that examine the patterns of discourse that occur in these groups indicate that members' communication is similar to that found in face-to-face support groups (e.g., high levels of mutual support, acceptance, positive feelings).

Only a few controlled studies have examined the effects of Internet-based support programs. One such study investigated the effects of a program named Bosom Buddies on reducing psychosocial distress in women with breast cancer (Winzelberg et al., in press). Compared with a wait-list control group, the intervention group reported significantly reduced depression, cancer-related trauma, and perceived stress.

On-Line Consultation

On-line consultation with "experts" is readily available on the Internet. There are organizations for on-line therapists (e.g., the International Society for Mental Health Online, www.ismpo.org) and sites that verify the credentials of on-line providers. However, little is known about the efficacy, reach, utility, or other aspects of on-line consultation.

Advocacy

The Internet has become an important medium for advocacy and political issues. Many organizations use the Internet to facilitate communication among members and to encourage members to support public policy (e.g., the National Alliance for the Mentally III, www.nami.org).

Internet-Based Psychotherapy

The Internet facilitates the creation of treatment programs that combine a variety of interactive components. The basic components that can be combined include psychoeducation; social support; chat groups; monitoring of symptoms, progress, and use of the program; feedback; and interactions with providers. Although many psychotherapy programs developed for desktop computers and manuals are readily translatable to the Internet format, surprisingly few have been adapted in this way, and almost none have been evaluated. Studies show that Internet-based treatments are effective for reducing symptoms of panic disorder. Compared with patients in a wait-list control group, those who participated in an Internet-based posttraumatic stress group reported significantly greater improvements on trauma-related symptoms. During the initial 6-month period of operation, an Australian CBT program for depression, MoodGYM, had more than 800,000 hits (Christensen, Griffiths, & Korten, 2002). In an uncontrolled study of a small subsample of participants who registered on this site, program use was associated with significant decreases in anxiety and depression. Internet-based programs also have been shown to reduce symptoms of eating disorders and associated behaviors. Users consistently report high satisfaction with these programs.

Treatment programs for depression, mood swings, and other mental health disorders are being designed to blend computer-assisted psychotherapy and psychoeducation with case management (in which a therapist helps to manage a client's problems by following treatment and therapy guidelines) and telephone-based care. These programs might also include limited face-to-face interventions, medication, and support groups. The effectiveness of these programs remains to be demonstrated.

Eventually, the most important use of the Internet might be to deliver integrated, home-based, case-managed, psychoeducational programs that are combined with some face-to-face contact and support groups. Unfortunately, all though a number of such programs are "under development," none have been evaluated in controlled trials.

ETHICAL AND PROFESSIONAL ISSUES

Web-based interventions present a number of ethical and professional issues (Hsiung, 2001). Privacy is perhaps the most significant concern. The Internet creates an environment where information about patients can be easily accessed and disseminated. Patients may purposely or inadvertently disclose private information about themselves and, in on-line support groups, about their peers. Although programs can be password-protected, and electronic records must follow federal privacy guidelines, participants must be clearly informed that confidentiality of records cannot be guaranteed.

Internet interventions create the potential that services will be provided to patients who have not been seen by a professional or who live in other states or countries where the professionals providing the services are not licensed to provide therapy. Professional organizations are struggling to develop guidelines to address these concerns (e.g., Hsiung, 2001; Kane & Sands, 1998).

Because of its accessibility and relative anonymity, patients may use the Internet during crises and report suicidal and homicidal thoughts. Although providers who use Internet support groups develop statements to clearly inform patients that the medium is not to be used for psychiatric emergencies, patients may ignore these instructions. Thus, providers need to identify ancillary procedures to reduce and manage potential crises.

Given the continuing advances in technology and the demonstrated effectiveness and advantages of computer- and Internet-based interventions, one might expect that providers would readily integrate these programs into their standard care practice. Yet few do, in part because programs that are easy to install and use are not available, there is no professional or market demand for the use of computer-assisted therapy, and practitioners may have ethical and professional concerns about applying this technology in their clinical practice. Thus, in the near future this technology may primarily be used for situations in which the cost-effectiveness advantages are particularly great.

CONCLUSION

Computers have the potential to make psychological assessments more efficient, more accurate, and less expensive. Computer-assisted therapy appears to be as effective as face-to-face therapy for treating anxiety disorders and depression and can be delivered at lower cost. However, applications of this technology are in the early stages.

A high priority is to clearly demonstrate the efficacy of this approach, particularly compared with standard face-to-face, "manualized" treatments that have been shown to be effective for common mental health disorders. Studies that compare two potentially efficacious treatments require large samples for us to safely conclude that the therapies are comparable if no statistically significant differences are found. Kenardy et al. (2002) demonstrated that multisite, international studies sampling large populations could be conducted relatively inexpensively, in part because the intervention they examined was standardized. If a treatment's efficacy is demonstrated, the next step would be to determine if the therapy, provided by a range of mental health professionals, is useful in large, diverse populations. Examination of combinations of therapies (e.g., CBT plus medication) and treatment modalities (Taylor, Cameron, Newman, & Junge, 2002) should follow. As the empirical study of this technology advances, research might examine the utility and cost-effectiveness of adapting these approaches to treating everyone in a community who wants therapy.

Continued use of the Internet to provide psychosocial support and group therapy is another promising avenue. As in the case of individual therapy, research is needed to compare the advantages and disadvantages between Internet and face-to-face groups, determine which patients benefit from which modality, compare the effectiveness of professionally moderated groups and self- or peer-directed groups, and compare the effectiveness of synchronous and asynchronous groups.

As research progresses, new and exciting applications can be explored. Because on-line text is stored, word content can be examined. This information may teach us more about the therapeutic process or may automatically alert providers to patients who are depressed, dangerous, or deteriorating.

Although research in many aspects of computer-assisted therapy is needed, and the professional and ethical concerns are substantial, computers and the Internet are likely to play a progressively important role in providing mental health assessment and interventions to clients. Thus, mental health professionals will need to decide how they will incorporate such programs into their practices.

Recommended Reading

Taylor, C.B., Winzelberg, A.J., & Celio, A.A. (2001). The use of interactive media to prevent eating disorders. In R.H. Striegal-Moore & L. Smolak (Eds.), *Eating disorders: Innovative directions in research and practice* (pp. 255–269). Washington, DC: American Psychological Association.

Yellowlees, P. (2001). *Your guide to e-health: Third millennium medicine on the Internet.* Brisbane, Australia: University of Queensland Press.

Note

1. Address correspondence to C. Barr Taylor, Department of Psychiatry, Stanford University Medical Center, Stanford, CA 94305-5722; e-mail: btaylor@stanford.edu.

References

Christensen, H., Griffiths, K.M., & Korten, A. (2002). Web-based cognitive behavior therapy: Analysis of site usage and changes in depression and anxiety scores. *Journal of Medical Internet Research, 4*(1), Article e3. Retrieved July 16, 2002, from http://www.jmir.org/2002/1/e3

Fletcher-Flinn, C.M., & Gravatt, B. (1995). The efficacy of computer assisted instruction (CAI): A meta-analysis. *Journal of Educational Computing Research,* 3, 219–241.

Houston, T.K., Cooper, L.A., Vu, H.T., Kahn, J., Toser, J., & Ford, D.E. (2001). Screening the public for depression through the Internet. *Psychiatric Services,* 52, 362–367.

Hsiung, R.C. (2001). Suggested principles of professional ethics for the online provision of mental health services. *Medinfo, 10,* 296–300.

Kane, B., & Sands, D.Z. (1998). Guidelines for the clinical use of electronic mail with patients: The AMIA Internet Working Group, Task Force on Guidelines for the Use of Clinic-Patient Electronic Mail. *Journal of the American Medical Informatics Association,* 5, 104–111.

Kenardy, J.A., Dow, M.G.T., Johnston, D.W., Newman, M.G., Thompson, A., & Taylor, C.B. (2002). *A comparison of delivery methods of cognitive behavioural therapy for panic disorder: An international multicentre trial.* Manuscript submitted for publication.

Newman, M.G., Consoli, A., & Taylor, C.B. (1997). Computers in assessment and cognitive behavioral treatment of clinical disorders: Anxiety as a case in point. *Behavior Therapy,* 28, 211–235.

Ogles, B.M., France, C.R., Lunnen, K.M., Bell, M.T., & Goldfarb, M. (1998). Computerized depression screening and awareness. *Community Mental Health Journal,* 34(1), 27–38.

Selmi, P.M., Klein, M.H., Greist, J.H., Sorrell, S.P., & Erdman, H.P. (1990). Computer-administered cognitive-behavioral therapy for depression. *American Journal of Psychiatry,* 147, 51–56.

Taylor, C.B., Cameron, R., Newman, M., & Junge, J. (2002). Issues related to combining risk factor reduction and clinical treatment for eating disorders in defined populations. *The Journal of Behavioral Health Services and Research,* 29, 81–90.

Winzelberg, A.J., Classen, C., Alpers, G., Roberts, H., Koopman, C., Adams, R., Ernst, H., Dev, P., & Taylor, C.B. (in press). An evaluation of an Internet support group for women with primary breast cancer. *Cancer.*

Depression, Anxiety, Dissociative Disorders, and Responses to Stress

The papers in this section of the reader are concerned with a variety of phenomena that are associated with anxiety and mood disorders. In one way or another, most focus on ways in which people respond to stressful experiences. All emphasize the combined effects of biological, psychological and social systems.

One interesting and important feature of both mood disorders and anxiety disorders is the fact that women are at least twice as likely as men to develop these problems. In her paper, Susan Nolen-Hoeksema reviews several possible explanations for these differences as they pertain to depression. She argues that women are more likely to become depressed because, in comparison to men, they are more often exposed to stressful experiences, such as sexual assault and harassment, and because these events lead to different patterns of response in women than in men. According to this perspective, women differ from men both in terms of their biological responses to stress as well as their typical ways of coping with stressful events.

The second paper, by Thomas Joiner, considers the possible impact of stressful events on one extreme form of behavior that is frequently associated with depression, i.e., suicide. Suicide takes many forms, and rates of suicide are influenced by many psychological and biological variables. Joiner's paper is concerned with a phenomenon that has been observed in some cases of suicide—clustering. Why do two or more people commit suicide at roughly the same time and place? Joiner's explanation points toward the joint effects of personal vulnerability factors and negative life events.

The third paper in this section is concerned with factors that are involved in the origins of anxiety disorders. Arne Öhman and Susan Mineka summarize their fascinating work which suggests that certain types of phobic disorders may involve a circuit in the brain that they call an "evolved fear module." In other words, people learn very quickly to associate intense fear with objects and situations, such as snakes, that have historically presented a severe threat to their survival.

The next papers are both concerned with one of the most controversial topics of our time: the effects of childhood sexual abuse. Many clinicians have argued that people who are sexually abused as children are more vulnerable to a number of mental disorders, including depression, anxiety, and dissociative disorders. The fourth and fifth papers in this section are concerned with one very specific debate about the consequences of sexual abuse. Can the person's memory for sexual abuse be repressed (become inaccessible to conscious awareness) for an extended period of time and then later be recovered? We have included two papers that address this issue because we believe that they will stimulate interesting discussions and encourage critical thinking. The first paper, by Jean Arrigo and Kathy Pezdek, reports several documented examples of memory disturbances following traumatic events, such as disasters, accidents, and combat. Of course, it risky to draw general conclusions about psychological processes from case studies, no matter how compelling the examples may be. The fact that some people have experienced amnesia following documented traumatic events does not prove that other undocumented examples of repressed memories are valid.

The other paper about repressed and recovered memories, written by Richard McNally, considers evidence from a number of studies that used personality questionnaires and cognitive tasks to compare four groups of women: those who suspected that they had repressed memories of prior abuse, those who had recovered explicit memories of abuse after long periods of not thinking about it, those with continuous memories who had never forgotten that they were abused, and a group of women who had not been abused. Data from these studies are discussed with regard to the possibility that, in some cases, recovered memories may be false.

The final paper in this section, by Susan Folkman and Judith Tedlie Moskowitz, takes an interesting and different perspective on the issue of reactions to stress. A course on abnormal psychology is primarily concerned with the negative impact of stressful life experiences. There are also times, however, when people are able to experience positive emotions in the face of chronic stress. How do they do it? Why is it sometimes possible to view negative experiences as a challenge rather than a threat? Folkman and Moskowitz have identified three types of coping that are associated with this adaptive response style.

Gender Differences in Depression

Susan Nolen-Hoeksema[1]

Department of Psychology, University of Michigan, Ann Arbor, Michigan

Abstract

From early adolescence through adulthood, women are twice as likely as men to experience depression. Many different explanations for this gender difference in depression have been offered, but none seems to fully explain it. Recent research has focused on gender differences in stress responses, arid in exposure to certain stressors. I review this research and describe how gender differences in stress experiences and stress reactivity may interact to create women's greater vulnerability to depression.

Keywords

gender; depression; stress

Across many nations, cultures, and ethnicities , women are about twice as likely as men to develop depression (Nolen-Hoeksema, 1990; Weissman et al., 1996). This is true whether depression is indexed as a diagnosed mental disorder or as subclinical symptoms. Diagnosable depressive disorders are extraordinarily common in women, who have a lifetime prevalence for major depressive disorder of 21.3%, compared with 12.7% in men (Kessler, McGonagle, Swartz, Blazer, & Nelson, 1993).

Most explanations for the gender difference in depression have focused on individual variables, and studies have attempted to show that one variable is better than another in explaining the difference. In three decades of research, however, no one variable has single-handedly accounted for the gender difference in depression. In recent years, investigators have moved toward more integrated models, taking a transactional, developmental approach. Transactional models are appropriate because it is clear that depression impairs social and occupational functioning, and thus can have a major impact on an individual's environment. Developmental models are appropriate because age groups differ markedly in the gender difference in depression. Girls are no more likely than boys to evidence depression in childhood, but by about age 13, girls' rates of depression begin to increase sharply, whereas boys' rates of depression remain low, and may even decrease. By late adolescence, girls are twice as likely as boys to be depressed, and this gender ratio remains more or less the same throughout adulthood. The absolute rates of depression in women and men vary substantially across the life span, however.

In this review, I focus on two themes in recent research. First, because women have less power and status than men in most societies, they experience certain traumas, particularly sexual abuse, more often than men. They also experience more chronic strains, such as poverty, harassment, lack of respect, and constrained choices. Second, even when women and men experience the same stressors, women may be more likely than men to develop depression because of gender differences in biological responses to stressors, self-concepts, or coping styles.

Frequent stressful experiences and reactivity to stress are likely to have reciprocal effects on each other. Stressful experiences can sensitize both biological and psychological systems to future stress, making it more likely that individuals will react with depression. In turn, reactivity to stress is associated with impaired problem solving, and, as a result, with the accumulation or generation of new stressors, which may contribute to more depression.

STRESSFUL LIFE EVENTS

Women's lack of social power makes them more vulnerable than men to specific major traumas, particularly sexual abuse. Traumas may contribute directly to depression, by making women feel they are helpless to control their lives, and may also contribute indirectly, by increasing women's reactivity to stress. Women's social roles also carry a number of chronic strains that might contribute directly or indirectly to depression. Major changes in the frequency of traumatic events and in social roles coincide with the emergence of gender differences in depression in adolescence, and may help to explain this emergence.

Victimization

Women are the victims of sexual assault—defined as being pressured or forced into unwanted sexual contact—at least twice as often as men, and people with a history of sexual assault have increased rates of depression (see Weiss, Longhurst, & Mazure, 1999). Sexual assault during childhood has been more consistently linked with the gender difference in depression than sexual assault that first occurs during adulthood. Estimates of the prevalence of childhood sexual assault range widely. Cutler and I reviewed the most methodologically sound studies including both male and female participants and found rates of childhood sexual assault between 7 and 19% for females and between 3 and 7% for males (Cutler & Nolen-Hoeksema, 1991). We estimated that, in turn, as much as 35% of the gender difference in adult depression could be accounted for by the higher incidence of assault of girls relative to boys. A few studies have examined whether depression might be an antecedent rather than a consequence of sexual assault. Depression does appear to increase risk for sexual assault in women and men, but sexual assault significantly increases risk for first or new onsets of depression.

Childhood sexual assault may increase risk for depression throughout the life span because abuse experiences negatively alter biological and psychological responses to stress (Weiss et al., 1999). Children and adolescents who have been abused, particularly those who have been repeatedly abused over an extended period of time, tend to have poorly regulated biological response to stress. Abuse experiences can also negatively alter children's and adolescents' perspectives on themselves and others, contributing to their vulnerability to depression (Zahn-Waxler, 2000).

Chronic Strains

Women face a number of chronic burdens in everyday life as a result of their social status and roles relative to men, and these strains could contribute to their higher rates of depression (see Nolen-Hoeksema, 1990). Women make less money than men, and are much more likely than men to live in poverty. Women are more likely than men to be sexually harassed on the job. Women often have full-time paid jobs and also do nearly all the child care and domestic work of the home. In addition, women are increasingly "sandwiched" between caring for young children and caring for sick and elderly family members. This role overload is said to contribute to a sense of "burn out" and general distress, including depressive symptoms, in women.

In the context of heterosexual relationships, some women face inequities in the distribution of power over important decisions that must be made, such as the decision to move to a new city, or the decision to buy an expensive item such as a car (Nolen-Hoeksema, Larson, & Grayson, 1999). Even when they voice their opinions, women may feel these opinions are not taken seriously, or that their viewpoints on important issues are not respected and affirmed by their partners. My colleagues and I measured chronic strain by grouping inequities in workload and heterosexual relationships into a single variable, and found that this variable predicted increases in depression over time, and partially accounted for the gender difference in depression (Nolen-Hoeksema et al., 1999). Depression also contributed to increased chronic strain over time, probably because it was associated with reductions in perceptions of control and effective problem solving.

Gender Intensification in Adolescence

Social pressure to conform to gender roles is thought to increase dramatically as children move through puberty. For girls, this may mean a reduction in their opportunities and choices, either real or perceived. According to adolescents' own reports, parents restrict girls' more than boys' behaviors and have lower expectations for girls' than for boys' competencies and achievements. Girls also feel that if they pursue male-stereotyped activities and preferences, such as interests in math and science or in competitive sports, they are rejected by their peers. For many girls, especially white girls, popularity and social acceptance become narrowly oriented around appearance.

This narrowing of acceptable behavior for girls in early adolescence may contribute to the increase in depression in girls at this time, although this popular theory has been the focus of remarkably little empirical research (Nolen-Hoeksema & Girgus, 1994). There is substantial evidence that excessive concern about appearance is negatively associated with wellbeing in girls, but these findings may apply primarily to white girls. In addition, very little research has examined whether appearance concerns and gender roles are risk factors for depression or only correlates.

REACTIVITY TO STRESS

Even when women and men are confronted with similar stressors, women may be more vulnerable than men to developing depression and related anxiety disorders such as posttraumatic stress disorder (Breslau, Davis, Andreski, Peterson, & Schultz, 1997). Women's greater reactivity compared with men's has been attributed to gender differences in biological responses, self-concepts, and coping styles.

Biological Responses to Stress

For many years, the biological explanations for women's greater vulnerability to depression focused on the direct effects of the ovarian hormones (especially estrogen and progesterone) on women's moods. This literature is too large and complicated to review here (but see Nolen-Hoeksema, 1990,1995). Simply put, despite widespread popular belief that women are more prone to depression than men because of direct negative effects of estrogen or progesterone on mood, there is little consistent scientific evidence to support this belief. Although some women do become depressed during periods of hormonal change, including puberty, the premenstrual period of the menstrual cycle, menopause, and the postpartum period, it is unclear that these depressions are due to the direct effects of hormonal changes on mood, or that depressions during these periods of women's lives account for the gender differences in rates of depression.

More recent biological research has focused not on direct effects of ovarian hormones on moods, but on the moderating effects of hormones, particularly adrenal hormones, on responses to stress. The hypothalamic-pituitary-adrenal (HPA) axis plays a major role in regulating stress responses, in part by regulating levels of a number of hormones, including cortisol, which is released by the adrenal glands in response to chemicals secreted by the brain's hypothalamus and then the pituitary. In turn, cortisol levels can affect other biochemicals known to influence moods. People with major depressive disorder often show elevated cortisol responses to stress, indicating dysregulation of the HPA response.

An intriguing hypothesis is that women are more likely than men to have a dysregulated HPA response to stress, which makes them more likely to develop depression in response to stress (Weiss et al., 1999). Women may be more likely to have a dysregulated HPA response because they are more likely to have suffered traumatic events, which are known to contribute to HPA dysregulation. In addition, ovarian hormones modulate regulation of the HPA axis (Young & Korszun, 1999). Some women may have depressions during periods of rapid change in levels of ovarian hormones (the postpartum period, premenstrual period, menopause, and puberty) because hormonal changes trigger dysregulation of the stress response, making these women more vulnerable to depression, particularly when they are confronted with stress. The causal relationship between HPA axis regulation and the gender difference in depression has not been established but is likely to be a major focus of future research.

Self-Concept

Although the idea that girls have more negative self-concepts than boys is a mainstay of the pop-psychology literature, empirical studies testing this hypothesis have produced mixed results (Nolen-Hoeksema & Girgus, 1994). Several studies have found no gender differences in self-esteem, self-concept, or dysfunctional attitudes. Those studies that do find gender differences, however, tend to show that girls have poorer self-concepts than boys. Again, negative self-concepts could contribute directly to depression, and could interact with stressors to contribute to depression. Negative self-concept has been shown to predict increases in depression in some studies of children (Nolen-Hoeksema & Girgus, 1994).

One consistent difference in males' and females' self-concepts concerns interpersonal orientation, the tendency to be concerned with the status of one's relationships and the opinions others hold of oneself. Even in childhood, girls appear more interpersonally oriented than boys, and this gender difference increases in adolescence (Zahn-Waxler, 2000). When interpersonal orientation leads girls and women to subordinate their own needs and desires completely to those of others, they become excessively dependent on the good graces of others (Cyranowski, Frank, Young, & Shear, 2000). They may then be at high risk for depression when conflicts arise in relationships, or relationships end. Several recent studies have shown that girls and women are more likely than boys and men to develop depression in response to interpersonal stressors. Because depression can also interfere with interpersonal functioning, an important topic for future research is whether the gender difference in depression is a consequence or cause of gender differences in interpersonal strain.

Coping Styles

By adolescence, girls appear to be more likely than boys to respond to stress and distress with rumination—focusing inward on feelings of distress and personal concerns rather than taking action to relieve their distress. This gender difference in rumination then is maintained throughout adulthood. Several longitudinal and experimental studies have shown that people who ruminate in response to stress are at increased risk to develop depressive symptoms and depressive disorders over time (Nolen-Hoeksema et al., 1999). In turn, the gender difference in rumination at least partially accounts for the gender difference in depression. Rumination may not only contribute directly to depression, but may also contribute indirectly by impairing problem solving, and thus preventing women from taking action to overcome the stressors they face.

AN INTEGRATIVE MODEL

Women suffer certain stressors more often than men and may be more vulnerable to develop depression in response to stress because of a number of factors. Both stress experiences and stress reactivity contribute directly to women's greater rates of depression compared with men. Stress experiences and stress reactivity also feed on each other, however. The more stress women suffer, the more hyperresponsive they may be to stress, both biologically and psychologically. This hyperresponsiveness may undermine women's ability to control their environments and overcome their stress, leading to even more stress in the future. In addition, depression contributes directly to more stressful experiences, by interfering with occupational and social functioning, and to vulnerability to stress, by inciting rumination, robbing the individual of any sense of mastery she did have, and possibly sensitizing the biological systems involved in the stress response.

Important advances will be made in explaining the gender difference in depression as we understand better the reciprocal effects of biological, social, and psychological systems on each other. Key developmental transitions, particularly the early adolescent years, are natural laboratories for observing the establishment of these processes, because so much changes during these transitions, and these transitions are times of increased risk.

Additional questions for future research include how culture and ethnicity affect the gender difference in depression. The gender difference is found across most cultures and ethnicities, but its size varies considerably, as do the absolute percentages of depressed women and men. The processes contributing to the gender difference in depression may also vary across cultures and ethnicities.

Understanding the gender difference in depression is important for at least two reasons. First, women's high rates of depression exact tremendous costs in quality of life and productivity, for women themselves and their families. Second, understanding the gender difference in depression will help us to understand the causes of depression in general. In this way, gender provides a valuable lens through which to examine basic human processes in psychopathology.

Recommended Reading

Cyranowski, J.M., Frank, E., Young; E., & Shear; K. (2000). (See References)
Nolen-Hoeksema, S. (1990). (See References)
Nolen-Hoeksema, S., & Girgus, J.S. (1994). (See References)
Nolen-Hoeksema, S., Larson, J., & Grayson, C., (1999). (See References)
Young, E., & Korszun, A. (1999). (See References)

Note

1. Address correspondence to Susan Nolen-Hoeksema, Department of Psychology, University of Michigan, 525 E. University Ave., Ann Arbor, MI 48109; e-mail: nolen@umich.edu.

References

Breslau, N., Davis, G.C., Andreski, P., Peterson, E.L., & Schultz, L. (1997). Sex differences in posttraumatic stress disorder. *Archives of General Psychiatry, 54*, 1044–1048.

Cutler, S., & Nolen-Hoeksema, S. (1991). Accounting for sex differences in depression through female victimization: Childhood sexual abuse. *Sex Roles, 24*, 425–438.

Cyranowski, J.M., Frank, E., Young, E., & Shear, K. (2000). Adolescent onset of the gender difference in lifetime rates of major depression. *Archives of General Psychiatry, 57*, 21–27.

Kessler, R.C., McGonagle, K.A., Swartz, M., Blazer, D.G., & Nelson, C.B. (1993). Sex and depression in the National Comorbidity Survey 1: Lifetime prevalence, chronicity, and recurrence. *Journal of Affective Disorders, 29*, 85–96.

Nolen-Hoeksema, S. (1990). *Sex differences in depression*. Stanford, CA: Stanford University Press.

Nolen-Hoeksema, S. (1995). Gender differences in coping with depression across the lifespan. *Depression, 3*, 81–90.

Nolen-Hoeksema, S., & Girgus, J.S. (1994). The emergence of gender differences in depression in adolescence. *Psychological Bulletin, 115*, 424–443.

Nolen-Hoeksema, S., Larson, J., & Grayson, C. (1999). Explaining the gender difference in depression. *Journal of Personality and Social Psychology, 77*, 1061–1072.

Weiss, E.L., Longhurst, J.G., & Mazure, C.M. (1999). Childhood sexual abuse as a risk factor for depression in women: Psychosocial and neurobiological correlates. *American Journal of Psychiatry, 156*, 816–828.

Weissman, M.M., Bland, R.C., Canino, G.J., Faravelli, C., Greenwald, S., Hwu, H.-G., Joyce, P.R., Karam, E.G., Lee, C.-K., Lellouch, J., Lepine, J.-P., Newman, S.C., Rubio-Stipc, M., Wells, E., Wickramaratne, P.J., Wittchen, H.-U., & Yeh, E.-K. (1996). Cross-national epidemiology of major depression and bipolar disorder. *Journal of the American Medical Association, 276*, 293–299.

Young, E., & Korszun, A. (1999). Women, stress, and depression: Sex differences in hypothalamic-pituitary-adrenal axis regulation. In E. Leibenluft (Ed.), *Gender differences in mood and anxiety disorders: From bench to bedside* (pp. 31–52). Washington, DC: American Psychiatric Press.

Zahn-Waxler, C. (2000). The development of empathy, guilt, and internalization of distress: Implications for gender differences in internalizing and externalizing problems. In R. Davidson (Ed.), *Wisconsin Symposium on Emotion: Vol. 1. Anxiety, depression, and emotion* (pp. 222–265). Oxford, England: Oxford University Press.

The Clustering and Contagion of Suicide

Thomas E. Joiner, Jr.[1]
Department of Psychology, Florida State University, Tallahassee, Florida

Abstract

Two general types of suicide cluster have been discussed in the literature; roughly, these can be classified as mass clusters and point clusters. Mass clusters are media related, and the evidence for them is equivocal; point clusters are local phenomena, and these do appear to occur. Contagion has not been conceptually well developed nor empirically well supported as an explanation for suicide clusters. An alternative explanation for why suicides sometimes cluster is articulated: People who are vulnerable to suicide may cluster well before the occurrence of any overt suicidal stimulus, and when they experience severe negative events, including but not limited to the suicidal behavior of one member of the cluster, all members of the cluster are at increased risk for suicidality (a risk that may be offset by good social support).

Keywords

suicide clusters; suicide contagion

The phenomena of attempted and completed suicide are troubling and mysterious enough in themselves; the possibility that suicide is socially contagious, even more so. This article considers whether suicide clusters exist, and if so, whether "contagion" processes can account for them.

There is a potentially important distinction between the terms *suicide cluster* and *suicide contagion*. A cluster refers to the factual occurrence of two or more completed or attempted suicides that are nonrandomly "bunched" in space or time (e.g., a series of suicide attempts in the same high school or a series of completed suicides in response to the suicide of a celebrity). The term *cluster* implies nothing about why the cluster came to be, only that it came to be. By contrast, *contagion* refers to a possible explanation (as I argue later, a fairly vague explanation) of why a cluster developed. Clusters (of a sort) appear to occur, but the status of contagion as the reason for such occurrences is more equivocal.

CLUSTERS—OF A SORT—APPEAR TO OCCUR

Given that attempted and completed suicides are relatively rare, and given that they tend to be more or less evenly distributed in space and time (e.g., suicides occur at roughly the same rate in various regions of the United States and occur at roughly the same rate regardless of the day of the week or the month), it is statistically unlikely that suicides would cluster by chance alone. Yet cluster they do, at least under some circumstances. (Such clustering is often termed the "Werther effect," after a fictional character of Goethe's whose suicide purportedly inspired actual suicides in 18th-century Europe.) Two general types of suicide cluster have been discussed in the literature: mass clusters and point clusters. Mass clusters are media related; point clusters, local.

Point Clusters

Point clusters occur locally, involving victims who are relatively contiguous in both space and time. The prototypical setting is institutional (i.e., a school or a hospital). Probably the best documented example was reported by Brent and his colleagues (Brent, Kerr, Goldstein, & Bozigar, 1989). In a high school of approximately 1,500 students, 2 students committed suicide within 4 days. During an 18-day span that included the 2 completed suicides, 7 other students attempted suicide and an additional 23 reported having suicidal thoughts. It is important to note, though, that Brent and his colleagues found that 75% of the members of the cluster had at least one major psychiatric disorder, which had existed before the students' exposure to the suicides (i.e., they were vulnerable to begin with). Also, victims' close friends appeared to develop suicidal symptoms more readily than students who were less close to victims. In other words, social contiguity was an important factor.

Haw (1994) described a point cluster of 14 suicides within a 1-year period among patients of a London psychiatric unit. Thirteen of the 14 patients suffered from severe, chronic mental illness (e.g., schizophrenia), and most had ongoing therapeutic contact with the psychiatric unit. The author reported that the point cluster's occurrence may have stemmed from patients' valid perceptions that the future of the hospital was uncertain and that their access to medical staff was decreasing and ultimately threatened. Several other point clusters have also been described (see, e.g., Gould, Wallenstein, & Davidson, 1989).

When Point Clusters Do Not Occur

Given that suicidality runs in families, and that the suicide of a family member is an enormously traumatic event, one might imagine that point clusters would be particularly likely within a given family (e.g., the suicide of one family member might be followed closely by the suicide of another family member). However, within family point clusters appear to be very rare. (Although certainly at least one has occurred, I could find no documented case in the literature. It is possible, however, that they are underreported or underpublicized.) Point clusters also appear not to occur within groupings beyond the institutional (e.g., at the level of a large community; cf. Chiu, 1988)—except, that is, in the (possible) case of mass clusters.

Mass Clusters

Unlike point clusters, mass clusters are media-related phenomena. They are grouped more in time than in space, and are purportedly in response to the publicizing of actual or fictional suicides. Phillips and his colleagues have examined the possible relation of suicide-related media events and the rate of subsequent suicides (see, e.g., Phillips & Carstensen, 1986, 1988). These researchers have argued that the suicide rate in the population increases in the days after descriptions of suicides appear in televised news reports and in newspapers. Indeed, in many of these studies, the suicide rate did appear to rise after a publicized suicide, although the effect did not always occur, and it appeared to be primarily applicable to adolescent suicide. Interestingly, these researchers also found that accidents, such as motor vehicle fatalities, may increase in the days following a publicized suicide, apparently because many such accidents are actually intentional suicides.

However, a study by Kessler, Downey, Milavsky, and Stipp (1988) cast doubt on the conclusion that mass clusters exist. Examining adolescent suicides from 1973 to 1984, the authors found no reliable relation between suicide-related newscasts and the subsequent adolescent suicide rate. Similarly, these researchers obtained no evidence that the number of teenagers viewing the newscasts (as determined by Neilsen ratings) was correlated with the number of adolescent suicides.

In the case of fictional portrayals of suicide (e.g., a television movie in which a character commits suicide), the evidence indicates, at most, a weak effect. Schmidtke and Haefner (1988) studied responses to a serial, broadcast twice in Germany, showing the railway suicide of a young man. After each broadcast, according to these researchers, railway suicides among young men (but not among other groups) increased sharply. However, several other researchers have conducted similar studies and concluded that there was no relation between fictionalized accounts of suicide and the subsequent suicide rate, for adolescents in particular (Phillips & Paight, 1987; Simkin, Hawton, Whitehead, & Fagg, 1995), as well as for people in general (Berman, 1988).

Clustering Does Not Contagion Make

If suicide clusters exist (and it appears that point clusters do, although mass clusters may not), contagion—the social, or interpersonal, transmission of suicidality from one victim to another—may or may not be involved. With regard to an array of unfortunate events (e.g., disasters, accidents, even illnesses), it is easy to imagine that there would be point clusters of victims without contagion of any sort. For example, the victims of the Chernobyl nuclear disaster were point-clustered, not because of any type of contagion between victims, but because of victims' simultaneous exposure to radiation. Even cases of mass suicide, the victims of which are point-clustered, are best viewed as instances of mass delusion (e.g., Heaven's Gate) or of a combination of delusion and coercion (e.g., Jonestown), rather than of contagion. In cases such as Chernobyl and even Jonestown, the point-clustering of victims may be seen as due to the simultaneous effects of some pernicious, external influence, such as radiation, on a preexisting, socially contiguous group of people, such as those working at or living near the Chernobyl plant.

In disease, the agent of contagion (e.g., some microbial pathogen) is specified, and its mechanism of action delineated. By contrast, no persuasive agent or mechanism of suicide contagion has been articulated. Indeed, with one exception, the very definition of suicide contagion has been so vague as to defy analysis. The one exception is behavioral imitation, which, although clearly defined, lacks explanatory power (e.g., in a school, what determines who, among all the students, imitates a suicide?).

A SPECULATION REGARDING POINT-CLUSTERED SUICIDES

I suggest that the concepts of imitation or contagion may not be needed to explain point-clustered suicides. Rather, four sets of findings, taken together, indicate an alternative view. First, severe negative life events are risk factors for suicidality (and the suicidal behavior of a friend or peer qualifies as one of a large array of severe negative life events). Second, good social support (e.g., healthy family functioning) buffers people against developing suicidal symptoms. Third, there exists an array of person-based risk factors for suicidality (e.g., personality disorder or other psychiatric disorder). Fourth, people form relationships *assortatively*—that is, people who possess similar qualities or problems, including suicide risk factors, may be more likely to form relationships with one another. Therefore, it is possible that people who are vulnerable to suicide may cluster well before the occurrence of any overt suicidal stimulus (i.e., suicide point clusters may be, in a sense, prearranged), and when they experience severe negative events, including but not limited to the suicidal behavior of one member of the cluster, all members of the cluster are at increased risk for suicidality (a risk that may be offset by good social support).

Consider, for example, the point cluster described by Haw (1994), in which victims were assortatively related on the basis of, at least in part, shared suicide risk factors (e.g., the chronic mental illness that brought them all to the same psychiatric unit). Vulnerable people were brought together (through contact with the agency), were exposed to severe stress (potential for dissolution of the agency; lack of access to important caregivers; for some, suicides of peers), and may not have been well buffered by good social support (the chronically mentally ill often have low social support; a main source of support may have been the agency, which was threatened).

Or consider the example of point clusters within high schools. In this case, the assortative relationships—the prearrangement of clusters—may occur in one or both of two ways. First, because they have mutual interests, compatible qualities, or similar problems (including vulnerability to and experience of psychopathology), vulnerable adolescents may gravitate toward one another. A point cluster reported by Robbins and Conroy (1983) demonstrates this possibility. In this cluster, two adolescent suicides were followed by five attempts (all five teenagers were subsequently admitted to the hospital) and one hospital admission for having suicidal thoughts. Of the six hospitalized teens, all had regularly socialized with each other, and all visited each other during their hospitalizations. Second, having social contact (for whatever reason, assortative or not) with an adolescent who completes or attempts suicide appears to lower the threshold at which a teen becomes suicidal (Brent et al., 1989). The mere occurrence, then, of suicidality in one adolescent may automatically arrange a potential cluster.

Although the empirical facts on point clusters are limited, they appear to be consistent with my speculation that severe negative life events, person-based risk, social contiguity (perhaps as a function of assortative relationships), and lack of buffering by social support, taken together, explain the phenomenon. In an effort to provide further empirical support for this view, I conducted an analogue study among college roommates. College roommates provide an interesting "natural laboratory" for studying issues involving assortative relationships, because in many large universities, a sizable proportion of roommates are randomly assigned to each other (by the university housing agency) and the rest assortatively choose to room with each other. I predicted that suicidality levels would be more similar among roommates who chose to room together than among those randomly paired together. Moreover, I predicted that suicidality levels would be particularly consonant among pairs who both chose one another and, by their own reports, had been experiencing negative life events that affected both of them. Results supported the view that prearranged point clusters (in this case, arranged by people choosing to live together) would share suicide-related features (in this case, symptoms), and that clustered suicidality was particularly likely in those prearranged clusters that had been affected by negative life events. It must be emphasized that this study was an analogue study, and that, in general, students' levels of suicidality were quite low, making the generalization to attempted or completed suicide questionable. The results, however, converge with those from reports on actual point clusters to make the explanation offered here, at the least, a candidate for further study.

ADDRESSING POTENTIAL CRITICISMS OF THIS EXPLANATION

Why Don't Point Clusters Happen All the Time?

According to my speculation about why point clusters develop, at least two concepts are key to understanding why they are relatively rare. First, my explanation involves the joint operation of several phenomena that themselves are infrequent in occurrence. Severe negative events, high person-based risk, suicidality itself, and low social support—all jointly operating ingredients of my explanation—are relatively rare; their confluence is even more so. Second, even given the confluence of these factors, attempted or completed suicides represent an extreme and severe psychopathology, the threshold for which is presumably quite high. Thus, even when life events are severely negative, person-based risk is high, and social support is low, the threshold may not be reached.

Why Don't Point Clusters Occur Within Families?

Because suicidality and suicide risk run in families, because the suicide of a family member is arguably the most severe of negative events, and because family members are socially contiguous, families would appear to be likely sources for point-clustered suicides. Apparently, however, they are not. This may be because of the protective action of social support. Social support is, in general, pervasive (indeed, the need to belong has been proposed as a fundamental human motive; Baumeister & Leary, 1995), and it is intensified for families in mourning. Increased social support thus may offset families' risk for additional suicides among family members.

CONCLUSIONS

The evidence for mass clusters is weak or equivocal, whereas point clusters appear to occur. But clustering does not contagion make. By implication at least, suicide clusters often have been explained as analogous to miniepidemics of contagious illness. I have suggested, however, that a more apt analogy is disasters or industrial accidents, in which simultaneous exposure to some external, pernicious agent (e.g., radiation) is the mechanism of action, a mechanism that is particularly harmful to already vulnerable people. Point-clustered suicides may occur similarly: Contiguous people, if exposed to noxious stimuli (e.g., a severe negative life event, such as the suicide of a peer), and if vulnerable but unprotected (by social support), may simultaneously develop suicidal symptoms.

Recommended Reading

Brent, D.A., Kerr, M.M., Goldstein, C., & Bozigar, J. (1989). (See References)
Gould, M.S., Wallenstein, S., Davidson, L. (1989). (See References)
Kessler, R.C., Downey, G., Milavsky, J.R., & Stipp, H. (1988). (See References)

Note

1. Address correspondence to Thomas Joiner, Department of Psychology, Florida State University, Tallahassee, FL 32306-1270; e-mail: joiner@psy.fsu.edu.

References

Baumeister, R.F., & Leary, M.R. (1995). The need to belong: Desire for interpersonal attachments as a fundamental human motivation. *Psychological Bulletin, 117*, 497–529.

Berman, A.L. (1988). Fictional depiction of suicide in television films and imitation effects. *American Journal of Psychiatry, 145*, 982–986.

Brent, D.A., Kerr, M.M., Goldstein, C., & Bozigar, J. (1989). An outbreak of suicide and suicidal behavior in a high school. *Journal of the American Academy of Child & Adolescent Psychiatry, 28*, 918–924.

Chiu, L.P. (1988). Do weather, day of the week, and address affect the rate of attempted suicide in Hong Kong? *Social Psychiatry & Psychiatric Epidemiology, 23*, 229–235.

Gould, M.S., Wallenstein, S., & Davidson, L. (1989). Suicide clusters: A critical review. *Suicide & Life-Threatening Behavior, 19*, 17–29.

Haw, C.M. (1994). A cluster of suicides at a London psychiatric unit. *Suicide & Life-Threatening Behavior, 24*, 256–266.

Kessler, R.C., Downey, G., Milavsky, J.R., & Stipp, H. (1988). Clustering of teenage suicides after television news stories about suicides: A reconsideration. *American Journal of Psychiatry, 145*, 1379–1383.

Phillips, D.P., & Carstensen, L.L. (1986). Clustering of teenage suicides after television news stories about suicide. *New England Journal of Medicine, 315*, 685–689.

Phillips, D.P., & Carstensen, L.L. (1988). The effect of suicide stories on various demographic groups, 1968–1985. *Suicide & Life-Threatening Behavior, 18*, 100–114.

Phillips, D.P., & Paight, D.J. (1987). The impact of televised movies about suicide: A replicative study. *New England Journal of Medicine, 317*, 809–811.

Robbins, D., & Conroy, R.C. (1983). A cluster of adolescent suicide attempts: Is suicide contagious? *Journal of Adolescent Health Care, 3*, 253–255.

Schmidtke, A., & Haefner, H. (1988). The Werther effect after television films: New evidence for an old hypothesis. *Psychological Medicine, 18*, 665–676.

Simkin, S., Hawton, K., Whitehead, L., & Fagg, J. (1995). Media influence on parasuicide: A study of the effects of a television drama portrayal of paracetamol self-poisoning. *British Journal of Psychiatry, 167*, 754–759.

The Malicious Serpent: Snakes as a Prototypical Stimulus for an Evolved Module of Fear

Arne Öhman[1] and Susan Mineka

Department of Clinical Neuroscience, Karolinska Institute, Stockholm, Sweden (A.Ö.), and Department of Psychology, Northwestern University, Evanston, Illinois (S.M.)

Abstract

As reptiles, snakes may have signified deadly threats in the environment of early mammals. We review findings suggesting that snakes remain special stimuli for humans. Intense snake fear is prevalent in both humans and other primates. Humans and monkeys learn snake fear more easily than fear of most other stimuli through direct or vicarious conditioning. Neither the elicitation nor the conditioning of snake fear in humans requires that snakes be consciously perceived; rather, both processes can occur with masked stimuli. Humans tend to perceive illusory correlations between snakes and aversive stimuli, and their attention is automatically captured by snakes in complex visual displays. Together, these and other findings delineate an evolved fear module in the brain. This module is selectively and automatically activated by once-threatening stimuli, is relatively encapsulated from cognition, and derives from specialized neural circuitry.

Keywords

evolution; snake fear; fear module

Snakes are commonly regarded as shiny, slithering creatures worthy of fear and disgust. If one were to believe the Book of Genesis, humans' dislike for snakes resulted from a divine intervention: To avenge the snake's luring of Eve to taste the fruit of knowledge, God instituted eternal enmity between their descendants. Alternatively, the human dislike of snakes and the common appearances of reptiles as the embodiment of evil in myths and art might reflect an evolutionary heritage. Indeed, Sagan (1977) speculated that human fear of snakes and other reptiles may be a distant effect of the conditions under which early mammals evolved. In the world they inhabited, the animal kingdom was dominated by awesome reptiles, the dinosaurs, and so a prerequisite for early mammals to deliver genes to future generations was to avoid getting caught in the fangs of Tyrannosaurus rex and its relatives. Thus, fear and respect for reptiles is a likely core mammalian heritage. From this perspective, snakes and other reptiles may continue to have a special psychological significance even for humans, and considerable evidence suggests this is indeed true. Furthermore, the pattern of findings appears consistent with the evolutionary premise.

THE PREVALENCE OF SNAKE FEARS IN PRIMATES

Snakes are obviously fearsome creatures to many humans. Agras, Sylvester, and Oliveau (1969) interviewed a sample of New Englanders about fears, and found snakes to be clearly the most prevalent object of intense fear, reported by 38% of females and 12% of males.

Fear of snakes is also common among other primates. According to an exhaustive review of field data (King, 1997), 11 genera of primates showed fear-related responses (alarm calls, avoidance, mobbing) in virtually all instances in which they were observed confronting large snakes. For studies of captive primates, King did not find consistent evidence of snake fear. However, in direct comparisons, rhesus (and squirrel) monkeys reared in the wild were far more likely than lab-reared monkeys to show strong phobiclike fear responses to snakes (e.g., Mineka, Keir, & Price, 1980). That this fear is adaptive in the wild is further supported by independent field reports of large snakes attacking primates (M. Cook & Mineka, 1991).

This high prevalence of snake fear in humans as well as in our primate relatives suggests that it is a result of an ancient evolutionary history. Genetic variability might explain why not all individuals show fear of snakes. Alternatively, the variability could stem from differences in how easily individuals learn to fear reptilian stimuli when they are encountered in aversive contexts. This latter possibility would be consistent with the differences in snake fear between wild- and lab-reared monkeys.

LEARNING TO FEAR SNAKES

Experiments with lab-reared monkeys have shown that they can acquire a fear of snakes vicariously, that is, by observing other monkeys expressing fear of snakes. When nonfearful lab-reared monkeys were given the opportunity to observe a wild-reared "model" monkey displaying fear of live and toy snakes, they were rapidly conditioned to fear snakes, and this conditioning was strong and persistent. The fear response was learned even when the fearful model monkey was shown on videotape (M. Cook & Mineka, 1990).

When videos were spliced so that identical displays of fear were modeled in response to toy snakes and flowers, or to toy crocodiles and rabbits (M. Cook & Mineka, 1991), the lab-reared monkeys showed substantial conditioning to toy snakes and crocodiles, but not to flowers and toy rabbits. Toy snakes and flowers served equally well as signals for food rewards (M. Cook & Mineka, 1990), so the selective effect of snakes appears to be restricted to aversive contexts. Because these monkeys had never seen any of the stimuli used prior to these experiments, the results provide strong support for an evolutionary basis to the selective learning.

A series of studies published in the 1970s (see Öhman & Mineka, 2001) tested the hypothesis that humans are predisposed to easily learn to fear snakes. These studies used a discriminative Pavlovian conditioning procedure in which various pictures served as conditioned stimuli (CSs) that predicted the presence and absence of mildly aversive shock, the unconditioned stimulus (US). Participants for whom snakes (or spiders) consistently signaled shocks showed stronger and more lasting conditioned skin conductance responses (SCRs; palmar sweat responses that index emotional activation) than control participants for whom flowers or mushrooms signaled shocks. When a nonaversive US was used, however, this difference disappeared. E.W. Cook, Hodes, and Lang (1986) demonstrated that qualitatively different responses were conditioned to snakes (heart rate acceleration, indexing fear) than to flowers and mushrooms (heart rate deceleration, indexing attention to the eliciting stimulus). They also reported superior conditioning to snakes than to gun stimuli paired with loud noises. Such results suggest that the selective association between snakes and aversive USs reflects evolutionary history rather than cultural conditioning.

NONCONSCIOUS CONTROL OF RESPONSES TO SNAKES

If the prevalence and ease of learning snake fear represents a core mammalian heritage, its neural machinery must be found in brain structures that evolved in early mammals. Accordingly, the fear circuit of the mammalian brain relies heavily on limbic structures such as the amygdala, a collection of neural nuclei in the anterior temporal lobe. Limbic structures emerged in the evolutionary transition from reptiles to mammals and use preexisting structures in the "reptilian brain" to control emotional output such as flight/fight behavior and cardiovascular changes (see Ohman & Mineka, 2001).

From this neuroevolutionary perspective, one would expect the limbically controlled fear of snakes to be relatively independent of the most recently evolved control level in the brain, the neocortex, which is the site of advanced cognition. This hypothesis is consistent with the often strikingly irrational quality of snake phobia. For example, phobias may be activated by seeing mere pictures of snakes. Backward masking is a promising methodology for examining whether phobic responses can be activated without involvement of the cortex. In this method, a brief visual stimulus is blanked from conscious perception by an immediately following masking stimulus. Because backward masking disrupts visual processing in the primary visual cortex, responses to backward-masked stimuli reflect activation of pathways in the brain that may access the fear circuit without involving cortical areas mediating visual awareness of the stimulus.

In one study (Öhman & Soares, 1994), pictures of snakes, spiders, flowers, and mushrooms were presented very briefly (30 ms), each time immediately followed by a masking stimulus (a randomly cut and reassembled picture). Although the participants could not recognize the intact pictures, participants who were afraid of snakes showed enhanced SCRs only to masked snakes, whereas participants who were afraid of spiders responded only to spiders. Similar results were obtained (Öhman & Soares, 1993) when nonfearful participants, who had been conditioned to unmasked snake pictures by shock USs, were exposed to masked pictures without the US. Thus, responses to conditioned snake pictures survived backward masking; in contrast, masking eliminated conditioning effects in another group of participants conditioned to neutral stimuli such as flowers or mushrooms.

Furthermore, subsequent experiments (Öhman & Soares, 1998) also demonstrated conditioning to masked stimuli when masked snakes or spiders (but not masked flowers or mushrooms) were used as CSs followed by shock USs. Thus, these masking studies show that fear responses (as indexed by SCRs) can be learned and elicited when backward masking prevents visually presented snake stimuli from accessing cortical processing. This is consistent with the notion that responses to snakes are organized by a specifically evolved primitive neural circuit that emerged with the first mammals long before the evolution of neocortex.

ILLUSORY CORRELATIONS BETWEEN SNAKES AND AVERSIVE STIMULI

If expression and learning of snake fear do not require cortical processing, are people's cognitions about snakes and their relationships to other events biased and irrational? One example of such biased processing occurred in experiments on illusory correlations: Participants (especially those who were afraid of snakes) were more likely to perceive that slides of fear-relevant stimuli (such as snakes) were paired with shock than to perceive that slides of control stimuli (flowers and mushrooms) were paired with shock. This occurred even though there were no such relationships in the extensive random sequence of slide stimuli and aversive and nonaversive outcomes (tones or nothing) participants had experienced (Tomarken, Sutton, & Mineka, 1995).

Similar illusory correlations were not observed for pictures of damaged electrical equipment and shock even though they were rated as belonging together better than snakes and shock (Tomarken et al., 1995). In another experiment, participants showed exaggerated expectancies for shock to follow both snakes and damaged electrical equipment before the experiment began (Kennedy, Rapee, & Mazurski, 1997), but reported only the illusory correlation between snakes and shock after experiencing the random stimulus series. Thus, it appears that snakes have a cognitive affinity with aversiveness and danger that is resistant to modification by experience.

AUTOMATIC CAPTURE OF ATTENTION BY SNAKE STIMULI

People who encounter snakes in the wild may report that they first froze in fear, only a split second later realizing that they were about to step on a snake. Thus, snakes may automatically capture attention. A study supporting this hypothesis (Öhman, Flykt, & Esteves, 2001) demonstrated shorter detection latencies for a discrepant snake picture among an array of many neutral distractor stimuli (e.g., flower pictures) than vice versa. Furthermore, "finding the snake in the grass" was not affected by the number of distractor stimuli, whereas it took longer to detect discrepant flowers and mushrooms among many than among few snakes when the latter served as distractor stimuli. This suggests that snakes, but not flowers and mushrooms, were located by an automatic perceptual routine that effortlessly found target stimuli that appeared to "pop out" from the matrix independently of the number of distractor stimuli. Participants who were highly fearful of snakes showed even superior performance in detecting snakes. Thus, when snakes elicited fear in participants, this fear state sensitized the perceptual apparatus to detect snakes even more efficiently.

THE CONCEPT OF A FEAR MODULE

The evidence we have reviewed shows that snake stimuli are strongly and widely associated with fear in humans and other primates and that fear of snakes is relatively independent of conscious cognition. We have proposed the concept of an evolved fear module to explain these and many related findings (Öhman & Mineka, 2001). The fear module is a relatively independent behavioral, mental, and neural system that has evolved to assist mammals in defending against threats such as snakes. The module is selectively sensitive to, and automatically activated by, stimuli related to recurrent survival threats, it is relatively encapsulated from more advanced human cognition, and it relies on specialized neural circuitry.

This specialized behavioral module did not evolve primarily from survival threats provided by snakes during human evolution, but rather from the threat that reptiles have provided through mammalian evolution. Because reptiles have been associated with danger throughout evolution, it is likely that snakes represent a prototypical stimulus for activating the fear module. However, we are not arguing that the human brain has a specialized module for automatically generating fear of snakes. Rather, we propose that the blueprint for the fear module was built around the deadly threat that ancestors of snakes provided to our distant ancestors, the early mammals. During further mammalian evolution, this blueprint was modified, elaborated, and specialized for the ecological niches occupied by different species. Some mammals may even prey on snakes, and new stimuli and stimulus features have been added to reptiles as preferential activators of the module. For example, facial threat is similar to snakes when it comes to activating the fear module in social primates (Öhman & Mineka, 2001). Through Pavlovian conditioning, the fear module may come under the control of a very wide range of stimuli signaling pain and danger. Nevertheless, evolutionarily derived constraints have afforded stimuli once related to recurrent survival threats easier access for gaining control of the module through fear conditioning (Öhman & Mineka, 2001).

ISSUES FOR FURTHER RESEARCH

The claim that the fear module can be conditioned without awareness is a bold one given that there is a relative consensus in the field of human conditioning that awareness of the CS-US contingency is required for acquiring conditioned responses. However, as we have extensively argued elsewhere (Öhman & Mineka, 2001; Wiens & Öhman, 2002), there is good evidence that conditioning to nonconsciously presented CSs is possible if they are evolutionarily fear relevant. Other factors that might promote such nonconscious learning include intense USs, short CS-US intervals, and perhaps temporal overlap between the CS and the US. However, little research on these factors has been reported, and there is a pressing need to elaborate their relative effectiveness in promoting conditioning of the fear module outside of awareness.

One of the appeals of the fear module concept is that it is consistent with the current understanding of the neurobiology of fear conditioning, which gives a central role to the amygdala (e.g., Öhman & Mineka, 2001). However, this understanding is primarily based on animal data. Even though the emerging brain-imaging literature on human fear conditioning is consistent with this database, systematic efforts are needed in order to tie the fear module more convincingly to human brain mechanisms. For example, a conspicuous gap in knowledge concerns whether the amygdala is indeed specially tuned to conditioning contingencies involving evolutionarily fear-relevant CSs such as snakes.

An interesting question that can be addressed both at a psychological and at a neurobiological level concerns the perceptual mechanisms that give snake stimuli privileged access to the fear module. For example, are snakes detected at a lower perceptual threshold relative to non-fear-relevant objects? Are they identified faster than other objects once detected? Are they quicker to activate the fear module and attract attention once identified? Regardless of the locus of perceptual privilege, what visual features of snakes make them such powerful fear elicitors and attention captors? Because the visual processing in pathways preceding the cortical level is crude, the hypothesis that masked presentations of snakes directly access the amygdala implies that the effect is mediated by simple features of snakes rather than by the complex configuration of features defining a snake. Delineating these features would allow the construction of a "super fear stimulus." It could be argued that such a stimulus would depict "the archetypical evil" as represented in the human brain.

Recommended Reading

Mineka, S. (1992). Evolutionary memories, emotional processing, and the emotional disorders. *The Psychology of Learning and Motivation, 28*, 161–206.

Öhman, A., Dimberg, U., & Öst, L.-G. (1985). Animal and social phobias: Biological constraints on learned fear responses. In S. Reiss & R.R. Bootzin (Eds.), *Theoretical issues in behavior therapy* (pp. 123–178). New York: Academic Press.

Öhman; A.,,& Mineka, S. (2001). (See References)

Note

1. Address correspondence to Arne Öhman, Psychology Section, Department of Clinical Neuroscience, Karolinska Institute and Hospital, Z6:6, S-171 76 Stockholm, Sweden; e-mail: arne.ohman@cns.ki.se.

References

Agras, S., Sylvester, D., & Oliveau, D. (1969). The epidemiology of common fears and phobias. *Comprehensive Psychiatry, 10*, 151–156.

Cook, E.W., Hodes, R.L., & Lang, P.J. (1986). Preparedness and phobia: Effects of stimulus content on human visceral conditioning. *Journal of Abnormal Psychology, 95*, 195–207.

Cook, M., & Mineka, S. (1990). Selective associations in the observational conditioning of fear in rhesus monkeys. *Journal of Experimental Psychology: Animal Behavior Processes, 16*, 372–389.

Cook, M., & Mineka, S. (1991). Selective associations in the origins of phobic fears and their implications for behavior therapy. In P. Martin (Ed.), *Handbook of behavior therapy and psychological science: An integrative approach* (pp. 413–434). Oxford, England: Pergamon Press.

Kennedy, S.J., Rapee, R.M., & Mazurski, E.J. (1997). Covariation bias for phylogenetic versus ontogenetic fear-relevant stimuli. *Behaviour Research and Therapy, 35*, 415–422.

King, G.E. (1997, June). *The attentional basis for primate responses to snakes.* Paper presented at the annual meeting of the American Society of Primatologists, San Diego, CA.

Mineka, S., Keir, R., & Price, V. (1980). Fear of snakes in wild- and laboratory-reared rhesus monkeys (*Macaca mulatta*). *Animal Learning and Behavior, 8*, 653–663.

Öhman, A., Flykt, A., & Esteves, F. (2001). Emotion drives attention: Detecting the snake in the grass. *Journal of Experimental Psychology: General, 131*, 466–478.

Öhman, A., & Mineka, S. (2001). Fear, phobias and preparedness: Toward an evolved module of fear and fear learning. *Psychological Review, 108*, 483–522.

Öhman, A., & Soares, J.J.F. (1993). On the automatic nature of phobic fear: Conditioned electrodermal responses to masked fear-relevant stimuli. *Journal of Abnormal Psychology, 102*, 121–132.

Öhman, A., & Soares, J.J.F. (1994). "Unconscious anxiety": Phobic responses to masked stimuli. *Journal of Abnormal Psychology, 103*, 231–240.

Öhman, A., & Soares, J.J.F. (1998). Emotional conditioning to masked stimuli: Expectancies for aversive outcomes following nonrecognized fear-irrelevant stimuli. *Journal of Experimental Psychology: General, 127*, 69–82.

Sagan, C. (1977). *The dragons of Eden: Speculations on the evolution of human intelligence.* London: Hodder and Stoughton.

Tomarken, A.J., Sutton, S.K., & Mineka, S. (1995). Fear-relevant illusory correlations: What types of associations promote judgmental bias? *Journal of Abnormal Psychology, 104*, 312–326.

Wiens, S., & Öhman, A. (2002). Unawareness is more than a chance event: Comment on Lovibond and Shanks (2002). *Journal of Experimental Psychology: Animal Behavior Processes, 28*, 27–31.

Lessons From the Study of Psychogenic Amnesia

Jean Maria Arrigo and Kathy Pezdek[1]
Department of Psychology, Claremont Graduate University, Claremont, California

Many people who have experienced traumatic events report that their memory for these events is completely inaccessible to them for extended periods of their lives; this phenomenon has been referred to as memory repression. Some of these people report that later in life they recover memory for the previously repressed trauma. Articles debating the veracity of repressed memory and recovered memory have flooded the psychology literature in recent years (for reviews, see Loftus, 1993; Pezdek & Banks, 1996; Pressley & Grossman, 1994), but political conflict has plagued progress in the field. Most scientists who have engaged the issue recently have done so within the specific arena of memory for childhood sexual abuse (but see Cohen, 1996). Unfortunately, the debate has elicited the personal views of the researchers regarding victimization of children and women, domestic violence, and the feminist issues of power more generally—that is, core beliefs recognized as intractable by policy analysts. Even the American Psychological Association's six-person Working Group on Investigation of Memories of Childhood Abuse could not agree on the content of a final report; rather, the group split and drafted two final reports.

Our purpose is to expand the study of repression and recovery of memory beyond the circumscribed realm of childhood sexual abuse, to reduce the political heat surrounding this area of study and to promote cooperative scientific pursuit. In this article, instead of the designations repressed memory and recovered memory, we use the more general terms amnesia and recovery so as not to presume the mechanism for amnesia. The thesis of this article is that amnesia for sexual abuse is just one specific type of psychogenic amnesia, a deficit in memory that is precipitated by psychological stressors rather than by structural brain damage and that has as its major symptom the loss of memory for information acquired normally prior to the onset of amnesia. In addition, we suggest that researchers interested in psychogenic amnesia more generally should be familiar with a wider range of types of psychogenic amnesia. We assert that the models, processes, and mechanisms developed to account for amnesia and recovery of memory for sexual abuse should account, as well, for psychogenic amnesia from a wide range of sources. Alternatively, constraints on the general models of psychogenic amnesia should be developed to explain why processes that operate on amnesia for and recovery of other types of traumatic memories do not operate on memory for sexual abuse.

As is the literature on childhood sexual abuse, the case literature on other types of trauma is skeptical of self-reported claims of amnesia and recovery. However, although investigators' own judgments of amnesia and recovery are often questioned in cases of childhood sexual abuse, such judgments tend not to be questioned when it comes to other types of trauma. Our second assertion, then, is that the same critical eye that is often applied to reports of childhood sexual abuse should be similarly applied to cases involving other types of trauma, for which even more vigorous memory recovery techniques are typical.

This article is not intended to provide a comprehensive review of the literature on psychogenic amnesia. Rather, we have widely sampled the extensive but amorphous case literature on psychogenic amnesia and report here some examples of six major classes of events that have been documented as sources of psychogenic amnesia: disasters and accidents, combat, attempted suicide, criminal acts, experiencing the violent death of a parent during childhood, and adult rape. Each case we present was independently documented or otherwise compellingly credited by the investigators. To foster neutrality and bring historical perspective, we have preferred sources that predate the recovered memory—false memory debate regarding childhood sexual abuse.

DISASTERS AND ACCIDENTS

To provide a baseline for the extreme cases of psychogenic amnesia, we first describe ordinary memory disturbances resulting from impersonal disasters and accidents. In such cases, the availability of public information and reminders of the event would presumably enhance memory.

Impersonal disasters and accidents reveal memory disturbances as very ordinary responses to emotional trauma. Survivors of automobile accidents have shown extreme misperceptions, hallucinations, and amnesia, even after minor rear-end collisions. It can be several weeks before symptoms occur, and after they disappear they may return periodically (Quirk, 1985). Significant proportions of survivors (25%–80%) of various earthquakes, fires, and airplane crash landings have reported memory impairments (Koopman, Classen, Etzel, & Spiegel, 1995), as well as derealization ("this is not happening") and depersonalization ("this is not me here"). Survivors of the 1972 Buffalo Creek flood had cloudy memories and magical fantasies and dreams of undoing the disaster; some identified with the dead in their dreams, behaviors, and attitudes; and some denied they had been personally altered by the flood that left 125 people dead and 4,000 homeless in a small community (Titchener & Kapp, 1976). In 1984, an airplane carrying the East Tennessee University basketball team and support staff crash-landed. Although the passengers had no serious physical injuries, they exhibited a wide range of memory disturbances, including memory impairment (79%), thoughts about the accident that intruded unexpectedly into daily life (71%), depersonalization or derealization (54%), and dreams about the crash (50%), with a few cases of loss of affective responses. These symptoms diminished rapidly over the first 2 months after the crash for most but not all survivors. One month afterward, there was an unrelated fatal airplane crash on the campus. Most survivors of the first crash showed strong reactions in interviews. The gravity of symptoms did not correspond to players' subsequent performance playing basketball nor to fear of flying (Sloan, 1988).

COMBAT

The military context provides a vast laboratory for the study of psychogenic amnesia. In World War II, 14% of the first thousand military cases admitted to the neurological unit of a British hospital exhibited psychogenic amnesia, and

35% of the patients arriving from severe combat conditions were classified amnesic (Sargant & Slater, 1941). Investigators advanced a wide range of root causes for combat amnesia and the encompassing syndrome now called post-traumatic stress disorder: constitutional inferiority (Sargant & Slater, 1941), anxiety evoked by separation from primary attachment figures (Torrie, 1944), neurotic mother-son relationship (Henderson & Moore, 1944), conflict between what one wants to do (flight) and what one "should" do (fight) (Fisher, 1945), malingering (Kalman, 1977; Parfitt & Gall, 1944), and trauma that occurred from combat (Grinker & Spiegel, 1943). Working from a field hospital during the Tunisian Campaign, Grinker and Spiegel explained the range of symptoms and the proposed etiologies of war neuroses in terms of the distance of patient and diagnostician from the combat zone. The same combatants who exhibited severe amnesia in the forward areas of combat exhibited instead psychotic reactions and chronic anxiety states at safe ports of embarkation. Therefore, these researchers warned that analyses of diagnoses should take into account the location of the patient; general statistical reports of clinical syndromes and predisposing causes can otherwise be misleading. The ensuing "false amnesia controversy" (Parfitt & Gall, 1944) has continued into the debate over dissociation (psychologically removing oneself to escape intolerable fear) in Vietnam combat veterans (Bremner et al., 1992).

World War II military psychologists employed high-speed techniques of abreaction (cathartic reliving of traumatic experience), instead of psychoanalysis, to restore memory and to return the soldier to duty, ideally within 3 weeks. The main agents were hypnosis, "truth serum" drugs such as pentothal and amytal barbiturates, and forceful suggestion, with some use of group discussion, free association, dream analysis, memory triggers, and electroconvulsive shock treatments. Two notable risks in application of these techniques were subsequent amnesia for the abreacted combat experience and unintentional evocation of childhood traumas (commonly sexual) instead of combat experience (Grinker & Spiegel, 1943; Rosen & Myers, 1947).

More recent literature has explored the phenomenon of long delay in recovery of combat memories. In one case, a World War II veteran had amnesia for his service as an intelligence agent, including his capture, torture, and escape in the Far East in 1951. Thirty-seven years later, hospitalized with a neurological impairment, he recalled these traumas, speaking an Asian dialect during flashbacks (Cassiday & Lyons, 1992). The sociologist Wilbur J. Scott was amnesic for his entire tour of duty as an infantry platoon leader in Vietnam in 1968–1969, but during the stress of a divorce in 1983, a flashback of jungle combat and discovery of his medals and souvenirs from Vietnam restored his memory (Peterson, 1995).

ATTEMPTED SUICIDE

Suicide researchers have conceptualized psychogenic amnesia as an individual coping mechanism, an alternative to suicide. Takahashi's (1988) case studies of "Suicide and Amnesia in Mt. Fuji's Black Forest" represent this view. Mr. A, 21 years of age, attempted suicide after the loss of his fiancée, whom his parents had forbidden him to marry. He was amnesic when rescued by police. He showed a normal range of emotional reactions and normal intelligence, and he had no physiological disorders nor signs of drug abuse to explain his amnesia. His family recognized him through a television program and took him home, but he left again. When his sister found him in a hotel 3 months later and tried to persuade him to return, without a word he threw himself through a window to his death. In another case, Domb and Beaman's (1991) Mr. X suffered complete loss of identity after the death of his wife, even when exposed to people and places he had previously known. After 2 months, he suddenly recalled he had promised his wife that he would kill himself from grief if she died. Amnesia had substituted for suicide.

CRIMINAL ACTS

Defendants claim amnesia in a quarter to a half of homicide cases (Gudjonsson, 1992; Kopelman, 1987). Although the ready explanation is simulation of amnesia to mitigate punishment, many amnesic defendants have reported their own crimes, made no effort to escape, or persisted in amnesia that delayed their acquittal. Kopelman (1987) cited the case of an elderly man who had amnesia after battering his wife to death without evident motive. When he saw her corpse, he reasoned that he must have been the assailant and turned himself in to the police. In another case, a young woman, a wife of a firefighter, was found taking a shower while her living room burned. Subsequently, she was charged with arson in connection with a rash of neighborhood fires. Her amnesia and anxiety led to her confinement in a state mental hospital. In the course of hypnosis sessions for relief of anxiety, she suddenly recalled setting the fire in her own house, thereby incriminating herself (MacHovec, 1981).

VIOLENT DEATH OF A PARENT IN CHILDHOOD

Cain and Fast (1966) studied 45 children who had witnessed, discovered, or otherwise observed a parental suicide. The trauma in these cases was confounded by the fact that almost all of the surviving parents had grossly lied to the children about the suicide and demanded that the children not know or not tell about the event they had witnessed. For example, a boy who saw his father kill himself with a shotgun was told by his mother the death was due to a heart attack. The investigators reported the children's sense of unreality surrounding the suicide and a tendency to systematic "not knowing" that manifested itself in learning disabilities, "conditions of pseudostupidity," stutters, and loss of speech despite having the physiological ability to speak (Cain & Fast, 1966, p. 879).

Memory impairment resulting from a parent's violent death may persist into adulthood. A 58-year-old Israeli social worker, with long-standing bodily complaints, sought therapy for insomnia, depression, and rage. She could not remember much of her childhood or her 1-year internment in Auschwitz at age 11, where she had been adopted by a non-Jewish physician to work in the infirmary. When her therapist introduced hypnosis as a therapeutic technique in the 19th session, the woman recalled her train trip to Auschwitz and the final moment with her parents before they were selected for extermination. After 18 months of treatment, her symptoms abated (Somer, 1994).

ADULT RAPE

Two extensively documented cases illustrate the power of a rape experience to produce amnesia, even when secrecy is no longer possible. A 27-year-old man was found lying in a busy intersection and was brought to a hospital, disoriented and hopeless, completely unable to remember autobiographical information. Sexual assault was suspected from psychological testing. During the course of five daily hypnosis sessions with relaxation and mental imagery techniques, the man pieced together his background and his recent rape at gunpoint by two men. He discovered his own identity last, on the 10th day after the assault (Kaszniak, Berren, & Santiago, 1988). In another case, a 23-year-old Swedish woman was raped while jogging. Found by another runner, she could not explain her bruises or shock. The rapist, however, confessed to police. When police accompanied her to the scene of the assault about 5 and 11 weeks afterward, she responded emotionally at appropriate locations. She first remembered the assault while jogging again. She regained all her personal memory, beginning with the rapist's odor of beer, within 4 or 5 months after the attack (Christianson & Nilsson, 1989).

CONCLUSION

The purpose of this review is to expand the study of amnesia and recovery of memory beyond the domain of childhood sexual abuse by offering researchers a sense of the broader range of traumatic events for which psychogenic amnesia has been documented. We have presented evidence from six classes of traumatic events to support the psychogenic origin of many cases of amnesia and to illustrate strategies of memory recovery. Unfortunately, the incidence of amnesia and recovery is largely unstudied except for criminal and combat cases.

There are certain to be some differences in the specific mechanisms underlying amnesia for childhood sexual abuse and other types of traumas, but significant similarities may be expected, as well. Across a range of types of traumatic events, implicit memory for the traumatic event has been documented despite the absence of explicit (conscious) memory for it. Memory recovery has been aided by exposing individuals to contextual cues as well as by forceful techniques of abreaction, for example, with combat amnesia and police investigation of homicide. Also, the degree of amnesia generally relates to the severity of trauma but may vary according to the circumstances operative when the memory is prompted. There are also lessons for evaluating investigators' possible bias or incompetence. Identification of symptoms has been found to differ with the assessment criteria used. For example, after the airplane accident involving the East Tennessee University basketball team, the players exhibited memory problems but no impairment in athletic performance. Also, malingerers showed gradations and variability in malingering. Investigators' attributions of motives have generally corresponded poorly to amnesiacs' behavior. And, especially for combat amnesia, the institutional role of the investigator with respect to the amnesic has affected the symptomatology.

Although in the literature, traumatic events are classified by the stories surrounding the events, such a classification of cases may not facilitate the cognitive study of amnesia. In any case, some of the conceptual roadblocks that have impeded researchers studying amnesia and recovery of memory for childhood sexual abuse could be circumvented by considering, as points of reference, these other types of real-life traumatic event that have produced psychogenic amnesia.

Recommended Reading

Anderson, D. (1994). *The moon reflected fire.* Cambridge, MA: Alice James Books.
Herman, J.L. (1992). *Trauma and recovery.* New York: Basic Books.
Pezdek, K., & Banks, W.P. (Eds.). (1996). (See References)
Shay, J. (1994). *Achilles in Vietnam.* New York: Atheneum.

Acknowledgments—We are extremely grateful to Kim Finger for her assistance compiling the published sources on which this article was based.

Note

1. Address correspondence to Kathy Pezdek, Department of Psychology, Claremont Graduate University, Claremont, CA 91711-3955; e-mail: kathy.pezdek@cgu.edu.

References

Bremner, J.D., Southwick, S., Brett, E., Fontana, A., Rosenheck, R., & Charney, D. (1992). Dissociation and posttraumatic stress disorder in Vietnam combat veterans. *American Journal of Psychiatry, 149*, 328–332.

Cain, A.C., & Fast, I., (1966). Children's disturbed reactions to parent suicide. *American Journal of Orthopsychiatry,* 36, 873–880.

Cassiday, K.L., & Lyons, J.A. (1992). Recall of traumatic memories following cerebral vascular accident. *Journal of Traumatic Stress,* 5, 627–631.

Christianson, S., & Nilsson, L. (1989). Hysterical amnesia: A case of aversively motivated isolation of memory. In T. Archer & L. Nilsson (Eds.), *Aversion, avoidance, and anxiety: Perspectives on aversively motivated behavior* (pp. 289–310). Hillsdale, NJ: Erlbaum.

Cohen, N.J. (1996). Functional retrograde amnesia as a model of amnesia for childhood sexual abuse. In K. Pezdek & W.P. Banks (Eds.), *The recovered memory/false memory debate* (pp. 81–95). San Diego: Academic Press.

Domb, Y., & Beaman, K. (1991). Mr X—A case of amnesia. *British Journal of Psychiatry, 158*, 423–425.

Fisher, C. (1945). Amnesic states in war neuroses: The psychogenesis of fugues. *Psychoanalytic Quarterly, 14*, 437–468.

Grinker, R.R., & Spiegel, J.P. (1943). *War neuroses in North Africa: The Tunisian Campaign, January–May 1943* (Restricted). New York: Josiah Macy.

Gudjonsson, G.H. (1992). *The psychology of interrogations, confessions and testimony.* New York: Wiley.

Henderson, J.L., & Moore, M. (1944). The psychoneuroses of war. *The New England Journal of Medicine, 230*, 273–278.

Kalman, G. (1977). On combat-neurosis: Psychiatric experience during the recent Middle-East War. *International Journal of Social Psychiatry,* 23, 195–203.

Kaszniak, N., Berren, M.R., & Santiago, J. (1988). Amnesia as a consequence of male rape: A case report. *Journal of Abnormal Psychology,* 97, 100–104.

Koopman, C., Classen, C., Etzel, C., & Spiegel, C. (1995). When disaster strikes, acute distress disorder may follow. *Journal of Traumatic Stress, 8*, 29–46.

Kopelman, M.D. (1987). Crime and amnesia: A review. *Behavioral Sciences & the Law,* 5, 323–342.

Loftus, E. (1993). The reality of repressed memory. *American Psychologist, 48*, 518–537.

MacHovec, F.J. (1981). Hypnosis to facilitate recall in psychogenic amnesia and fugue states: Treatment variables. *The American Journal of Clinical Hypnosis, 24*, 7–13.

Parfitt, D.N., & Gall, C.M.C. (1944). Psychogenic amnesia: The refusal to remember. *The Journal of Mental Science, 90*, 513–531.

Peterson, M.A. (1995, May 1–7). Veteran, sociologist looks at Vietnam veterans. [Review of the book *The politics of readjustment: Vietnam veterans since the war*]. *The Stars and Stripes*, p. 15.

Pezdek, K., & Banks, W.P. (Eds.). (1996). *The recovered memory/false memory debate*. San Diego: Academic Press.

Pressley, M., & Grossman, L.R, (Eds.). (1994). Recovery of memories of childhood sexual abuse [Special issue]. *Applied Cognitive Psychology,* 8(4).

Quirk, D.A. (1985). Motor vehicle accidents and post-traumatic anxiety conditioning. *The Ontario Psychologist, 17*, 11–18.

Rosen, H., & Myers, H. (1947). Abreaction in the military setting. *Archives of Neurology and Psychiatry*, 557, 162–172.

Sargant, W., & Slater, E. (1941). Amnesic syndromes in war. *Proceedings of the Royal Society of Medicine, 34*, 757–764.

Sloan, P. (1988). Post-traumatic stress in survivors of an airplane crash-landing: A clinical and exploratory research intervention. *Journal of Traumatic Stress Studies, 1*, 211–229.

Somer, E. (1994). Hypnotherapy and unregulated uncovering in the treatment of older survivors of Nazi persecution. *Clinical Gerontologist, 14*, 47–65.

Takahashi, Y. (1988). Aokigahara-jukai: Suicide and amnesia in Mt. Fuji's Black Forest. *Suicide and Life-Threatening Behavior, 18*, 164–175.

Titchener, J.L., & Kapp, F.T. (1976). Family and character change at Buffalo Creek. *American Journal of Psychiatry, 133*, 295–299.

Torrie, A. (1944). Psychosomatic casualties in the Middle East, *The Lancet, 29*, 139–143.

Recovering Memories of Trauma: A View From the Laboratory

Richard J. McNally[1]
Department of Psychology, Harvard University, Cambridge, Massachusetts

Abstract

The controversy over the validity of repressed and recovered memories of childhood sexual abuse (CSA) has been extraordinarily bitter. Yet data on cognitive functioning in people reporting repressed and recovered memories of trauma have been strikingly scarce. Recent laboratory studies have been designed to test hypotheses about cognitive mechanisms that ought to be operative if people can repress and recover memories of trauma or if they can form false memories of trauma. Contrary to clinical lore, these studies have shown, that people reporting CSA histories are not characterized by a superior ability to forget trauma-related material. Other studies have shown that individuals reporting recovered memories of either CSA or abduction by space aliens are characterized by heightened proneness to form false memories in certain laboratory tasks. Although cognitive psychology methods cannot distinguish true memories from false ones, these methods can illuminate mechanisms for remembering and forgetting among people reporting histories of trauma.

Keywords

recovered memories; trauma; repression; sexual abuse; dissociation

How victims remember trauma is among the most explosive issues facing psychology today. Most experts agree that combat, rape, and other horrific experiences are unforgettably engraved on the mind (Pope, Oliva, & Hudson, 1999). But some also believe that the mind can defend itself by banishing traumatic memories from awareness, making it difficult for victims to remember them until many years later (Brown, Scheflin, & Hammond, 1998).

This controversy has spilled out of the clinics and cognitive psychology laboratories, fracturing families, triggering legislative change, and determining outcomes in civil suits and criminal trials. Most contentious has been the claim that victims of childhood sexual abuse (CSA) often repress and then recover memories of their trauma in adulthood.[2] Some psychologists believe that at least some of these memories may be false—inadvertently created by risky therapeutic methods (e.g., hypnosis, guided imagery; Ceci & Loftus, 1994).

One striking aspect of this controversy has been the paucity of data on cognitive functioning in people reporting repressed and recovered memories of CSA. Accordingly, my colleagues and I have been conducting studies designed to test hypotheses about mechanisms that might enable people either to repress and recover memories of trauma or to develop false memories of trauma.

For several of our studies, we recruited four groups of women from the community. Subjects in the *repressed-memory group* suspected they had been sexually abused as children, but they had no explicit memories of abuse. Rather, they inferred their hidden abuse history from diverse indicators, such as depressed mood, interpersonal problems with men, dreams, and brief, recurrent visual images (e.g., of a penis), which they interpreted as "flashbacks" of early trauma. Subjects in the *recovered-memory group* reported having remembered their abuse after long periods of not having thought about it.[3] Unable to corroborate their reports, we cannot say whether the memories were true or false. Lack of corroboration, of course, does not mean that a memory is false. Subjects in the *continuous-memory group* said that they had never forgotten their abuse, and subjects in the *control group* reported never having been sexually abused.

PERSONALITY TRAITS AND PSYCHIATRIC SYMPTOMS

To characterize our subjects in terms of personality traits and psychiatric symptoms, we asked them to complete a battery of questionnaires measuring normal personality variation (e.g., differences in absorption, which includes the tendency to fantasize and to become emotionally engaged in movies and literature), depressive symptoms, posttraumatic stress disorder (PTSD) symptoms, and dissociative symptoms (alterations in consciousness, such as memory lapses, feeling disconnected with one's body, or episodes of "spacing out"; McNally, Clancy, Schacter, & Pitman, 2000b).

There were striking similarities and differences among the groups in terms of personality profiles and psychiatric symptoms. Subjects who had always remembered their abuse were indistinguishable from those who said they had never been abused on all personality measures. Moreover, the continuous-memory and control groups did not differ in their symptoms of depression, posttraumatic stress, or dissociation. However, on the measure of negative affectivity—proneness to experience sadness, anxiety, anger, and guilt—the repressed-memory group scored higher than did either the continuous-memory or the control group, whereas the recovered -memory group scored midway between the repressed-memory group on the one hand and the continuous-memory and control groups on the other.

The repressed-memory subjects reported more depressive, dissociative, and PTSD symptoms than did continuous-memory and control subjects. Repressed-memory subjects also reported more depressive and PTSD symptoms than did recovered-memory subjects, who, in turn, reported more dissociative and PTSD symptoms than did control subjects. Finally, the repressed- and recovered-memory groups scored higher than the control group on the measure of fantasy proneness, and the repressed-memory group scored higher than the continuous-memory group on this measure.

This psychometric study shows that people who believe they harbor repressed memories of sexual abuse are more psychologically distressed than those who say they have never forgotten their abuse.

FORGETTING TRAUMA-RELATED MATERIAL

Some clinical theorists believe that sexually molested children learn to disengage their attention during episodes of abuse and allocate it elsewhere (e.g., Terr,

1991). If CSA survivors possess a heightened ability to disengage attention from threatening cues, impairing their subsequent memory for them, then this ability ought to be evident in the laboratory. In our first experiment, we used directed-forgetting methods to test this hypothesis (McNally, Metzger, Lasko, Clancy, & Pitman, 1998). Our subjects were three groups of adult females: CSA survivors with PTSD, psychiatrically healthy CSA survivors, and nonabused control subjects. Each subject was shown, on a computer screen, a series of words that were either trauma related (e.g., *molested*), positive (e.g., *charming*), or neutral (e.g., *mailbox*). Immediately after each word was presented, the subject received instructions telling her either to remember the word or to forget it. After this encoding phase, she was asked to write down all the words she could remember, irrespective of the original instructions that followed each word.

If CSA survivors, especially those with PTSD, are characterized by heightened ability to disengage attention from threat cues, thereby attenuating memory for them, then the CSA survivors with PTSD in this experiment should have recalled few trauma words, especially those they had been told to forget. Contrary to this hypothesis, this group exhibited memory deficits for positive and neutral words they had been told to remember, while demonstrating excellent memory for trauma words, including those they had been told to forget. Healthy CSA survivors and control subjects recalled remember-words more often than forget-words regardless of the type of word. Rather than possessing a superior ability to forget trauma-related material, the most distressed survivors exhibited difficulty banishing this material from awareness.

In our next experiment, we used this directed-forgetting approach to test whether repressed- and recovered-memory subjects, relative to nonabused control subjects, would exhibit the hypothesized superior ability to forget material related to trauma (McNally, Clancy, & Schacter, 2001). If anyone possesses this ability, it ought to be such individuals. However, the memory performance of the repressed- and recovered-memory groups was entirely normal: They recalled remember-words better than forget-words, regardless of whether the words were positive, neutral, or trauma related.

INTRUSION OF TRAUMATIC MATERIAL

The hallmark of PTSD is involuntary, intrusive recollection of traumatic experiences. Clinicians have typically relied on introspective self-reports as confirming the presence of this symptom. The emotional Stroop color-naming task provides a quantitative, nonintrospective measure of intrusive cognition. In this paradigm, subjects are shown words varying in emotional significance, and are asked to name the colors the words are printed in while ignoring the meanings of the words. When the meaning of a word intrusively captures the subject's attention despite the subject's efforts to attend to its color, Stroop interference—delay in color naming—occurs. Trauma survivors with PTSD take longer to name the colors of words related to trauma than do survivors without the disorder, and also take longer to name the colors of trauma words than to name the colors of positive and neutral words or negative words unrelated to their trauma (for a review, see McNally, 1998).

Using the emotional Stroop task, we tested whether subjects reporting either continuous, repressed, or recovered memories of CSA would exhibit interference for trauma words, relative to nonabused control subjects (McNally, Clancy, Schacter, & Pitman, 2000a). If severity of trauma motivates repression of traumatic memories, then subjects who cannot recall their presumably repressed memories may nevertheless exhibit interference for trauma words. We presented a series of trauma-related, positive, and neutral words on a computer screen, and subjects named the colors of the words as quickly as possible. Unlike patients with PTSD, including children with documented abuse histories (Dubner & Motta, 1999), none of the groups exhibited delayed color naming of trauma words relative to neutral or positive ones.

MEMORY DISTORTION AND FALSE MEMORIES IN THE LABORATORY

Some psychotherapists who believe their patients suffer from repressed memories of abuse will ask them to visualize hypothetical abuse scenarios, hoping that this guided-imagery technique will unblock the presumably repressed memories. Unfortunately, this procedure may foster false memories.

Using Garry, Manning, Loftus, and Sherman's (1996) methods, we tested whether subjects who have recovered memories of abuse are more susceptible than control subjects to this kind of memory distortion (Clancy, McNally, & Schacter, 1999). During an early visit to the laboratory, subjects rated their confidence regarding whether they had experienced a series of unusual, but non-traumatic, childhood events (e.g., getting stuck in a tree). During a later visit, they performed a guided-imagery task requiring them to visualize certain of these events, but not others. They later rerated their confidence that they had experienced each of the childhood events. Nonsignificant trends revealed an inflation in confidence for imagined versus nonimagined events. But the magnitude of this memory distortion was more than twice as large in the control group as in the recovered-memory group, contrary to the hypothesis that people who have recovered memories of CSA would be especially vulnerable to the memory-distorting effects of guided imagery.

To use a less-transparent paradigm for assessing proneness to develop false memories, we adapted the procedure of Roediger and McDermott (1995). During the encoding phase in this paradigm, subjects hear word lists, each consisting of semantically related items (e.g., *sour*, *bitter*, *candy*, *sugar*) that converge on a nonpresented word—the *false target*—that captures the gist of the list (e.g., *sweet*). On a subsequent recognition test, subjects are given a list of words and asked to indicate which ones they heard during the previous phase. The false memory effect occurs when subjects "remember" having heard the false target. We found that recovered-memory subjects exhibited greater proneness to this false memory effect than did subjects reporting either repressed memories of CSA, continuous memories of CSA, or no abuse (Clancy, Schacter, McNally, & Pitman, 2000). None of the lists was trauma related, and so we cannot say whether the effect would have been more or less pronounced for words directly related to sexual abuse.

In our next experiment, we tested people whose memories were probably false: individuals reporting having been abducted by space aliens (Clancy, McNally, Schacter, Lenzenweger, & Pitman, 2002). In addition to testing these individuals (and control subjects who denied having been abducted by aliens), we tested individuals who believed they had been abducted, but who had no memories of encountering aliens. Like the repressed-memory subjects in our previous studies, they inferred their histories of trauma from various "indicators" (e.g., a passion for reading science fiction, unexplained marks on their bodies). Like subjects with recovered memories of CSA, those reporting recovered memories of alien abduction exhibited pronounced false memory effects in the laboratory. Subjects who only believed they had been abducted likewise exhibited robust false memory effects.

CONCLUSIONS

The aforementioned experiments illustrate one way of approaching the recovered-memory controversy. Cognitive psychology methods cannot ascertain whether the memories reported by our subjects were true or false, but these methods can enable testing of hypotheses about mechanisms that ought to be operative if people can repress and recover memories of trauma or if they can develop false memories of trauma.

Pressing issues remain unresolved. For example, experimentalists assume that directed forgetting and other laboratory methods engage the same cognitive mechanisms that generate the signs and symptoms of emotional disorder in the real world. Some therapists question the validity of this assumption. Surely, they claim, remembering or forgetting the word *incest* in a laboratory task fails to capture the sensory and narrative complexity of autobiographical memories of abuse. On the one hand, the differences between remembering the word *incest* in a directed-forgetting experiment, for example, and recollecting an episode of molestation do, indeed, seem to outweigh the similarities. On the other hand, laboratory studies may underestimate clinical relevance. For example, if someone cannot expel the word *incest* from awareness during a directed-forgetting experiment, then it seems unlikely that this person would be able to banish autobiographical memories of trauma from consciousness. This intuition notwithstanding, an important empirical issue concerns whether these tasks do, indeed, engage the same mechanisms that figure in the cognitive processing of traumatic memories outside the laboratory.

A second issue concerns attempts to distinguish subjects with genuine memories of abuse from those with false memories of abuse. Our group is currently exploring whether this might be done by classifying trauma narratives in terms of how subjects describe their memory-recovery experience. For example, some of the subjects in our current research describe their recovered memories of abuse by saying, "I had forgotten about that. I hadn't thought about the abuse in years until I was reminded of it recently." The narratives of other recovered-memory subjects differ in their experiential quality. These subjects, as they describe it, suddenly realize that they are abuse survivors, sometimes attributing current life difficulties to these long-repressed memories. That is, they do not say that they have remembered forgotten events they once knew, but rather indicate that they have learned (e.g., through hypnosis) the abuse occurred. It will be important to determine whether these two groups of recovered-memory subjects differ cognitively. For example, are subjects exemplifying the second type of recovered-memory experience more prone to develop false memories in the laboratory than are subjects exemplifying the first type of experience?

Recommended Reading

Lindsay, D.S., & Read, J.D. (1994). Psychotherapy and memories of childhood sexual abuse: A cognitive perspective. *Applied Cognitive Psychology, 8*, 281–338.

McNally, R.J. (2001). The cognitive psychology of repressed and recovered memories of childhood sexual abuse: Clinical implications. *Psychiatric Annals, 31*, 509–514.

McNally, R.J. (2003). Progress and controversy in the study of posttraumatic stress disorder. *Annual Review of Psychology, 54*, 229–252.

McNally, R.J. (2003). *Remembering trauma.* Cambridge, MA: Belknap Press/Harvard University Press.

Piper, A., Jr., Pope, H.G., Jr., & Borowiecki, J.J., III. (2000). Custer's last stand: Brown, Scheflin, and Whitfield's latest attempt to salvage "dissociative amnesia." *Journal of Psychiatry and Law, 28*, 149–213.

Acknowledgments—Preparation of this article was supported in part by National Institute of Mental Health Grant MH61268.

Notes

1. Address correspondence to Richard J. McNally, Department of Psychology, Harvard University, 1230 William James Hall, 33 Kirkland St., Cambridge, MA 02138; e-mail: rjm@wjh.harvard.edu.

2. Some authors prefer the term *dissociation* (or *dissociative amnesia*) to *repression*. Although these terms signify different proposed mechanisms, for practical purposes these variations make little difference in the recovered-memory debate. Each term implies a defensive process that blocks access to disturbing memories.

3. However, not thinking about a disturbing experience for a long period of time must not be equated with an inability to remember it. Amnesia denotes an inability to recall information that has been encoded.

References

Brown, D., Scheflin, A.W., & Hammond, D.C. (1998). *Memory, trauma treatment, and the law.* New York: Norton.

Ceci, S.J., & Loftus, E.F. (1994). 'Memory work': A royal road to false memories? *Applied Cognitive Psychology, 8*, 351–364.

Clancy, S.A., McNally, R.J., & Schacter, D.L. (1999). Effects of guided imagery on memory distortion in women reporting recovered memories of childhood sexual abuse. *Journal of Traumatic Stress, 12*, 559–569.

Clancy, S.A., McNally, R.J., Schacter, D.L., Lenzenweger, M.F., & Pitman, R.K. (2002). Memory distortion in people reporting abduction by aliens. *Journal of Abnormal Psychology, 111*, 455–461.

Clancy, S.A., Schacter, D.L., McNally, R.J., & Pitman, R.K. (2000). False recognition in women reporting recovered memories of sexual abuse. *Psychological Science, 11*, 26–31.

Dubner, A.E., & Motta, R.W. (1999). Sexually and physically abused foster care children and posttraumatic stress disorder. *Journal of Consulting and Clinical Psychology, 67*, 367–373.

Garry, M., Manning, C.G., Loftus, E.F., & Sherman, S.J. (1996). Imagination inflation: Imagining a childhood event inflates confidence that it occurred. *Psychonomic Bulletin & Review, 3*, 208–214.

McNally, R.J. (1998). Experimental approaches to cognitive abnormality in posttraumatic stress disorder. *Clinical Psychology Review, 18*, 971–982.

McNally, R.J., Clancy, S.A., & Schacter, D.L. (2001). Directed forgetting of trauma cues in adults reporting repressed or recovered memories of childhood sexual abuse. *Journal of Abnormal Psychology, 110*, 151–156.

McNally, R.J., Clancy, S.A., Schacter, D.L., & Pitman, R.K. (2000a). Cognitive processing of trauma cues in adults reporting repressed, recovered, or continuous memories of childhood sexual abuse. *Journal of Abnormal Psychology, 109*, 355–359.

McNally, R.J., Clancy, S.A., Schacter, D.L., & Pitman, R.K. (2000b). Personality profiles, dissociation, and absorption in women reporting repressed, recovered, or continuous memories of childhood sexual abuse. *Journal of Consulting and Clinical Psychology, 68*, 1033–1037.

McNally, R.J., Metzger, L.J., Lasko, N.B., Clancy, S.A., & Pitman, R.K. (1998). Directed forgetting of trauma cues in adult survivors of childhood sexual abuse with and without posttraumatic stress disorder. *Journal of Abnormal Psychology, 107*, 596–601.

Pope, H.G., Jr., Oliva, P.S., & Hudson, J.I. (1999). Repressed memories: The scientific status. In D.L. Faigman, D.H. Kaye, M.J. Saks, & J. Sanders (Eds.), *Modern scientific evidence: The law and science of expert testimony* (Vol. 1, pocket part, pp. 115–155). St. Paul, MN: West Publishing.

Roediger, H.L., III, & McDermott, K.B. (1995). Creating false memories: Remembering words not presented in lists. *Journal of Experimental Psychology: Learning, Memory, and Cognition, 21*, 803–814.

Terr, L.C. (1991). Childhood traumas: An outline and overview. *American Journal of Psychiatry, 148*, 10–20.

Stress, Positive Emotion, and Coping

Susan Folkman[1] and Judith Tedlie Moskowitz
Center for AIDS Prevention Studies, University of California-San Francisco, San Francisco, California

Abstract

There is growing interest in positive aspects of the stress process, including positive outcomes (if stress and antecedents that dispose individuals to appraise stressful situations more as a challenge than as a threat. Less attention has been given to the adaptational significance of positive emotions during stress or to the coping processes that sustain positive emotions. We review evidence for the occurrence of positive emotions under conditions of stress, discuss the functional role that positive emotions play under such conditions, and present three types of coping that are associated with positive emotion during chronic stress. These findings point to new research questions about the role of positive emotions during stress and the nature of the coping processes that generate these positive emotions.

Keywords

coping; positive emotion; chronic stress

Decades of research have shown that stress is associated with a wide array of negative outcomes, such as depression, anxiety, physical symptoms, disease, and even death in extreme cases. In recent years, however, there has been a growing interest in positive aspects of the stress process, including positive outcomes such as personal transformation or growth (for review, see Tedeschi, Park, & Calhoun, 1998) and antecedents that dispose individuals to appraise situations more as a challenge than as a threat. With the exception of a few investigators such as Affleck and Tennen (1996), however, researchers have not given much attention to the actual coping mechanisms that link the positive dispositions, on the one hand, and the positive outcomes of stressful situations, on the other.

The growing interest in positive aspects of the stress process is paralleled by a growing interest in positive emotions and, of particular relevance here, the possibility that they may have important adaptational significance during the stress process. Fredrickson (1998), for example, cited evidence that positive emotions broaden the scope of attention, cognition, and action, and help build physical, intellectual, and social resources. Her "Broaden and Build Model of Positive Emotions," which is premised on this evidence, raises the possibility that positive emotions are important facilitators of adaptive coping and adjustment to acute and chronic stress and may underlie the beneficial effects of interventions such as relaxation therapies (Fredrickson, 2000). Twenty years ago, we (Lazarus, Kanner, & Folkman, 1980) suggested that positive emotions may have three important adaptive functions during stress: sustaining coping efforts, providing a "breather," and restoring depleted resources. However, until recently, there has been little effort to provide empirical support for these ideas.

The idea that people even experience positive emotions in the midst of acute or chronic stress may at first seem counterintuitive. But people do experience these emotions, even under the most difficult of circumstances. For example, when we monitored gay men who were the primary informal caregivers of partners with AIDS for up to 5 years, the caregivers reported levels of depressed mood that were more than one standard deviation above levels in the general population, and increased to more than two standard deviations above the general population's levels during periods of crisis. Throughout the study, with the exception of the weeks immediately preceding and following their partners' deaths, however, the caregivers also reported experiencing positive mood at a frequency comparable to the frequency of their negative mood (Folkman, 1997).

COPING AND POSITIVE EMOTION

Given data demonstrating that positive emotions occur even under the most dire of circumstances, the compelling question becomes not whether people experience positive emotions during long periods of severe stress, but rather, how they do it. In our study of caregivers, we identified three classes of coping mechanisms that help answer this question: positive reappraisal, problem-focused coping, and the creation of positive events (Folkman, 1997; Folkman & Moskowitz, in press).

Positive Reappraisal

Positive reappraisal is a cognitive process through which people focus on the good in what is happening or what has happened. Forms of positive reappraisal include discovering opportunities for personal growth, perceiving actual personal growth, and seeing how one's own efforts can benefit other people. Through the process of positive reappraisal, the meaning of a situation is changed in a way that allows the person to experience positive emotion and psychological well-being. In our study of AIDS-related caregiving, we found that positive reappraisal was consistently associated with positive emotion both during caregiving and after the death of the partner. This association remained significant even when emotion at the previous interview and the other types of coping were statistically controlled (Moskowitz, Folkman, Collette, & Vittinghoff, 1996).

Not all forms of positive reappraisal necessarily generate positive emotion. For example, a cognitive reappraisal through which an individual devalues an important goal that has proven to be unrealistic, such as gaining admission to a prestigious Ivy League school, may be positive in that it lessens the personal significance of failing to achieve the goal, but it may do more to reduce distress than to enhance positive emotion.

Problem-Focused Coping

Problem-focused coping includes thoughts and instrumental behaviors that manage or solve the underlying cause of distress. It tends to be used more in situations in which there is personal control over an outcome and less in situations in which there is an absence of personal control. Problem-focused coping is usually considered maladaptive when there is no personal control (Lazarus & Folkman, 1984), but this general formula may be overly simplified; a situation that appears on its surface to be uncontrollable may still have controllable aspects.

In our research, for example, we found a significant increase in problem-focused coping by caregivers during the weeks leading up to the partner's death, a period of profound lack of control. A review of narrative data showed that during this period caregivers were often creating the proverbial "to-do" list, usually comprising seemingly mundane tasks such as getting a prescription filled, successfully administering a medication, or changing the partner's bed linens. Such lists served multiple purposes: In attending to even the most trivial task, the caregiver had an opportunity to feel effective and in control, thereby helping to combat the feelings of helplessness and lack of control that often characterized the overall situation; working on tasks helped the caregiver feel mobilized and focused, which was energizing; and the successful accomplishment of the various tasks was often helpful, in which case the caregiver often benefited from positive feedback from his partner or other people involved in the partner's care. An important finding was that this type of coping was responsible for increases in positive mood (as distinct from decreases in distress) during these weeks (Moskowitz et al., 1996).

Creation of Positive Events

This coping mechanism involves creating a positive psychological time-out by infusing ordinary events with positive meaning (Folkman, Moskowitz, Ozer, & Park, 1997), as when a person reflects on a compliment that was offered in passing, or pauses to take note of a beautiful sunset. Such time-outs provide momentary respite from the ongoing stress. In our study of caregivers, we were struck by the pervasiveness of this method of coping throughout caregiving and bereavement. Month after month, for example, more than 99% of the caregivers noted and remembered positive events in the midst of some of the most psychologically stressful circumstances people encounter. For the most part, these events were ordinary events of daily life that in less stressful moments might not even have been noted. We believe the occurrence of these positive events was not random. Rather, caregivers created them deliberately by planning positive events, noting positive events when they occurred serendipitously, or infusing neutral events with positive meaning, as a way of having a few moments of relief from the intense stress.

Sometimes the creation of these meaningful events depended on the caregiver's ability to find humor in the situation. Humor, which has long been recognized for its tension-reducing properties (e.g., Menninger, 1963), has the added benefit of generating positive emotion in the very darkest of moments, which may, in turn, help build social bonds that can be beneficial under conditions of stress. The term gallows humor attests to the widespread use of humor in situations that are particularly grim. Humor was common in the accounts provided by caregivers, even the accounts that described partners' deaths. The humor usually managed to capture positive qualities of the dying partner in a loving manner, which had the additional benefit of helping the caregiver create images of the partner that he wanted to remember.

COMPELLING UNANSWERED QUESTIONS

Research on coping and positive emotions is still in its earliest stages, and each new finding raises new questions. For example, researchers have only begun to understand the adaptive functions of positive emotions in the midst of stressful circumstances. Laboratory studies have provided provocative suggestions regarding the ways positive emotions may help people endure stress (e.g., Fredrickson & Levenson, 1998). But because constraints of the laboratory limit researchers' ability to simulate the meaning or duration of serious real-life stressors, we strongly encourage pursuing research under real-life circumstances, with all their complexity. In our newly launched study of maternal caregivers, for example, we are investigating positive emotions and relevant coping processes in the daily lives of women providing care for a child with HIV or other serious chronic illness.

There are several issues regarding measurement and conceptualization of emotion that need to be addressed in order to advance knowledge of the role of positive emotion in the stress process. At this point, there is little in the literature about the intensity and duration of positive emotions necessary to activate their adaptive functions during stress. In our study of AIDS-related caregiving, the quantitative measures assessed the frequency of emotions, not their duration or intensity. But qualitative data suggested that positive emotions were less intense and less enduring than negative emotions (Folkman et al., 1997). It may be that it is the frequency of positive emotion, and not its intensity or duration, that confers benefits on the individual.

A related issue has to do with whether different positive emotions are differentially effective with respect to motivating and sustaining coping, and if so, under what circumstances. For example, is excitement more adaptive than happiness at the outset of a stressful undertaking, but less so while the situation unfolds?

Answering these questions regarding intensity, duration, and differential effects of positive emotions will require close attention to the measurement and conceptualization of emotion. Recent debates regarding whether positive and negative emotion are independent or bipolar constructs (i.e., opposite extremes of the same construct) have reignited interest in these issues (see Russell & Carroll, 1999, for a review). As Russell and Carroll (1999) noted, when all the measurement issues are considered, a bipolar model fits the data best. By making the assertion that both positive and negative emotion occur in chronically stressful situations, we are not implying that they are independent and that at any given moment high levels of negative emotion co-occur with high levels of positive emotion. Rather, our point is that over a period of time, people in stressful situations experience not only negative emotion, but also positive emotion. Thus, in the case of our caregiver study, when participants reported their emotions over the previous week, as expected, they indicated that they experienced frequent negative affect, but they also experienced fairly frequent positive affect.

The coping processes that are associated with positive emotion involve another set of questions. Are the coping processes that generate positive emotion truly different from those that regulate distress? If so, how are they different? For example, many of the positive reappraisal processes that generate positive emotion depend on the individual's ability to access deeply held values that enhance the personal significance of ongoing coping activity. In contrast, coping processes that people are more likely to use to regulate distress (such as escape-avoidance or distancing), or even strategies that are intended to reduce tension (such as relaxation or meditation), do not seem to depend on accessing values in the same way. Further work that specifically addresses the distinction between coping processes that are associated with positive as opposed to negative emotions is clearly needed. If the ways of coping that decrease negative emotion differ from those that increase positive emotion, it may be necessary for researchers to expand the repertoire of coping measures in order to more fully tap into these positive ways of coping.

Another set of questions concerns the importance of the duration of stress, and whether the capacity or need for positive emotions differs in acute versus chronic stressful situations. Does the novelty, immediacy, or urgency of the demands of an acute stressful situation reduce the person's capacity for engaging in the coping strategies that generate positive emotions? Or perhaps it is not as important to generate positive emotions during an acute, time-limited situation as it is when a stressful situation persists over time, and the person needs to have respite from distress to become rededicated to the coping efforts in order to keep going. Studies directly comparing coping with acute, relatively short-lived stressors and coping with chronic stressors are necessary to answer this question.

Finally, to what extent can people be taught to generate positive emotions while they are also regulating distress? Is the ability to generate positive emotions attached to underlying personality dimensions, such as optimism, that may be relatively immutable? Or are there teachable skills that are independent of the underlying personality dimensions? Lewinsohn and his colleagues recognized the importance of pleasant events (and the associated positive emotions) in the treatment of depression years ago (e.g., Lewinsohn, Sullivan, & Grosscup, 1980). More recent work has pursued the idea that helping clients identify thoughts and beliefs that interfere with positive experiences is an important component of therapy (Fava, Rafanelli, Cazzaro, Conti, & Grandi, 1998).

We have highlighted some of the exciting new developments in the areas of stress, positive emotions, and coping. These developments point the way for systematic, programmatic research that may help explain the fascinating, fundamental question, namely, why it is that some people not only survive adversity mentally and physically, but manage somehow even to thrive.

Recommended Reading

Folkman, S. (1997). (See References) Fredrickson, B.L. (1998). (See References) Tedeschi, R.G., Park, C.L., & Calhoun, L.G. (Eds.). (1998). (See References)

Acknowledgments—This research was supported by Grants 49985 and 52517 from the National Institute of Mental Health, and by Grant 58069 from the National Institute of Mental Health and the National Institute of Nursing Research.

Note

1. Address correspondence to Susan Folkman, 74 New Montgomery, Suite 600, San Francisco, CA 94105; e-mail: sfolkman@psg.ucsf.edu.

References

Affleck, G., & Tennen, H. (1996). Construing benefits from adversity: Adaptational significance and dispositional underpinnings. *Journal of Personality, 64,* 899–922.

Fava, G.A., Rafanelli, C., Cazzaro, M., Conti, S., & Grandi, S. (1998). Well-being therapy: A novel psychotherapeutic approach for residual symptoms of affective disorders. *Psychological Medicine, 28,* 475–480.

Folkman, S. (1997). Positive psychological states and coping with severe stress. *Social Science and Medicine, 45,* 1207–1221.

Folkman, S., & Moskowitz, J.T. (in press). Positive affect and the other side of coping. *American Psychologist.*

Folkman, S., Moskowitz, J.T., Ozer, E.M., & Park, C.L. (1997). Positive meaning" events and coping in the context of HIV/AIDS. In B.H. Gottlieb (Ed.), *Coping with chronic stress* (pp. 293–314). New York: Plenum Press.

Fredrickson, B.L. (1998). What good are positive emotions? *Review of General Psychology, 2,* 300–319.

Fredrickson, B.L. (2000). Cultivating positive emotions to optimize health and well-being. *Prevention and Treatment* [On-line], 3. Available: http://journals.apa.org.prevention

Fredrickson, B.L., & Levenson, R.W. (1998). Positive emotions speed recovery from the cardiovascular sequelae of negative emotions. *Cognition and Emotion, 12,* 191–220.

Lazarus, R.S., & Folkman, S. (1984). *Stress, appraisal, and coping.* New York: Springer.

Lazarus, R.S., Kanner, A.D., & Folkman, S. (1980). Emotions: A cognitive-phenomenological analysis. In R. Plutchik & H. Kellerman (Eds.), *Theories of emotion* (pp. 189–217). New York: Academic Press.

Lewinsohn, P.M., Sullivan, J.M., & Grosscup, S.J. (1980). Changing reinforcing events: An approach to the treatment of depression. *Psychotherapy: Theory, Research, and Practice, 17,* 322–334.

Menninger, K. (1963). *The vital balance: The life process in mental health and illness.* New York: Viking.

Moskowitz, J.T., Folkman, S., Collette, L., & Vittinghoff, E. (1996). Coping and mood during AIDS-related caregiving and bereavement. *Annals of Behavioral Medicine, 18,* 49–57.

Russell, J.A., & Carroll, J.M. (1999). On the bipolarity of positive and negative affect. *Psychological Bulletin, 125,* 3–30.

Tedeschi, R.G., Park, C.L., & Calhoun, L.G. (Eds.). (1998). *Posttraumatic growth.* Mahwah, NJ: Erlbaum.

Personality Disorders, Sexual and Eating Disorders, Schizophrenia, and Dementia

This section of the reader includes papers that address a range of issues from personality and sexual behavior to psychosis and dementia. Again, these papers are included for a variety of reasons. They present specific examples of cutting-edge ideas about the development of problem behaviors. Most also provide accessible descriptions of current research methods that are being used to advance our knowledge of these disorders. These are the findings that, in a few short years, will likely become standard knowledge about abnormal psychology.

The first paper, by Roy Baumeister, Brad Bushman, and W. Keith Campbell, is concerned with narcissism, a fascinating and vexing personality problem that has not been studied extensively. Personality disorders are defined not only by a set of traits and characteristics but also in terms of their negative impact on interpersonal relationships and social adjustment. Baumeister and his colleagues have explored the connection between narcissism and violent behavior. When you read this paper, you might want to ask yourself about similarities between this approach and the view of personality that is suggested by Mischel and his colleagues in an earlier paper in this reader. How do personality characteristics interact with situational contexts to influence behavior?

In the next paper, J. Kevin Thompson and Eric Stice discuss their work regarding eating disorders and the internalization of societal standards of attractiveness. They suggest that women who accept socially defined ideals of attractiveness are more likely to diet and to experience more negative emotion because the ideal is impossible for most women to achieve. This program of research has generated interesting ideas about ways of treating and preventing eating disorders.

The third paper in this section, by Danielle Dick and Richard Rose, provides an accessible and exciting description of cutting edge research methods that are being used to explore the impact of genetic factors on the development of mental disorders, especially substance use disorders. The field has moved beyond the point at which investigators wanted to know whether genetic factors influence psychopathology (see earlier paper by Turkheimer). The answer to that question is definitely "yes," but the real challenge is to move beyond that finding. This paper suggests, for example, that the impact of genetic vulnerability can be influenced by changes in environmental circumstances. These findings raise new questions about the causes of alcoholism and other kinds of substance use disorders.

We have included two papers that are concerned with sexual behavior. Both address important and timely topics and go beyond the level of information that can be provided in most textbooks. The paper by Letitia Peplau is concerned with gender differences in sexual interests and behavior. The system that is currently used to classify sexual dysfunctions is based largely on the assumption that patterns of sexual response are quite similar for men and women. Some experts have recently questioned this view and its implications for defining sexual problems. Peplau provides a compelling summary of several ways in which men and women may differ with regard to sexuality. Ask yourself how these differences might lead to changes in way that sexual dysfunctions are classified when DSM-V is produced.

The second paper on sexual disorders was written by R. Karl Hanson, whose research is concerned with the prediction of new sexual offenses among those with previous convictions. The issues addressed in this paper highlight the importance of methods used to assess patterns of abnormal sexual arousal (paraphilias). Hanson's analyses also illustrate the challenges faced by investigators who want to predict future problems, such as repeated sexual offenses.

We have included two papers that are concerned with schizophrenia. The first, by Heather Conklin and William Iacono, provides a broad model for the development of schizophrenia, taking into account factors such as genetic vulnerability and neurological abnormalities. The authors discuss a number of ideas and research methods that help to place current thinking about this disorder in better perspective. The second paper, by Deanna Barch, explores in greater detail one particular type of cognitive problem—deficits in working memory—that seems to play a central role in this disorder. If we use the terms suggested by Miller and Keller (first article in this reader), Barch suggests that specific cognitive problems are *implemented* in dopamine pathways of the prefrontal cortex.

The final paper in this section, written by Robert Wilson and David Bennett, is concerned with Alzheimer's disease. More specifically, it reviews evidence regarding a phenomenon that has been observed in epidemiological studies: higher levels of educational achievement are associated with reduced risk for developing this form of dementia. Wilson and Bennett consider various explanations for this finding, including the possibility that increased cognitive activity may improve structural and functional organization in the brain.

Self-Esteem, Narcissism, and Aggression: Does Violence Result From Low Self-Esteem or From Threatened Egotism?

Roy F. Baumeister,[1] Brad J. Bushman, and W. Keith Campbell
Department of Psychology, Case Western Reserve University, Cleveland, Ohio (R.F.B., W.K.C.), and Department of Psychology, Iowa State University, Ames, Iowa (B.J.B.)

Abstract

A traditional view holds that low self-esteem causes aggression, but recent work has not confirmed this. Although aggressive people typically have high self-esteem, there are also many nonaggressive people with high self-esteem, and so newer constructs such as narcissism and unstable self-esteem are most effective at predicting aggression. The link between self-regard and aggression is best captured by the theory of threatened egotism, which depicts aggression as a means of defending a highly favorable view of self against someone who seeks to undermine or discredit that view.

Keywords

aggression; violence; self-esteem; narcissism

For decades, the prevailing wisdom has held that low self-esteem causes aggression. Many authors have cited or invoked this belief or used it as an implicit assumption to explain their findings regarding other variables (e.g., Gondolf, 1985; Levin & McDevitt, 1993; Staub, 1989). The origins of this idea are difficult to establish. One can search the literature without finding any original theoretical statement of that view, nor is there any seminal investigation that provided strong empirical evidence that low self-esteem causes aggression. Ironically, the theory seemed to enter into conventional wisdom without ever being empirically established.

The view of low self-esteem that has emerged from many research studies does not, however, seem easily reconciled with the theory that low self-esteem causes aggression. A composite of research findings depicts people with low self-esteem as uncertain and confused about themselves, oriented toward avoiding risk and potential loss, shy, modest, emotionally labile (and having tendencies toward depression and anxiety), submitting readily to other people's influence, and lacking confidence in themselves (see compilation by Baumeister, 1993).

None of these patterns seems likely to increase aggression, and some of them seem likely to discourage it. People with low self-esteem are oriented toward avoiding risk and loss, whereas attacking someone is eminently risky. People with low self-esteem lack confidence of success, whereas aggression is usually undertaken in the expectation of defeating the other person. Low self-esteem involves submitting to influence, whereas aggression is often engaged in to resist and reject external influence. Perhaps most relevant, people with low self-esteem are confused and uncertain about who they are, whereas aggression is likely to be an attempt to defend and assert a strongly held opinion about oneself.

PAINTING THE PICTURE OF VIOLENT MEN

An alternative to the low-self-esteem theory emerges when one examines what is known about violent individuals. Most research has focused on violent men, although it seems reasonable to assume that violent women conform to similar patterns. Violent men seem to have a strong sense of personal superiority, and their violence often seems to stem from a sense of wounded pride. When someone else questions or disputes their favorable view of self, they lash out in response.

An interdisciplinary literature review (Baumeister, Smart, & Boden, 1996) found that favorable self-regard is linked to violence in one sphere after another. Murderers, rapists, wife beaters, violent youth gangs, aggressive nations, and other categories of violent people are all marked by strongly held views of their own superiority. When large groups of people differ in self-esteem, the group with the higher self-esteem is generally the more violent one.

When self-esteem rises or falls as a by-product of other events, aggressive tendencies likewise tend to covary, but again in a pattern precisely opposite to what the low-self-esteem theory predicts. People with manic depression, for example, tend to be more aggressive and violent during their manic stage (marked by highly favorable views of self) than during the depressed phase (when self-esteem is low). Alcohol intoxication has been shown to boost self-esteem temporarily, and it also boosts aggressive tendencies. Changes in the relative self-esteem levels of African-American and white American citizens have been accompanied by changes in relative violence between the groups, and again in the direction opposite to the predictions of the low-self-esteem view. Hence, it appears that aggressive, violent people hold highly favorable opinions of themselves. Moreover, the aggression ensues when these favorable opinions are disputed or questioned by other people. It therefore seems plausible that aggression results from threatened egotism.

AGGRESSION, HOSTILITY, AND SELF-REGARD

Thus, the low-self-esteem theory is not defensible. Should behavioral scientists leap to the opposite conclusion, namely, that high self-esteem causes violence? No. Although clearly many violent individuals have high self-esteem, it is also necessary to know whether many exceptionally nonviolent individuals also have high self-esteem.

Perhaps surprisingly, direct and controlled studies linking self-esteem to aggression are almost nonexistent. Perhaps no one has ever bothered to study the question, but this seems unlikely. Instead, it seems more plausible that such investigations have been done but have remained unpublished because they failed to find any clear or direct link. Such findings would be consistent with the view that the category of people with high self-esteem contains both aggressive and nonaggressive individuals.

One of the few studies to link self-esteem to hostile tendencies found that people with high self-esteem tended to cluster at both the hostile and the non-hostile extremes (Kernis, Grannemann, & Barclay, 1989). The difference lay in stability of self-esteem, which the researchers assessed by measuring self-esteem on several occasions and computing how much variability each individual showed over time. People whose self-esteem was high as well as stable—thus, people whose favorable view of self was largely impervious to daily events—were the least prone to hostility of any group. In contrast, people with high but unstable self-esteem scored highest on hostility. These findings suggest that violent individuals are one subset of people with high self-esteem. High self-esteem may well be a mixed category, containing several different kinds of people. One of those kinds is very nonaggressive, whereas another is quite aggressive.

The view that individuals with high self-esteem form a heterogeneous category is gaining ground among researchers today. Some researchers, like Kernis and his colleagues, have begun to focus on stability of self-esteem. Others are beginning to use related constructs, such as narcissism. Narcissism is defined by grandiose views of personal superiority, an inflated sense of entitlement, low empathy toward others, fantasies of personal greatness, a belief that ordinary people cannot understand one, and the like (American Psychiatric Association, 1994). These traits seem quite plausibly linked to aggression and violence, especially when the narcissist encounters someone who questions or disputes his or her highly favorable assessment of self. Narcissism has also been linked empirically to high but unstable self-esteem, so narcissism seems a very promising candidate for aggression researchers to study.

We have recently undertaken laboratory tests of links among self-esteem, narcissism, and aggression (Bushman & Baumeister, 1998). In two studies, participants were insulted (or praised) by a confederate posing as another participant, and later they were given an opportunity to aggress against that person (or another person) by means of sounding an aversive blast of loud noise. In both studies, the highest levels of aggression were exhibited by people who had scored high on narcissism and had been insulted. Self-esteem by itself had no effect on aggression, and neither did either high or low self-esteem in combination with receiving the insult. These results confirmed the link between threatened egotism and aggression and contradicted the theory that low self-esteem causes violence.

Narcissism has thus taken center stage as the form of self-regard most closely associated with violence. It is not, however, entirely fair to depict narcissists as generally or indiscriminately aggressive. In our studies (Bushman & Baumeister, 1998), narcissists' aggression did not differ from that of other people as long as there was no insulting provocation. Narcissism is thus not directly a cause of aggression and should instead be understood as a risk factor that can contribute to increasing a violent, aggressive response to provocation. The causal role of the provocation itself (in eliciting aggression by narcissists) is clearly established by the experimental findings.

Moreover, even when the narcissists were insulted, they were no more aggressive than anyone else toward an innocent third person. These patterns show that the aggression of narcissists is a specifically targeted, socially meaningful response. Narcissists are heavily invested in their high opinion of themselves, and they want others to share and confirm this opinion. When other people question or undermine the flattering self-portrait of the narcissist, the narcissist turns aggressive in response, but only toward those specific people. The aggression is thus a means of defending and asserting the grandiose self-view.

Do laboratory studies really capture what happens out in the real world, where violence often takes much more serious and deadly forms than pushing a button to deliver a blast of aversive noise? To answer this question, we conducted another study in which we obtained self-esteem and narcissism scores from incarcerated violent felons (Bushman, Baumeister, Phillips, & Gilligan, 1999). We assumed that the prisoners' responses to some items (e.g., "I certainly feel useless at times") would be affected by being in prison as well as by the salient failure experience of having been arrested, tried, convicted, and sentenced. These factors would be expected to push all scores toward low self-esteem and low narcissism.

Despite any such tendency, however, the prisoners' scores again pointed toward high narcissism as the major cause of aggression. The self-esteem scores of this group were comparable to the scores of published samples. The narcissism scores, meanwhile, were significantly higher than the published norms from all other studies. In particular, the prisoners outscored the baselines from other (nonincarcerated) groups to the largest degree on subscales measuring entitlement and superiority. (Again, though, the fact that the participants were in prison might have artificially lowered scores on some items, such as vanity, exhibitionism, and authority.) These findings suggest that the dangerous aspects of narcissism are not so much simple vanity and self-admiration as the inflated sense of being superior to others and being entitled to special privileges. It is apparently fine to love oneself quietly—instead, the interpersonal manifestations of narcissism are the ones associated with violence.

DEEP DOWN INSIDE

A common question raised about these findings is whether the apparent egotism of aggressive, violent people is simply a superficial form of bluster that is put on to conceal deep-rooted insecurities and self-doubts. This question is actually an effort to salvage the low-self-esteem theory, because it suggests that aggressive people really do have low self-esteem but simply act as if they do not. For example, perhaps murderers and wife beaters really perceive themselves as inferior beings, and their aggressive assertion of superiority is just a cover-up.

The question can be handled on either conceptual or empirical grounds. Empirically, some investigators have sought to find this inner core of self-doubt and reported that they could not do so. For example, Olweus (1994) specifically rejected the view that playground bullies secretly have low self-esteem, and Jankowski (1991) likewise concluded that members of violent gangs do not carry around a load of inner insecurities or self-doubts. Likewise, a number of experts who study narcissism have reported that they could not support the traditional clinical view of an egotistical outer shell concealing inner self-loathing. Virtually all studies that have measured self-esteem and narcissism have found positive correlations between the two, indicating that narcissists have high self-esteem.

Even if such evidence could be found, though, the view that low self-esteem causes aggression would still be wrong. It is by now clear that overt low self-esteem does not cause aggression. How can hidden low self-esteem cause aggression if nonhidden low self-esteem has no such effect? The only possible response is that the hidden quality of that low self-esteem would be decisive. Yet focusing the theory on the hidden quality of low self-esteem requires one to consider what it is that is hiding it—which brings the analysis back to the surface veneer of egotism. Thus, again, it would be the sense of superiority that is responsible for aggression, even if one could show that that sense of superiority is only on the surface and conceals an underlying low self-esteem. And no one has shown that, anyway.

CONCLUSION

It is time to abandon the quest for direct, simple links between self-esteem and aggression. The long-standing view that low self-esteem causes violence has been shown to be wrong, and the opposite view implicating high self-esteem is too simple. High self-esteem is a characteristic of both highly aggressive individuals and exceptionally nonaggressive ones, and so attempts at direct prediction tend to be inconclusive. Moreover, it is unwarranted to conclude that self-views directly cause aggression. At best, a highly favorable self-view constitutes a risk factor for turning violent in response to perceptions that one's favorable view of self has been disputed or undermined by others.

Researchers have started trying to look more closely at the people with high self-esteem in order to find the aggressive ones. Patterns of narcissism and instability of self-esteem have proven successful in recent investigations, although more research is needed. At present, the evidence best fits the view that aggression is most likely when people with a narcissistically inflated view of their own personal superiority encounter someone who explicitly disputes that opinion. Aggression is thus a means of defending a highly favorable view of self against someone who seeks (even unwittingly) to deflate it. Threatened egotism, rather than low self-esteem, is the most explosive recipe for violence.

Further research can benefit by discarding the obsolete view that low self-esteem causes violence and building on the findings about threatened egotism. It would be helpful to know whether a highly favorable view of self contributes to violent response by increasing the perception of insult (i.e., by making people oversensitive) or instead by simply producing a more aggressive response to the same perceived provocation. Further, research on whether narcissistic individuals would aggress against people who know bad information about them (but have not specifically asserted it themselves) would shed light on whether it is the critical view itself or the expression of it that is decisive. Another question is what exactly narcissistic people hope to accomplish by responding violently to an insult: After all, violence does not really refute criticism in any meaningful way, but it may discourage other people from voicing similar criticisms. The emotion processes involved in egotistical violence also need to be illuminated: How exactly do the shameful feelings of being criticized transform into aggressive outbursts, and does aggression genuinely make the aggressor feel better?

Recommended Reading

Baumeister, R. (1997). Evil: Inside human violence and cruelty. New York, W.H. Freeman.
Baumeister, R., Smart, L., & Boden, J. (1996). (See References)
Bushman, B., & Baumeister, R. (1998). (See References)
Kernis, K., Grannemann, B., & Barclay, L. (1989). (See References)

Note

1. Address correspondence to R. Baumeister, Department of Psychology, Case Western Reserve University, Cleveland, OH 44106-7123; e-mail: rfb2@po.cwru.edu.

References

American Psychiatric Association. (1994). *Diagnostic and statistical manual of mental disorders* (4th ed.). Washington, DC: Author.

Baumeister, R. (1993). *Self-esteem.* New York; Plenum Press.

Baumeister, R., Smart, L., & Boden, J. (1996). Relation of threatened egotism to violence and aggression: The dark side of high self-esteem. *Psychological Review, 103,* 5–33.

Bushman, B., & Baumeister, R. (1998). Threatened egotism, narcissism, self-esteem, and direct and displaced aggression: Does self-love or self-hate lead to violence? *Journal of Personality and Social Psychology,* 75, 219–229.

Bushman, B., Baumeister, R., Phillips, C., & Gilligan, J. (1999). *Narcissism and self-esteem among violent offenders in a prison population.* Manuscript submitted for publication.

Gondolf, E. (1985). *Men who batter.* Holmes Beach, FL: Learning Publications.

Jankowski, M.S. (1991). *Islands in the street: Gangs and American urban society.* Berkeley: University of California Press.

Kernis, M., Grannemann, B., & Barclay, L. (1989). Stability and level of self-esteem as predictors of anger arousal and hostility. *Journal of Personality and Social Psychology,* 56, 1013–1022.

Levin, J., & McDevitt, J. (1993), *Hate crimes.* New York: Plenum Press.

Olweus, D. (1994). Bullying at school: Long-term outcomes for the victims and an effective school-based intervention program. In R. Huesmann (Ed.), *Aggressive behavior: Current perspectives* (pp. 97–130). New York: Plenum Press.

Staub, E. (1989). *The roots of evil.* New York: Cambridge University Press.

Thin-Ideal Internalization: Mounting Evidence for a New Risk Factor for Body-Image Disturbance and Eating Pathology

J. Kevin Thompson[1] and Eric Stice

Department of Psychology, University of South Florida, Tampa, Florida (J.K.T.), and Department of Psychology, University of Texas at Austin, Austin, Texas (E.S.)

Abstract

Body-image disturbance and eating disorders are a Significant physical and mental health problem in Western countries. We describe emerging work on one newly identified variable that appears to be a potent risk factor for the development of these problems—internalization of societal standards of attractiveness. Work conducted independently in our labs over the past decade has included scale development, correlational studies, prospective risk-factor studies, randomized experiments, and randomized prevention trials. Findings collectively suggest that internalization is a causal risk factor for body-image and eating disturbances, and that it appears to operate in conjunction with other established risk factors for these outcomes, including dieting and negative affect. Future research is needed to examine the specific familial, peer, and media influences that promote internalization and to replicate and extend our prospective and experimental studies.

Keywords

internalization; body image; eating disturbance; risk factors; prevention

Eating disorders are one of the most common psychiatric problems faced by women, and are characterized by a persistent course, co-occurrence with other psychopathology, medical complications, and elevated mortality. Body-image disturbance, generally consisting of a subjective unhappiness with some aspect of one's appearance, is also extremely prevalent and may be associated with psychological distress (e.g., depression) and functional impairment (Thompson, Heinberg, Altabe, & Tantleff-Dunn, 1999). Exciting advances have recently occurred in social scientists' understanding of the risk factors that promote body-image and eating disturbances. One promising avenue of new research concerns the role of internalization of societal ideals of attractiveness (thin-ideal internalization[2]) in the development of these problems. Thin-ideal internalization refers to the extent to which an individual cognitively "buys into" socially defined ideals of attractiveness and engages in behaviors designed to produce an approximation of these ideals (Thompson et al., 1999).

Theoretically, thin-ideal internalization results because individuals internalize attitudes that are approved of by significant or respected others (Kandel, 1980). This process is referred to as social reinforcement. Specifically, family, peers, and media (i.e., the socialization agents) are thought to reinforce the thin-ideal body image for women through comments or actions that serve to support and perpetuate this ideal (e.g., criticism or teasing regarding weight, encouragement to diet, and glorification of ultra-slender models). These sources communicate expectations concerning the benefits of thinness, such as increased social acceptance, and these expectations likely play a key role in the propagation of this ideal (Hohlstein, Smith, & Atlas, 1998).

Thin-ideal internalization is thought to directly foster body dissatisfaction because this ideal is virtually unattainable for most females (Thompson et al., 1999). Additionally, thin-ideal internalization is thought to work in conjunction with other established risk factors for eating pathology, including body dissatisfaction, dieting, and negative affect (e.g., Killen et al., 1996), in promoting eating-disordered symptoms. Specifically, the body dissatisfaction that is thought to result from thin-ideal internalization theoretically promotes dieting and negative affect, which in turn increase the risk for onset of bulimic symptoms (Stice, 2001). Body dissatisfaction putatively leads to dieting because of the common belief that this is an effective weight-control technique. Body dissatisfaction may also foster negative affect because appearance is a central evaluative dimension for women in our culture. Dieting is theorized to result in a greater risk for bulimic symptoms because individuals might binge-eat in an effort to counteract the effects of caloric deprivation. Finally, negative affect may increase the likelihood of bulimic symptoms because of the belief that eating provides comfort and distraction from negative emotions.

RESEARCH BACKGROUND

Our initial work on thin-ideal internalization focused on the operationalization of the internalization construct and an evaluation of the reliability and validity of the resulting measures. We asked young women and men to describe the current ideal for attractiveness for females in Western culture and used these qualitative responses to create our initial scales (Heinberg, Thompson, & Stormer, 1995; Stice, Schupak-Neuberg, Shaw, & Stein, 1994). These two paper-and-pencil questionnaires and their revisions have received extensive examination, with adult and child-adolescent samples, and have demonstrated strong internal consistencies, test-retest reliabilities, predictive validity, and convergent validity (i.e., they correlate significantly with other measures that are similar or that they should theoretically correlate with, such as measures of body image; Cusumano & Thompson, 2001; Heinberg et al., 1995; Stice, 2001; Stice & Agras, 1998; Stice, Mazotti, Weibel, & Agras, 2000). The convergent validity of our two internalization scales was supported by research indicating that they were highly correlated ($r = .69$) in a sample of young adult females (Stice et al., 2000). (See Table 1 for sample items from our two internalization scales.)

The second phase of our research consisted of preliminary studies that tested whether thin-ideal internalization is positively correlated with body-image and eating disturbances. Research with female college students confirmed these correlations (e.g., Stice et al., 1994). In addition, in studies that separated out the role of awareness of societal standards from internalization of such messages and images, internalization was a more potent correlate of eating and body-image problems (Cusumano & Thompson, 2001; Heinberg et al., 1995; Thompson et al., 1999).

Table 1. *Sample internalization items*

I would like my body to look like the women that appear in TV shows and movies.
I wish I looked like the women pictured in magazines that model underwear.
Music videos that show women who are in good physical shape make me wish that I were in better physical shape.
I do not wish to look like the female models that appear in magazines. (reverse-keyed)
From Thompson, Heinberg, Altabe, and Tantleff-Dunn (1999)
Slender women are more attractive.
Women with toned bodies are more attractive.
Women with long legs are more attractive.
From Stice and Agras (1998)

Our third line of research tested whether thin-ideal internalization prospectively predicts body-image and eating disturbances. It is important to demonstrate temporal precedence between a putative risk factor and the pathologic outcomes to rule out the possibility that the factor is simply a concomitant or consequence of the disorder (Kraemer et al., 1997). An initial prospective study found that thin-ideal internalization predicted the onset of bulimic symptoms among initially asymptomatic adolescent girls (Stice & Agras, 1998), thereby establishing that thin-ideal internalization is a risk factor for eating pathology. Two additional findings support the theorized mediational processes that link thin-ideal internalization to eating disturbances. First, analyses also revealed that internalization predicted increased dieting (Stice, Mazotti, Krebs, & Martin, 1998). Second, an independent study found that thin-ideal internalization predicted subsequent increases in body dissatisfaction, dieting, and negative affect, which in turn predicted subsequent increase in bulimic symptoms (Stice, 2001).

The fourth phase of our research used randomized experiments to reduce the impact of one major promoter of thin-ideal internalization: thin-ideal images portrayed in the media. Specifically, Stormer and Thompson (1998) developed a program to teach women how to be more critical consumers of the media so as to reduce thin-ideal internalization. For example, one component of this intervention provides information on the degree to which photographic images in magazines are altered through computer modification. Two controlled trials showed that this intervention reduced thin-ideal internalization (Stormer & Thompson, 1998), and the effect has been replicated in other independent trials (e.g., Irving, DuPen, & Berel, 1998).

The fifth phase in this line of research entailed the experimental manipulation of thin-ideal internalization in an effort to rule out potential third variables that might explain the prospective findings and to establish that internalization is a causal risk factor for body-image and eating disturbances (Kraemer et al., 1997). In a dissonance-based intervention, women with higher than average thin-ideal internalization were persuaded to voluntarily argue against this ideal through a series of verbal, written, and behavioral exercises. Assessments conducted both at the time the intervention ended and at a later follow-up indicated that this intervention resulted in reductions in level of internalization, as well as decreased body dissatisfaction, dieting, negative affect, and bulimic pathology (Stice et al., 2000). These findings were replicated in an independent randomized experiment (Stice, Chase, Stormer, & Appel, 2001). Because there is experimental evidence that a reduction in thin-ideal internalization resulted in decreased body dissatisfaction and bulimic symptoms, thin-ideal internalization can be considered a causal risk factor for these outcomes according to the criteria of Kraemer et al. (1997).

FUTURE DIRECTIONS

These preliminary findings suggest that thin-ideal internalization is an important risk factor for body-image and eating disturbances, but several avenues of future research are indicated. First, our findings appear to suggest that internalization is a causal risk factor, and not a proxy for some other variable. Manipulation of thin-ideal internalization would not have affected body image if a proxy effect were operating. Nonetheless, our confidence in this conclusion would be strengthened by replication from other laboratories. Second, further work is needed in the prevention area to verify that interventions targeting internalization do not inadvertently manipulate other variables, such as body dissatisfaction. A temporal analysis indicating that internalization decreased prior to any changes in eating or body-image measures would be a key demonstration. Third, it would be desirable to elucidate possible physiological and cognitive correlates of internalization, such as reaction time or processing biases in response to weight and shape stimuli.

Finally, additional theoretical work is needed to investigate the factors that promote thin-ideal internalization, as well as the factors that buffer and heighten the effects of this risk variable. Variables that have been hypothesized or found to moderate the pernicious effects of internalization include self-esteem, exposure to the media, and tendency to compare one's appearance with other people's appearance (Thompson et al., 1999). More theory-driven work based on social-comparison and cognitive-processing models may also yield important information about the dispositional and contextual factors related to internalization. Furthermore, as we noted at the outset of this article, social-reinforcement theory may help explain the development of internalization. However, prospective studies are needed to document that social reinforcement from family, peers, and the media predicts subsequent development of thin-ideal internalization. Research should also attempt to manipulate parental and peer social reinforcement of the thin-ideal, to generate experimental evidence that these processes foster thin-ideal internalization.

Recommended Reading

Piran, N., Levine, M.P., & Steiner-Adair, C. (Eds.). (1999). *Preventing eating disorders: A handbook of interventions and special challenges.* Philadelphia: Brunner/Mazel.

Stice, E. (2001). Risk factors for eating pathology: Recent advances and future directions. In R.H. Striegel-Moore & L. Smolak (Eds.), *Eating disorders: Innovative directions for research and practice* (pp. 51–73). Washington, DC: American Psychological Association.

Thompson, J.K., & Heinberg, L.J. (1999). The media's influence on body image disturbance and eating disorders: We've reviled them, now can we rehabilitate them? *Journal of Social Issues,* 55, 339–353.

Thompson, J.K., & Smolak, L. (Eds.). (2001). *Body image, eating disorders, and obesity in youth: Assessment, prevention and treatment.* Washington, DC: American Psychological Association.

Notes

1. Address correspondence to J. Kevin Thompson, Department of Psychology, University of South Florida, Tampa, FL 33620-8200; e-mail: jthompso@chuma1.cas.usf.edu.

2. The societal ideal of attractiveness encompasses more than just thinness. However, we use the term thin-ideal internalization because this is the convention in the literature. Furthermore, it is the weight component of the ideal that is thought to give rise to eating pathology.

References

Cusumano, D.L., & Thompson, J.K. (2001). Media influence and body image in 8–11 year old boys and girls: A preliminary report on the Multidimensional Media Influence Scale. *International Journal of Eating Disorders, 29*, 37–44.

Heinberg, L.J., Thompson, J.K., & Stormer, S. (1995). Development and validation of the Sociocultural Attitudes Towards Appearance Questionnaire (SATAQ). *International Journal of Eating Disorders, 17*, 81–89.

Hohlstein, L.A., Smith, G.T., & Atlas, J.G. (1998). An application of expectancy theory to eating disorders: Development and validation of measures of eating and dieting expectancies. *Psychological Assessment, 10*, 49–58.

Irving, L.M., DuPen, J., & Berel, S. (1998). A media literacy program for high school females. *Eating Disorders: The Journal of Treatment and Prevention, 6*, 119–131.

Kandel, D.B. (1980). Drug and drinking behavior among youth. *Annual Review of Sociology, 6*, 235–285.

Killen, J.D., Taylor, C.B., Hayward, C., Haydel, K.F., Wilson, D.M., Hammer, L., Kraemer, H., Blair-Greiner, A., & Strachowski, D. (1996). Weight concerns influence the development of eating disorders: A 4 year prospective study. *Journal of Consulting and Clinical Psychology, 64*, 936–940.

Kraemer, H.C., Kazdin, A.E., Offord, D.R., Kessler, R.C., Jensen, P.S., & Kupfer, D.J. (1997). Coming to terms with the terms of risk. *Archives of General Psychiatry, 54*, 337–343.

Stice, E. (2001). A prospective test of the dual pathway model of bulimic pathology: Mediating effects of dieting and negative affect. *Journal of Abnormal Psychology, 110*, 124–135.

Stice, E., & Agras, W.S. (1998). Predicting the onset and remission of bulimic behaviors in adolescence: A longitudinal grouping analysis. *Behavior Therapy, 29*, 257–276.

Stice, E., Chase, A., Stormer, S., & Appel, A. (2001). A randomized trial of a dissonance-based eating disorder prevention program. *International Journal of Eating Disorders, 29*, 247–262.

Stice, E., Mazotti, L., Krebs, M., & Martin, S. (1998). Predictors of adolescent dieting behaviors: A longitudinal study. *Psychology of Addictive Behaviors, 12*, 195–205.

Stice, E., Mazotti, L., Weibel, D., & Agras, W.S. (2000). Dissonance prevention program decreases thin-ideal internalization, body dissatisfaction, dieting, negative affect, and bulimic symptoms: A preliminary experiment. *International Journal of Eating Disorders, 27*, 206–217.

Stice, E., Schupak-Neuberg, E., Shaw, H.E., & Stein, R.I. (1994). Relation of media exposure to eating disorder symptomatology: An examination of mediating mechanisms. *Journal of Abnormal Psychology, 103*, 836–840.

Stormer, S.M., & Thompson, J.K. (1998, November). *Challenging media messages regarding appearance: A psychoeducational program for males and females.* Paper presented at the annual meeting of the Association for the Advancement of Behavior Therapy, Washington, DC.

Thompson, J.K., Heinberg, L.J., Altabe, M.N., & Tantleff-Dunn, S. (1999). *Exacting beauty: Theory, assessment and treatment of body image disturbance.* Washington, DC: American Psychological Association.

Behavior Genetics: What's New? What's Next?

Danielle M. Dick and Richard J. Rose[1]
Department of Psychology, Indiana University, Bloomington, Indiana

Abstract

What's new in behavior genetics? With widespread acceptance that nearly all behavioral variation reflects some genetic influence, current studies are investigating developmental changes in the nature and magnitude of genetic and environmental effects, the extent to which different behaviors are influenced by common genes, and different forms of gene-environment correlation and interaction. New designs, focused on assessment of unrelated children in the same households or neighborhood environments, and use of measured environmental variables within genetically informative designs, are yielding more incisive evidence of common environmental effects on behavior. What will be next? Behavior genetic techniques and analyses will be used to inform efforts to find genes altering susceptibility for disorder and dispositional genes affecting behavioral variation. The developing integration behavioral and molecular genetics will identify genes influencing specific behavioral variation and enhance understanding of how they do so. Psychologists will play a pivotal role in communicating that understanding to the public and in facilitating consideration of the inevitable ethical issues then to be confronted.

Keywords

behavior genetics; molecular genetics; development; environment interaction

Through most of its brief history, behavior genetics had a single and simple goal: to demonstrate that some of the variation in behavior is attributable to genetic variance. Now, a diverse array of behaviors has been investigated with twin and adoption designs, yielding evidence that genetic variation contributes to individual differences in virtually all behavioral domains (McGuffin, Riley, & Plomin, 2001). Is behavior genetics, then, a thing of the past, a field whose success makes it obsolete? Not at all: Never has behavior genetic research held more promise. Investigators now possess analytic tools to move from estimating latent, unmeasured sources of variance to specifying the genes and environments involved in behavioral development, and the ways in which they interact. Our modest aim in this essay is to describe the questions now asked by behavior geneticists and to sketch the role that the field will assume in the emerging era of behavioral genomics.

A DEVELOPMENTAL PERSPECTIVE

Traditional behavior genetic analyses divide observed behavioral variance into three unobserved (latent) sources: variance attributable to genetic effects, that due to environmental influences shared by siblings (e.g., family structure and status), and that arising in unshared environmental experience that makes siblings differ from one another. Estimates of the magnitude of these genetic and environmental effects are usually obtained from statistical path models that compare identical twins, who share all their genes, with fraternal twins, who like ordinary siblings, on average, share one half their genes. Behavior genetic research now identifies developmental changes in the importance of genetic dispositions and environmental contexts in accounting for individual differences in behavior. Such changes can be dramatic and rapid. For example, we assessed substance use in a sample of adolescent Finnish twins on three occasions from ages 16 to 18 1/2; we found that genetic contributions to individual differences in drinking frequency increased over time, accounting for only a third of the variation at age 16, but half of it just 30 months later (Rose, Dick, Viken, & Kaprio, 2001). Concurrently, the effects of sharing a common environment decreased in importance. Interestingly, parallel analyses of smoking found little change in the importance of genetic and environmental effects, illustrating the trait-specificity of gene-environment dynamics: Some effects are stable across a developmental period; others change.

DIFFERENT BEHAVIORS, SAME GENES?

It is well known that certain behaviors tend to co-occur, as do certain disorders, but the causes of such covariance are much less understood. Behavior genetic models assess the degree to which covariation of different disorders or behaviors is due to common genetic influences, common environmental influences, or both. An example can be found in the significant, albeit modest, correlations observed between perceptual speed (the minimum time required to make a perceptual discrimination, as assessed with computer display methods) and standard IQ test scores (Posthuma, de Geus, & Boomsma, in press); those correlations were found to be due entirely to a common genetic factor, hypothesized to reflect genetic influences on neural transmission. Another example is found in our study of behavioral covariance between smoking and drinking during adolescence. Genes contributing to the age when teens started smoking and drinking correlated nearly 1.0 (suggesting that the same genes influence an adolescent's decision to begin smoking and to begin drinking), but once smoking or drinking was initiated, genes influencing the frequency with which an adolescent smoked or drank were quite substance-specific, correlating only about .25.

GENE-ENVIRONMENT INTERACTION AND CORRECTION

The interaction of genes and environments has been difficult to demonstrate in human behavioral data, despite consensus that interaction must be ubiquitous. New behavior genetic methods are demonstrating what was long assumed. These methods use information from twins who vary in specified environmental exposure to test directly for the differential expression of genes across different environments. For example, genetic effects played a larger role in the use of alcohol among twin women who had been reared in nonreligious households than among those who had been reared in religious households (Koopmans, Slutske, van Baal, & Boomsma, 1999). Similarly, we found greater genetic effects on adolescent alcohol use among Finnish twins living in urban environments than among those living in rural environments (Rose, Dick, et al., 2001).

These demonstrations of gene-environment interaction used simple dichotomies of environmental measures. But subsequently, we explored underlying processes in the interaction effect of urban versus rural environments by employing new statistical techniques to accommodate more continuous measures of the characteristics of the municipalities in which the Finnish twins resided. We hypothesized that communities spending relatively more money on alcohol allow for greater access to it, and communities with proportionately more young adults offer more role models for adolescent twins, and that either kind of community enhances expression of individual differences in genetic predispositions. And that is what we found: up to a 5-fold difference in the importance of genetic effects among twins residing in communities at these environmental extremes (Dick, Rose, Viken, Kaprio, & Koskenvuo, 2001), suggesting that the influence of genetic dispositions can be altered dramatically by environmental variation across communities.

Analysis of gene-environment interaction is complemented by tests of gene-environment correlation. Individuals' genomes interact with the environmental contexts in which the individuals live their lives, but this process is not a passive one, for genetic dispositions lead a person to select, and indeed create, his or her environments. Perhaps the most salient environment for an adolescent is found in the adolescent's peer relationships. In a study of 1,150 sixth-grade Finnish twins, we (Rose, in press) obtained evidence that they actively selected their friends from among their classmates. This result is consistent with the inference that people's genetic dispositions play some role in their selection of friends. People like other people who are like themselves, and genetically identical co-twins make highly similar friendship selections among their classmates.

MEASURING EFFECTS OF THE ENVIRONMENT IN GENETICALLY INFORMATIVE DESIGNS

In traditional behavior genetic designs, environmental influences were modeled, but not measured. Environmental effects were inferred from latent models fit to data. Such designs understandably received much criticism. Now, behavior geneticists can incorporate specific environmental measures into genetically informative designs and, by doing so, are demonstrating environmental effects that latent models failed to detect. Thus, we have studied effects of parental monitoring and home atmosphere on behavior problems in 11- to 12-year-old Finnish twins; both parental monitoring and home atmosphere contributed significantly to the development of the children's behavior problems, accounting for 2 to 5% of the total variation, and as much as 15% of the total common environmental effect. Recent research in the United Kingdom found neighborhood deprivation influenced behavior problems, too, accounting for about 5% of the effect of shared environment. Incorporation of specific, measured environments into genetically informative designs offers a powerful technique to study and specify environmental effects.

In other work, new research designs have been used to directly assess environmental effects in studies of unrelated children reared in a common neighborhood or within the same home. We have investigated neighborhood environmental effects on behavior in a large sample of 11- to 12-year-old same-sex Finnish twins. For each twin, we included a control classmate of the same gender and similar age, thus enabling us to compare three kinds of dyads: co-twins, each twin and his or her control classmate, and the two control classmates for each pair of co-twins. These twin-classmate dyads were sampled from more than 500 classrooms throughout Finland. The members of each dyad shared the same neighborhood, school, and classroom, but only the co-twin dyads shared genes and common household experience. For some behaviors, including early onset of smoking and drinking, we found significant correlations for both control-twin and control-control dyads; fitting models to the double-dyads formed by twins and their controls documented significant contributions to behavioral variation from nonfamilial environments—schools, neighborhoods, and communities (Rose, Viken, Dick, Pulkkinen, & Kaprio, 2001).

A complementary study examined genetically unrelated siblings who were no more than 9 months apart in age and who had been reared together from infancy in the same household. An IQ correlation of .29 was reported for 50 such dyads, and in another analysis, 40 of these dyads were only slightly less alike than fraternal co-twins on a variety of parent-rated behaviors (Segal, 1999). Clearly, appropriate research designs can demonstrate effects of familial and extrafamilial environmental variation for some behavioral outcomes at specific ages of development.

INTEGRATING BEHAVIOR AND MOLECULAR GENETICS[2]

Where do the statistical path models of behavior geneticists fit into the emerging era of behavioral genomics (the application of molecular genetics to behavior)? In the same way that specific, measured environments can be incorporated into behavior genetic models, specific information about genotypes can be included, as well, to test the importance of individual genes on behavior. Additionally, the kinds of behavior genetic analyses we have described can be informative in designing studies that maximize the power to detect susceptibility genes. Many efforts to replicate studies identifying genes that influence clinically defined diagnoses have failed. Those failures have stimulated the study of alternatives to diagnoses. When several traits are influenced by the same gene (or genes), that information can be used to redefine (or refine) alternatives to study, to enhance gene detection. For example, because heavy smoking and drinking frequently co-occurred in the Collaborative Study of the Genetics of Alcoholism sample, combined smoking and alcohol dependence was studied (Beirut et al., 2000). The combined dependency yielded greater evidence of linkage with a chromosomal region than did either tobacco dependence or alcohol dependence alone.

This approach is not limited to co-occurring behavioral disorders. It applies to normative behavioral differences, as well: A multidisciplinary international collaboration (Wright et al., 2001) has initiated a study of covariation among traditional and experimental measures of cognitive ability and will employ the correlated measures, once found, in subsequent molecular genetic analyses. And in a complementary way, behavior genetic methods can be useful to identify behavioral outcomes that are highly heritable, because these outcomes are most likely informative for genetic studies: When the definition of major depression was broadened, genetic factors assumed a larger role in women's susceptibility to this disorder (Kendler, Gardner, Neale, & Prescott, 2001), and, interestingly, this broader definition of depression suggested that somewhat different genes may influence depression in men and women.

A second strategy to enhance the power of molecular genetic analyses is to more accurately characterize trait-relevant environmental factors and also incorporate them more accurately in the analyses. In searching for genes, traditional genetic research effectively ignored the interplay of genetic and environmental influences in behavioral and psychiatric traits. Now, new analytic methods are being developed to incorporate environmental information better (Mosley, Conti, Elston, & Witte, 2000). But which specific environmental information is pertinent to a particular disorder? And how does a specific risk-relevant environment interact with genetic dispositions? Behavioral scientists trained in the methods of behavior genetics will play a key role in answering these questions.

BEYOND FINDING GENES

The traditional endpoint for geneticists is finding the gene (or genes) involved in a behavior or disorder. At that point, psychologists should become instrumental in using this genetic information. Applying genetic research on complex disorders to clinical practice will be complicated, because gene-behavior correlations will be modest and nonspecific, altering risk, but rarely determining outcome. Genes confer dispositions, not destinies. Research examining how risk and protective factors interact with genetic predispositions is critical for understanding the development of disorders and for providing information to vulnerable individuals and their family members. Far from ousting traditional psychological intervention, advances in genetics offer opportunities to develop interventions tailored to individual risks in the context of individual lifestyles. Enhanced understanding of the interactions between genetic vulnerabilities and environmental variables may dispel public misconceptions about the nature of genetics and correct erroneous beliefs about genetic determinism. Informed psychologists can play a vital role in disseminating the benefits of genetic research to families whose members experience behavioral and psychiatric disorders, and to the public in general.

CONCLUSIONS

Research questions now addressed by behavior geneticists have grown dramatically in scope: The questions have expanded into developmental psychology and sociology, as researchers have employed measures of the home and community, and utilized longitudinal designs. And behavior geneticists now study the effect of measured genotypes, a study traditionally left to geneticists. These developments create new and compelling research questions and raise new challenges. One such challenge is in addressing the complexity of behavioral development despite current reliance on methods that largely assume additive, linear effects. People who appreciate the complex, interactive, and unsystematic effects underlying behavioral development may be skeptical that the genomic era will profoundly advance understanding of behavior. But there is a preliminary illustration that advance will occur, even within the constraints of additive models: the identification of a gene (ApoE) that increases risk for Alzheimer's disease, and the interaction of that gene with head trauma (Mayeux et al., 1995). Further, new analytic techniques are being developed to analyze simultaneously hundreds of genes and environments in attempts to understand how gene-gene and gene-environment interactions contribute to outcome (Moore & Hahn, 2000). These techniques are beginning to capture the systems-theory approach long advocated by many researchers as an alternative to linear additive models.

This is not to deny that unresolved problems remain. For example, we are enthusiastic about including measured environmental information in genetic research designs, but we note, with disappointment, that the magnitude of shared environmental effects detected to date has been modest. Equally disappointing are the results of recent research efforts to specify nonshared environmental effects (Turkheimer & Waldron, 2000). Such findings underscore a problem acutely evident in contemporary behavior genetics: an imperative need for better measures of trait-relevant environments. Now that researchers have tools to search for measured environmental effects, what aspects of the environment should they measure—and with what yardsticks? These are questions that psychologists are uniquely positioned to address.

Another set of challenging questions will arise from the ethical, legal, and social issues to be confronted once genes conferring susceptibility to disorders are identified. How should information about the nature and meaning of susceptibility genes be conveyed to the media, the public, and the courts? How can erroneous beliefs about genetic determinism be dispelled effectively? Such issues will be even more salient once dispositional genes for normal behavioral variation are identified: Ethical issues surrounding prevention of behavioral disorders are undeniably complex, but surely they are less so than the ethical issues surrounding enhancement of selected behavioral traits.

Results from the first phase of behavior genetics research convincingly demonstrated that genes influence behavioral development. In the next phase, that of behavioral genomics, psychologists will begin to identify specific genes that exert such influence, seek understanding of how they do so, and accept the challenge to interpret that understanding to the public.

Recommended Reading

The Human Genome [Special issue]. (2001, February 16). *Science, 291.*

Rutter, M., Pickles, A., Murray, R., & Eaves, L. (2001). Testing hypotheses on specific environmental causal effects on behavior. *Psychological Bulletin, 127,* 291–324.

Turkheimer, E. (1998). Heritability and biological explanation. *Psychological Review, 105,* 782–791.

Acknowledgments—We gratefully acknowledge the contributions of Lea Pulkkinen, Jaakko Kaprio, Markku Koskenvuo, and Rick Viken to FinnTwin research, and support from the National Institute on Alcohol Abuse and Alcoholism (AA00145, AA09203, and AA08315) awarded to R.J.R. Manuscript preparation was supported by the Indiana Alcohol Research Center (AA07611) and by a National Science Foundation Pre-Doctoral Fellowship awarded to D.M.D.

Notes

1. Address correspondence to Richard Rose, Indiana University, Department of Psychology, 1101 East 10th St., Bloomington, IN 47405.

2. We use the term molecular genetics broadly to include statistical genetic techniques that test for gene-behavior associations.

References

Beirut, L., Rice, J., Goate, A., Foroud, T., Edenberg, H., Crowe, R., Hesselbrock, V., Li, T.K., Numberger, J., Porjesz, B., Schuckit, M., Begleiter, H., & Reich, T. (2000). Common and specific factors in the familial transmission of substance dependence. *American Journal of Medical Genetics, 96*, 459.

Dick, D.M., Rose, R.J., Viken, R.J., Kaprio, J., & Koskenvuo, M. (2001). Exploring gene-environment interactions: Socio-regional moderation of alcohol use. *Journal of Abnormal Psychology, 110*, 625–632.

Kendler, K.S., Gardner, C.O., Neale, M.C., & Prescott, C.A. (2001). Genetic risk factors for major depression in men and women: Similar or different heritabilities and same or partly distinct genes? *Psychological Medicine, 31*, 605–616.

Koopmans, J.R., Slutske, W.S., van Baal, G.C.M., & Boomsma, D.I. (1999). The influence of religion on alcohol use initiation: Evidence for genotype X environment interaction. *Behavior Genetics, 29*, 445–453.

Mayeux, R., Ottman, R., Maestre, G., Ngai, C., Tang, M.X., Ginsberg, H., Chun, M., Tycko, B., & Shelanski, M. (1995). Synergistic effects of traumatic head injury and apolipoprotein-E4 in patients with Alzheimer's disease. *Neurology, 45*, 555–557.

McGuffin, P., Riley, B., & Plomin, R. (2001). Toward behavioral genomics. *Science, 291*, 1232–1249.

Moore, J.H., & Hahn, L.W. (2000). A cellular automata approach to identifying gene-gene and gene-environment interactions. *American Journal of Medical Genetics, 96*, 486–487.

Mosley, J., Conti, D.V., Elston, R.C., & Witte, J.S. (2000). Impact of preadjusting a quantitative phenotype prior to sib-pair linkage analysis when gene-environment interaction exists. *Genetic Epidemiology, 21*(Suppl. 1), S837–S842.

Posthuma, D., de Geus, E.J.C., & Boomsma, D.I. (in press). Perceptual speed and IQ are associated through common genetic factors. *Behavior Genetics.*

Rose, R.J. (in press). How do adolescents select their friends? A behavior-genetic perspective. In L. Pulkkinen & A. Caspi (Eds.), *Paths to successful development.* Cambridge, England: Cambridge University Press.

Rose, R.J., Dick, D.M., Viken, R.J., & Kaprio, J. (2001). Gene-environment interaction in patterns of adolescent drinking: Regional residency moderates longitudinal influences on alcohol use. *Alcoholism: Clinical and Experimental Research, 25*, 637–643.

Rose, R.J., Viken, R.J., Dick, D.M., Pulkkinen, L., & Kaprio, J. (2001, July). *Shared environmental effects on behavior: Distinguishing familial from non-familial sources with data from twins and their classmate controls.* Paper presented at the annual meeting of the Behavior Genetics Association, Cambridge, England.

Segal, N.L. (1999). *Entwined lives.* New York: Penguin Putnam.

Turkheimer, E., & Waldron, M. (2000). Nonshared environment: A theoretical, methodological, and quantitative review. *Psychological Bulletin, 126*, 78–108.

Wright, M., de Geus, E., Ando, J., Luciano, M., Posthuma, D., Ono, Y., Hansell, N., Van Baal, C., Hiraishi, K., Hasegawa, T., Smith, G., Geffen, G., Geffen, L., Kanba, S., Miyake, A., Martin, N., & Boomsma, D. (2001). Genetics of cognition: Outline of a collaborative twin study. *Twin Research, 4*, 48–56.

Human Sexuality: How Do Men and Women Differ?

Letitia Anne Peplau[1]
Psychology Department, University of California, Los Angeles, Los Angeles, California

Abstract

A large body of scientific research documents four important gender differences in sexuality. First, on a wide variety of measures, men show greater sexual desire than do women. Second, compared with men, women place greater emphasis on committed relationships as a context for sexuality. Third, aggression is more strongly linked to sexuality for men than for women. Fourth, women's sexuality tends to be more malleable and capable of change over time. These male female differences are pervasive, affecting thoughts and feelings as well as behavior, and they characterize not only heterosexuals but lesbians and gay men as well. Implications of these patterns are considered.

Keywords

human sexuality; sexual desire; sexual orientation; sexual plasticity

A century ago, sex experts confidently asserted that men and women have strikingly different sexual natures. The rise of scientific psychology brought skepticism about this popular but unproven view, and the pendulum swung toward an emphasis on similarities between men's and women's sexuality. For example, Masters and Johnson (1966) captured attention by proposing a human sexual response cycle applicable to both sexes. Feminist scholars cautioned against exaggerating male-female differences and argued for women's sexual equality with men. Recently, psychologists have taken stock of the available scientific evidence. Reviews of empirical research on diverse aspects of human sexuality have identified four important male-female differences. These gender differences are pervasive, affecting thoughts and feelings as well as behavior, and they characterize not only heterosexuals but lesbians and gay men as well.

SEXUAL DESIRE

Sexual desire is the subjective experience of being interested in sexual objects or activities or wishing to engage in sexual activities (Regan & Berscheid, 1999). Many lines of research demonstrate that men show more interest in sex than women (see review by Baumeister, Catanese, & Vohs, 2001). Compared with women, men think about sex more often. They report more frequent sex fantasies and more frequent feelings of sexual desire. Across the life span, men rate the strength of their own sex drive higher than do their female age-mates. Men are more interested in visual sexual stimuli and more likely to spend money on such sexual products and activities as X-rated videos and visits to prostitutes.

Men and women also differ in their preferred frequency of sex. When heterosexual dating and marriage partners disagree about sexual frequency, it is usually the man who wants to have sex more often than the woman does. In heterosexual couples, actual sexual frequency may reflect a compromise between the desires of the male and female partners. In gay and lesbian relationships, sexual frequency is decided by partners of the same gender, and lesbians report having sex less often than gay men or heterosexuals. Further, women appear to be more willing than men to forgo sex or adhere to religious vows of celibacy.

Masturbation provides a good index of sexual desire because it is not constrained by the availability of a partner. Men are more likely than women to masturbate, start masturbating at an earlier age, and do so more often. In a review of 177 studies, Oliver and Hyde (1993) found large male-female differences in the incidence of masturbation. In technical terms, the meta-analytic effect size[2] (*d*) for masturbation was 0.96, which is smaller than the physical sex difference in height (2.00) but larger than most psychological sex differences, such as the performance difference on standardized math tests (0.20). These and many other empirical findings provide evidence for men's greater sexual interest.

SEXUALITY AND RELATIONSHIPS

A second consistent difference is that women tend to emphasize committed relationships as a context for sexuality more than men do. When Regan and Berscheid (1999) asked young adults to define sexual desire, men were more likely than women to emphasize physical pleasure and sexual intercourse. In contrast, women were more likely to "romanticize" the experience of sexual desire, as seen in one young woman's definition of sexual desire as "longing to be emotionally intimate and to express love for another person" (p. 75). Compared with women, men have more permissive attitudes toward casual premarital sex and toward extramarital sex. The size of these gender differences is relatively large, particularly for casual premarital sex ($d = 0.81$; Oliver & Hyde, 1993). Similarly, women's sexual fantasies are more likely than men's to involve a familiar partner and to include affection and commitment. In contrast, men's fantasies are more likely to involve strangers, anonymous partners, or multiple partners and to focus on specific sex acts or sexual organs.

A gender difference in emphasizing relational aspects of sexuality is also found among lesbians and gay men (see review by Peplau, Fingerhut, & Beals, in press). Like heterosexual women, lesbians tend to have less permissive attitudes toward casual sex and sex outside a primary relationship than do gay or heterosexual men. Also like heterosexual women, lesbians have sex fantasies that are more likely to be personal and romantic than the fantasies of gay or heterosexual men. Lesbians are more likely than gay men to become sexually involved with partners who were first their friends, then lovers. Gay men in committed relationships are more likely than lesbians or heterosexuals to have sex with partners outside their primary relationship.

In summary, women's sexuality tends to be strongly linked to a close relationship. For women, an important goal of sex is intimacy; the best context for pleasurable sex is a committed relationship. This is less true for men.

SEXUALITY AND AGGRESSION

A third gendered pattern concerns the association between sexuality and aggression. This link has been demonstrated in many domains, including individuals' sexual self-concepts, the initiation of sex in heterosexual relationships, and coercive sex.

Andersen, Cyranowski, and Espindle (1999) investigated the dimensions that individuals use to characterize their own sexuality. Both sexes evaluated themselves along a dimension of being romantic, with some individuals seeing themselves as very passionate and others seeing themselves as not very passionate. However, men's sexual self-concepts were also characterized by a dimension of aggression, which concerned the extent to which they saw themselves as being aggressive, powerful, experienced, domineering, and individualistic. There was no equivalent aggression dimension for women's sexual self-concepts.

In heterosexual relationships, men are commonly more assertive than women and take the lead in sexual interactions (see review by Impett & Peplau, 2003). During the early stages of a dating relationship, men typically initiate touching and sexual intimacy. In ongoing relationships, men report initiating sex about twice as often as their female partners or age-mates. To be sure, many women do initiate sex, but they do so less frequently than their male partners. The same pattern is found in people's sexual fantasies. Men are more likely than women to imagine themselves doing something sexual to a partner or taking the active role in a sexual encounter.

Rape stands at the extreme end of the link between sex and aggression. Although women use many strategies to persuade men to have sex, physical force and violence are seldom part of their repertoire. Physically coercive sex is primarily a male activity (see review by Felson, 2002). There is growing recognition that stranger and acquaintance rape are not the whole story; some men use physical force in intimate heterosexual relationships. Many women who are battered by a boyfriend or husband also report sexual assaults as part of the abuse.

In summary, aggression is more closely linked to sexuality for men than for women. Currently, we know little about aggression and sexuality among lesbians and gay men; research on this topic would provide a valuable contribution to our understanding of gender and human sexuality.

SEXUAL PLASTICITY

Scholars from many disciplines have noted that, in comparison with men's sexuality, women's sexuality tends to have greater plasticity. That is, women's sexual beliefs and behaviors can be more easily shaped and altered by cultural, social, and situational factors. Baumeister (2000) systematically reviewed the scientific evidence on this point. In this section, I mention a few of the many supportive empirical findings.

One sign of plasticity concerns changes in aspects of a person's sexuality over time. Such changes are more common among women than among men. For example, the frequency of women's sexual activity is more variable than men's. If a woman is in an intimate relationship, she might have frequent sex with her partner. But following a breakup, she might have no sex at all, including masturbation, for several months. Men show less temporal variability: Following a romantic breakup, men may substitute masturbation for interpersonal sex and so maintain a more constant frequency of sex. There is also growing evidence that women are more likely than men to change their sexual orientation over time. In an illustrative longitudinal study (Diamond, 2003), more than 25% of 18- to 25-year-old women who initially identified as lesbian or bisexual changed their sexual identity during the next 5 years. Changes such as these are less common for men.

A further indication of malleability is that a person's sexual attitudes and behaviors are responsive to social and situational influences. Such factors as education, religion, and acculturation are more strongly linked to women's sexuality than to men's. For example, moving to a new culture may have more impact on women's sexuality than on men's. The experience of higher education provides another illustration. A college education is associated with more liberal sexual attitudes and behavior, but this effect is greater for women than for men. Even more striking is the association between college education and sexual orientation shown in a recent national survey (Laumann, Gagnon, Michael, & Michaels, 1994). Completing college doubled the likelihood that a man identified as gay or bisexual (1.7% among high school graduates vs. 3.3% among college graduates). However, college was associated with a 900% increase in the percentage of women identifying as lesbian or bisexual (0.4% vs. 3.6%).

CONCLUSION AND IMPLICATIONS

Diverse lines of scientific research have identified consistent male-female differences in sexual interest, attitudes toward sex and relationships, the association between sex and aggression, and sexual plasticity. The size of these gender differences tends to be large, particularly in comparison to other male-female differences studied by psychologists. These differences are pervasive, encompassing thoughts, feelings, fantasies, and behavior. Finally, these male-female differences apply not only to heterosexuals but also to lesbians and gay men.

Several limitations of the current research are noteworthy. First, much research is based on White, middle-class American samples. Studies of other populations and cultural groups would be valuable in assessing the generalizability of findings. Second, although research findings on lesbians and gay men are consistent with patterns of male-female difference among heterosexuals, the available empirical database on homosexuals is relatively small. Third, differences between women and men are not absolute but rather a matter of degree. There are many exceptions to the general patterns described. For instance, some women show high levels of sexual interest, and some men seek sex only in committed relationships. Research documenting male-female differences has advanced further than research systematically tracing the origins of these differences. We are only beginning to understand the complex ways in which biology, experience, and culture interact to shape men's and women's sexuality.

These four general differences between women's and men's sexuality can illuminate specific patterns of sexual interaction. For example, in heterosexual couples, it is fairly common for a partner to engage in sex when he or she is not really interested or "in the mood." Although both men and women sometimes consent to such unwanted sexual activity, women are more often the compliant sexual partner (see review by Impett & Peplau, 2003). Each of the gender differences I have described may contribute to this pattern. First, the stage is set by a situation in which partners have differing desires for sex, and the man is more often the partner desiring sex. Second, for compliant sex to occur, the more interested partner must communicate his or her desire. Men typically take the lead in expressing sexual interest. Third, the disinterested partner's reaction is pivotal: Does this partner comply or, instead, ignore or reject the request? If women view sex as a way to show love and caring for a partner, they may be more likely than men to resolve a dilemma about unwanted sex by taking their partner's welfare into account. In abusive relationships, women may fear physical or psychological harm from a male partner if they refuse. Finally, sexual compliance illustrates the potential plasticity of female sexuality. In this case, women are influenced by relationship concerns to engage in a sexual activity that goes against their personal preference at the time.

The existence of basic differences between men's and women's sexuality has implications for the scientific study of sexuality. Specifically, an adequate understanding of human sexuality may require separate analyses of sexuality in women and in men, based on the unique biology and life experiences of each sex. Currently, efforts to reconceptualize sexual issues have focused on women's sexuality. Three examples are illustrative.

Rethinking Women's Sexual Desire

How should we interpret the finding that women appear less interested in sex than men? One possibility is that researchers have inadvertently used male standards (e.g., penile penetration and orgasm) to evaluate women's sexual experiences and consequently ignored activities, such as intimate kissing, cuddling, and touching, that may be uniquely important to women's erotic lives. Researchers such as Wallen (1995) argue that it is necessary to distinguish between sexual desire (an intrinsic motivation to pursue sex) and arousability (the capacity to become sexually aroused in response to situational cues). Because women's sexual desire may vary across the menstrual cycle, it may be more appropriate to describe women's desire as periodic rather than weak or limited. In contrast, women's receptivity to sexual overtures and their capacity for sexual response may depend on situational rather than hormonal cues. Other researchers (e.g., Tolman & Diamond, 2001) argue that more attention must be paid to the impact of hormones that may have special relevance for women, such as the neuropeptide oxytocin, which is linked to both sexuality and affectional bonding.

Rethinking Women's Sexual Orientation

Some researchers have proposed new paradigms for understanding women's sexual orientation (e.g., Peplau & Garnets, 2000). Old models either assumed commonalities among homosexuals, regardless of gender, or hypothesized similarities between lesbians and heterosexual men, both of whom are attracted to women. In contrast, empirical research has documented many similarities in women's sexuality, regardless of their sexual orientation. A new model based on women's experiences might highlight the centrality of relationships to women's sexual orientation, the potential for at least some women to change their sexual orientation over time, and the importance of sociocultural factors in shaping women's sexual orientation.

Rethinking Women's Sexual Problems

Finally, research on women's sexuality has led some scientists to question current systems for classifying sexual dysfunction among women. The widely used *Diagnostic and Statistical Manual of Mental Disorders (DSM)* of the American Psychiatric Association categorizes sexual dysfunction on the basis of Masters and Johnson's (1966) model of presumed normal and universal sexual functioning. Critics (e.g., Kaschak & Tiefer, 2001) have challenged the validity of this model, its applicability to women, and its use as a basis for clinical assessment. They have also faulted the *DSM* for ignoring the relationship context of sexuality for women. Kaschak and Tiefer have proposed instead a new "woman-centered" view of women's sexual problems that gives prominence to partner and relationship factors that affect women's sexual experiences, and also to social, cultural, and economic factors that influence the quality of women's sexual lives.

Recommended Reading

Baumeister, R.F., & Tice, D.M. (2001). *The social dimension of sex.* Boston: Allyn and Bacon.

Kaschak, E., & Tiefer, L. (Eds.). (2001). (See References)

Peplau, L.A., & Garnets, L.D. (2000). (See References)

Regan, P.C., & Berscheid, 18. (1999). (See References)

Notes

1. Address correspondence to Letitia Anne Peplau, Psychology Department, Franz 1285, University of California, Los Angeles, CA 90095-1563; e-mail: lapeplau@ucla.edu.

2. In a meta-analysis, the findings of multiple studies are analyzed quantitatively to arrive at an overall estimate of the size of a difference between two groups, in this case, between men and women. This effect size (known technically as *d*) is reported using a common unit of measurement. By convention in psychological research, 0.2 is considered a small effect size, 0.5 is a moderate effect size, and 0.8 is a large effect size.

References

Andersen, B.L., Cyranowski, J.M., & Espindle, D. (1999). Men's sexual self-schema. *Journal of Personality and Social Psychology, 76*, 645–661.

Baumeister, R.F. (2000). Gender differences in erotic plasticity. *Psychological Bulletin, 126*, 347–374.

Baumeister, R.F., Catanese, K.R., & Vohs, K.D. (2001). Is there a gender difference in strength of sex drive? *Personality and Social Psychology Review,* 5, 242–273.

Diamond, L.M. (2003). Was it a phase? Young women's relinquishment of lesbian/bisexual identities over a 5-year period. *Journal of Personality and Social Psychology, 84*, 352–364.

Felson, R.B. (2002). *Violence and gender reexamined.* Washington, DC: American Psychological Association.

Impett, E., & Peplau, L.A. (2003). Sexual compliance: Gender, motivational, and relationship perspectives. *Journal of Sex Research, 40*, 87–100.

Kaschak, E., & Tiefer, L. (Eds.). (2001). *A new view of women's sexual problems.* New York: Haworth Press.

Laumann, E., Gagnon, J., Michael, R., & Michaels, S. (1994). *The social organization of sexuality.* Chicago: University of Chicago Press.

Masters, W.H., & Johnson, V.E. (1966). *Human sexual response.* Boston: Little, Brown, & Co.

Oliver, M.B., & Hyde, J.S. (1993). Gender differences in sexuality: A meta-analysis. *Psychological Bulletin, 114,* 29–51.

Peplau, L.A., Fingerhut, A., & Beals, K. (in press). Sexuality in the relationships of lesbians and gay men. In J. Harvey, A. Wenzel, & S. Sprecher (Eds.), *Handbook of sexuality in close relationships.* Mahwah, NJ: Erlbaum.

Peplau, L.A., & Garnets, L.D. (Eds.). (2000). Women's sexualities: New perspectives on sexual orientation and gender [Special issue]. *Journal of Social Issues, 56*(2).

Regan, P.C., & Berscheid, E. (1999). *Lust: What we know about human sexual desire.* Thousand Oaks, CA: Sage.

Tolman, D.L., & Diamond, L.M. (2001). Desegregating sexuality research: Cultural and biological perspectives on gender and desire. *Annual Review of Sex Research, 12,* 33–74.

Wallen, K. (1995). The evolution of female sexual desire. In P. Abramson & S.D. Pinkerton (Eds.), *Sexual nature/sexual culture* (pp. 57–79). Chicago: University of Chicago Press.

Will They Do It Again? Predicting Sex-Offense Recidivism

R. Karl Hanson[1]

Department of the Solicitor General of Canada, Ottawa, Ontario, Canada

Abstract

This article reviews the empirical research on the prediction of reoffending among sexual offenders. The major predictors of sexual-offense recidivism are factors related to sexual deviance (e.g., deviant sexual preferences, previous sex crimes) and, to a lesser extent, criminal lifestyle (e.g., antisocial personality disorder, total number of prior offenses). The factors that predict recidivism among sex offenders are the same as the factors that predict general recidivism among nonsexual criminals (e.g., juvenile delinquency, prior violent offenses). Given that there are special predictors of sexual recidivism, evaluators should consider separately the risk for sexual and nonsexual recidivism.

Keywords

sex offenders; recidivism; prediction

All too often, we hear about sexual offenders committing new crimes. Every sexual crime is worrisome, but we are particularly troubled when it seems that the new offense should have been predicted and could have been prevented. Perhaps the offender had a history of similar offenses or, worse, was currently under community supervision (probation or parole). The fear of recidivism (i.e., repeat offending) among sex offenders has resulted in a number of exceptional policy measures for sex offenders, such as indeterminate sentences, community notification, lifetime supervision, and postsentence detention.

All these policy initiatives assume the ability to accurately distinguish between those individuals who are at risk of committing another sexual offense and those who are not. Unfortunately, the methods most commonly used to assess recidivism risk among sex offenders have low levels of accuracy (only slightly above chance; see Hanson & Bussière, 1998). Recent research, however, has the potential of substantially improving such risk assessments.

One plausible approach to recidivism prediction is to assume that an individual offender will behave like other similar individuals. If, for example, research has found that 30% of "Type X" sex offenders commit another sexual offense, then an individual offender who matches the "Type X" profile would be expected to have a 30% chance of reoffending. Because individuals differ on any number of characteristics, evaluators need to know which characteristics are meaningfully related to recidivism. In other words, which differences make a difference?

HOW MANY SEX OFFENDERS REOFFEND?

Before considering characteristics that increase or decrease recidivism potential, it is useful to consider the expected recidivism rate for the average sex offender—the recidivism base rate. Contrary to common opinion, the observed recidivism rate of sexual offenders is relatively low. A review of 61 recidivism studies involving close to 24,000 sex offenders found that only 13.4% committed a new sexual offense within 4 to 5 years (Hanson & Bussière, 1998). Approximately 12% of sex offenders committed a new nonsexual violent offense (e.g., assault), with rapists violently reoffending more often (22%) than child molesters (10%). When recidivism was defined as any reoffense, then the rates were predictably higher (36% overall).

The observed recidivism rates are underestimates of the actual rates because many sexual offenses are never detected. The extent of the underestimation is the topic of active debate—a debate that is likely to remain active because definitive evidence is, by definition, unavailable. Nevertheless, we know that the observed recidivism rates for sexual offenses can increase to 30 to 40% as the follow-up period extends over 20 years (Hanson, Steffy, & Gauthier, 1993; Prentky, Lee, Knight, & Cerce, 1997). The inclusion of arrests and informal reports of criminal activity will also provide estimates substantially higher than those based solely on official convictions (e.g., Marshall & Barbaree, 1988; Prentky et al., 1997). However, even with long follow-up periods and thorough searches, studies rarely find sex-offense recidivism rates greater than 40%. Any recidivism is troubling, but the available evidence does not support the popular belief that sexual offenders inevitably reoffend. The overall recidivism rate of sex offenders is, on average, less than the rate for nonsexual criminals (Beck & Shipley, 1989).

RECIDIVISM RISK FACTORS

The best way to determine whether a particular characteristic is related to recidivism is to compare the recidivism rates of offenders with that characteristic (e.g., those who are single) and offenders without that characteristic (e.g., those who are married). Recently, Bussière and I reviewed 61 studies that examined 69 potential predictors of sexual-offense recidivism, 38 predictors of nonsexual violent recidivism, and 58 predictors of general (any) recidivism (total sample size of 28,972 sexual offenders). In general, the strongest predictors of sex-offense recidivism were factors related to sexual deviancy. These factors included deviant sexual preferences (according to clinical assessments); early onset of sex offending; and history of prior sex offenses, choosing strangers as victims, choosing males as victims, and committing diverse sexual crimes. The single strongest predictor of sex-offense recidivism was sexual interest in children, assessed phallometrically. Phallometric assessment involves direct monitoring of an individual's penile responses while he is viewing or listening to erotic stimuli (Launay, 1994). Apart from the sexual deviancy factors, the next most important predictors of sexual-offense recidivism were factors related to criminal lifestyle, such as antisocial personality disorder and the total number of prior offenses.

Our review also identified a number of factors that were not related to sexual-offense recidivism. These unrelated factors included being sexually abused as a child, having low self-esteem, denying the sex offense, and lacking empathy with the victim. Many of these characteristics are difficult to assess because there are obvious social consequences to appearing victimized and remorseful; consequently, it is possible that any potential relationships could have been obscured by measurement problems. In addition, verbal statements of sex offenders may have limited predictive value. A finding that supports this interpretation is that offenders' verbal statements concerning motivation for treatment were unrelated to sex-offense recidivism, but those offenders who actually followed through with treatment reoffended less often than offenders who failed to complete treatment.

In general, the predictors of nonsexual recidivism for sexual offenders were the same factors that predict nonsexual recidivism among nonsexual criminals (see Gendreau, Little, & Goggin, 1996). These factors include antisocial personality disorder, young age, juvenile delinquency, history of prior offenses, and minority race. Rapists were more likely than child molesters to recidivate with a nonsexual offense.

COMBINING RISK FACTORS

Although the research literature demonstrates a number of factors reliably related to recidivism risk among sexual offenders, the predictive accuracy of any single factor is modest. No single factor is sufficiently diagnostic that it could be used on its own. Consequently, evaluators wishing to estimate the recidivism risk of sexual offenders need to consider a range of relevant risk factors.

When considering multiple factors, evaluators need to use valid methods for translating the offender's pattern of risk factors into a recidivism prediction. This is not an easy task. For example, consider an evaluator who rates an offender on a set of 20 valid risk factors (young age, never married, prior sex offenses, diverse sex crimes, etc.). If the offender has none of the risk factors, the offender can safely be considered low risk. If the offender has all the risk factors, then the offender can be considered high risk. But what about the typical offender who has only some of the risk factors? How does this particular pattern translate into a risk prediction? Are some risk factors more important than others?

Such concerns have stimulated efforts to produce actuarial risk scales that not only specify the risk factors to consider, but also provide explicit rules for combining individual scores into probability estimates. For many years, actuarial risk scales have been routinely used to predict general criminal recidivism among nonsexual offenders (see Andrews & Bonta, 1998). The scales designed to predict general recidivism have been effective in predicting general recidivism among sexual offenders, but they have been less successful in predicting sexual-offense recidivism. It appears that the prediction of sexual-offense recidivism requires the consideration of special factors (e.g., sexual deviance) that are not included in the risk scales designed for general criminal offenders (e.g., thieves, drug dealers).

Several different research teams—notably, those led by Epperson in Minnesota and Thornton in England—have made significant progress in constructing risk scales specifically for sexual offenders, but many of their findings have yet to be fully cross-validated and are available only as unpublished conference presentations. My own work (with Thornton) suggests that it is possible to achieve moderate accuracy in predicting sexual-offense recidivism using a relatively simple list of demographic and offense-history variables (i.e., never married, any stranger victims, any male victims, any unrelated victims, age less than 25, any noncontact sex offense, total number of prior sexual offenses, any violent offenses, total number of prior offenses; Hanson & Thornton, 2000). Offenders are assigned points for each risk factor present, and the total number of points is used to classify offenders into relative risk categories. In our validation study, the sex-offense recidivism rate for the highest-risk categories was greater than 50%, whereas the rate for the lowest-risk categories was approximately 10% after 15 years.

STATIC AND DYNAMIC (CHANGEABLE) RISK FACTORS

Almost all the available research has focused on static, unchangeable factors. Static factors are useful for identifying long-term risk potential, but they provide no information concerning when offenders are likely to reoffend or how to intervene in order to reduce the potential for recidivism. My recent research with Harris (Hanson & Harris, 2000) suggests that a number of dynamic factors can usefully contribute to risk assessment of sexual offenders under community supervision. These factors include negative social influences, attitudes tolerant of sexual assault, sexual preoccupations, uncontrolled release environment (e.g., rooming house in a high-crime neighborhood), access to victims, and lack of cooperation with supervision. Further research is required, however, before we know how best to integrate these dynamic factors into applied risk assessments for sex offenders.

One consequence of our limited knowledge of dynamic risk factors is that we have better evidence for identifying offenders who are dangerous than we have for determining when offenders are safe to be released. Not all sex offenders reoffend, and even high-risk offenders can change their ways. Unfortunately, clinicians have achieved only limited accuracy in determining when offenders have benefited from treatment.

EXPLANATIONS FOR SEX OFFENDING

Evaluating change requires an accurate model of the causes of sexual offending. As in other areas of psychology, the major theories can be divided into those that emphasize nature versus those that emphasize nurture. On the nature side are theories that consider deviant sexual preferences to be linked to genetic or hormonal anomalies. No one seriously questions that normal sexual interests are biologically based, and the recent evidence linking homosexuality to the Xq28. region of the sex chromosome (Hamer & Copeland, 1994) has lent support to the belief in a genetic predisposition for pedophilia. Researchers, however, have yet to find any biological markers associated with sex offending.

Although biomedical research may eventually provide insights, most treatment programs for sex offenders are based on some form of social learning theory. Those offenders with the most well practiced patterns of deviant behavior, and the least ability to appropriately manage their impulses, are considered to be at the highest risk for recidivism. The validity of this model is currently being tested through cognitive-behavioral treatment programs that teach offenders relapse-prevention skills in the hope of reducing their long-term recidivism risk.

DIRECTIONS FOR FUTURE RESEARCH

The ongoing research challenge of all these treatment programs is determining when offenders have changed. For sex offenders, unlike individuals with other types of behavioral problems, it is difficult to provide realistic tests of their new coping skills. Depressed patients can monitor their mood, and agoraphobics can try to go out, but clinicians can never provide sex offenders with unsupervised access to vulnerable victims. Knowledge concerning sexual offending would likely advance quickly given a reliable analogue of sex offending. Imagine, for example, creating artificial situations in which individuals at risk would feel tempted to sexually offend. The success of phallometric assessment as a recidivism risk indicator may be due to its resemblance to such an analogue stress test.

One of the ongoing controversies concerns the role of low self-esteem and subjective distress in the recidivism process. Sex offenders are characterized by considerable anxiety, depression, and low self-regard. Moreover, their recidivism risk increases when their mood deteriorates (Hanson & Harris, 2000). What is surprising, however, is that subjective distress is unrelated to long-term recidivism. Those sex offenders who are chronically unhappy commit new offenses at the same rate as other sex offenders. Treatment programs that successfully raise offenders' self-esteem appear to have no impact on recidivism rates (Hanson et al., 1993).

It is possible that low self-esteem (like being sexually abused) is linked to the initiation of sex offending but is unrelated to recidivism. In addition, the level of subjective distress may matter less than attempts to escape distress by resorting to sexual fantasies or sexual activities (deviant or otherwise). Disentangling the factors that contribute to sexual recidivism will require detailed accounts from cooperative offenders, as well as prospective studies that monitor ongoing changes in the offenders' lives.

In conclusion, it is worth considering Grove and Meehl's (1996) caution about the use of unverified clinical opinion, which they compare to the Inquisition's methods for identifying witches. "All policymakers should know that a practitioner who claims not to need any statistical or experimental studies but relies solely on clinical experience as adequate justification, by that very claim is shown to be a nonscientifically minded person whose professional judgments are not to be trusted" (Grove & Meehl, 1996, p. 320). Not too long ago, the people who evaluate sexual offenders had little choice but to use unverified clinical opinion because the relevant research was unavailable. With recent advances, however, knowledgeable evaluators now have the potential of providing risk assessments worthy of serious consideration.

Recommended Reading

Hanson, R.K. (1998). What do we know about sex offender risk assessment? *Psychology, Public Policy, and Law, 4*, 50–72.

Hanson, R.K., & Bussière, M.T. (1998). (See References)

Quinsey, V.L., Lalumière, M.L., Rice, M.E., & Harris, G.T. (1995). Predicting sexual offenses. In J.C. Campbell (Ed.), *Assessing dangerousness: Violence by sexual offenders, batterers, and child abusers* (pp. 114–137). Thousand Oaks, CA: Sage.

Note

1. Address correspondence to R. Karl Hanson, Corrections Research, Department of the Solicitor General of Canada, 340 Laurier Ave., West, Ottawa, Ontario, Canada K1A 0P8.

References

Andrews, D.A., & Bonta, J. (1998). *The psychology of criminal conduct* (2nd ed.). Cincinnati, OH: Anderson.

Beck, A.J., & Shipley, B.E. (1989). *Recidivism of prisoners released in 1983* (U.S. Bureau of Justice Statistics Special Report). Washington, DC: U.S. Department of Justice.

Gendreau, P., Little, T., & Goggin, C. (1996). A meta-analysis of the predictors of adult offender recidivism: What works! *Criminology, 34*, 575–607.

Grove, W.M., & Meehl, P.E. (1996). Comparative efficiency of informal (subjective, impressionistic) and formal (mechanical, algorithmic) prediction procedures: The clinical-statistical controversy. *Psychology, Public Policy, & Law, 2*, 293–323.

Hamer, D., & Copeland, P. (1994). *The science of desire: The search for the gay gene and the biology of behavior.* New York: Simon & Schuster.

Hanson, R.K., & Bussière, M.T. (1998). Predicting relapse: A meta-analysis of sexual offender recidivism studies. *Journal of Consulting and Clinical Psychology, 66*, 348–362.

Hanson, R.K., & Harris, A.J.R. (2000). Where should we intervene? Dynamic predictors of sex offense recidivism. *Criminal Justice and Behavior, 27*, 6–35.

Hanson, R.K., Steffy, R.A., & Gauthier, R. (1993). Long-term recidivism of child molesters. *Journal of Consulting and Clinical Psychology, 61*, 646–652.

Hanson, R.K., & Thornton, D. (2000). Improving risk assessments for sex offenders: A comparison of three actuarial scales. *Law and Human Behavior, 24*, 119–136.

Launay, G. (1994). The phallometric assessment of sex offenders: Some professional and research issues. *Criminal Behaviour and Mental Health, 4*, 48–70.

Marshall, W.L., & Barbaree, H.E. (1988). The long-term evaluation of a behavioural treatment program. *Behaviour Research and Therapy, 26*, 499–511.

Prentky, R.A., Lee, A.F.S., Knight, R.A., & Cerce, D. (1997). Recidivism rates among child molesters and rapists: A methodological analysis. *Law and Human Behavior, 21*, 635–659.

Schizophrenia: A Neurodevelopmental Perspective

Heather M. Conklin and William G. Iacono[1]
Department of Psychology, University of Minnesota, Minneapolis, Minnesota

Abstract

Diverse lines of research suggest that schizophrenia is a genetically influenced neurodevelopmental disorder. Family, twin, and adoption studies suggest that most cases of schizophrenia involve a genetic diathesis that is necessary but not sufficient for development of the disorder. Histological, neuroimaging, and neuropsychological findings converge in providing evidence for medial-temporal and frontal lobe dysfunction that likely predates the onset of psychosis. Behavioral phenomenology and neurobiology suggest that dopamine plays a crucial moderating role between these structural abnormalities and functional impairment. Recently, investigators have used animal models and clinical syndromes to integrate these findings into neurodevelopmental models of schizophrenia that hold great potential for yielding etiological insight.

Keywords

schizophrenia; neurodevelopment; etiology; predisposition

The past decade has seen a proliferation of research findings in the field of schizophrenia, with provocative developments in molecular genetics, neurobiology, neuroimaging, neuropsychology, and studies of high-risk individuals. Although the etiology of schizophrenia remains enigmatic, scientists are gaining ground in developing plausible models of vulnerability to this disorder. In the past, most research findings have provided insights into selected aspects of the disorder without yielding a comprehensive theory that has received broad-based approval. Recently emerging neurodevelopmental models of schizophrenia, however, are capable of accommodating diverse findings and are receiving widespread support among schizophrenia investigators.

Neurodevelopmental models propose that vulnerability to schizophrenia results from a disruption in forebrain development during the perinatal period. A brain lesion that occurs early in development is hypothesized to lie dormant until normal brain maturational events trigger the appearance of traditional diagnostic signs, typically in adolescence or early adulthood (Weinberger, 1987). Such models are supported by reports of increased intrauterine and perinatal complications among individuals with schizophrenia, as well as by demonstrations that neurological, neuropsychological, and physical abnormalities predate the onset of psychosis. Although this evidence is far from conclusive, neurodevelopmental models hold immense promise as a heuristic for bridging research in multiple domains and posing questions central to discovering the etiology of this disorder.

GENETIC AND ENVIRONMENTAL VULNERABILITY

Well-replicated findings from family, twin, and adoption studies indicate that there is a substantial genetic component to the predisposition for schizophrenia. The likelihood that this genetic predisposition involves multiple genes and the possibility that different genetic variants underlie the risk for schizophrenia have made the search for genes via standard molecular techniques daunting. Although research findings have identified several chromosomal sites where there may be genes that confer susceptibility to schizophrenia (i.e., genetic linkage), a failure to replicate these findings has become the norm rather than the exception. A recent study, which examined the entire genome of individuals in families with high rates of schizophrenia, provided evidence for schizophrenia susceptibility on chromosome 1 (Brzustowicz, Hodgkinson, Chow, Honer, & Bassett, 2000). This finding is promising in that the evidence for genetic linkage was unusually strong, a factor that should facilitate the search for a specific gene on this chromosome in these families.

It is reasonable to propose that alteration of gene expression (i.e., production of proteins coded for by genes), during critical phases of early development, contributes to neurodevelopmental abnormalities seen in schizophrenia. Brain development is a delicate process that requires a precise cascade of events orchestrated by the timing and specificity of gene expression. However, until one or more schizophrenia-susceptibility genes have been identified, the link between genetic variations and neurodevelopmental abnormalities remains largely theoretical. For example, neurodevelopmental disturbances in schizophrenia may result from the improper function of proteins that regulate the movement of neurons to their final destination in the brain (neuronal migration) and the formation of neural connections (synaptogenesis).

If schizophrenia were entirely due to heredity, all identical twins with schizophrenia would have co-twins who also have the disorder because identical twins share all of their genes. In fact, the co-twins of affected identical twins develop schizophrenia only about half the time. Thus, environmental factors must also influence schizophrenia's development. From a neurodevelopmental perspective, events occurring early in life are of greatest interest as potential environmental risk factors. A higher rate of obstetric complications has been found for schizophrenia patients relative to normal comparison subjects, psychiatric comparison subjects, and well siblings. A recent report suggests that the risk for schizophrenia is correlated with the number of hypoxia-associated obstetric complications (i.e., complications that can result in oxygen deprivation) an individual may have experienced (Cannon, Rosso, Bearden, Sanchez, & Hadley, 1999). The risk for schizophrenia appears to be conferred from an interaction between genetic predisposition and obstetric complications, rather than obstetric complications alone. In addition, *in utero* viral exposure has been studied as an environmental risk factor for schizophrenia because of the higher number of winter births than births in other seasons among schizophrenia patients and the increased frequency of viral epidemics in the fall. For example, an increased rate of schizophrenia was demonstrated among individuals who were exposed during their second trimester to an influenza epidemic in Helsinki in 1957 (Mednick, Machon, Huttunen, & Bonett, 1988).

NEUROLOGICAL ABNORMALITIES

The longest-held finding in support of the neurodevelopmental model is the increased size of fluid-filled spaces (lateral ventricles) in the brain that is present in first-episode schizophrenia patients and appears to remain static over time. It appears, then, that brain abnormalities are not just an index of the disorder's progression, but more likely constitute a preexisting vulnerability to the disorder. Post mortem histological studies have produced convergent evidence for neurological anomalies at the cellular level. Cellular abnormalities in the brain, such as increased neuronal spacing and altered arrangement of neuronal layers in temporal and frontal lobes areas,[2] have suggested that the predisposition for schizophrenia may involve disruption in neuronal migration. Furthermore, histological studies have failed to find signs of gliosis (a neuronal indicator of injury to a mature brain or of a neuropathological process), again suggesting the cellular deviations occurred early in life.

Neuroimaging studies have demonstrated structural and metabolic abnormalities in the medial-temporal lobe and frontal lobe of schizophrenia patients. For example, reduced frontal cerebral blood flow (hypofrontality) during tasks that require frontal activation has been observed, with the degree of frontal blood flow correlating with task performance. Although a review of recent neuroimaging findings in schizophrenia is beyond the scope of this article, there have been increasing efforts to parse out specific areas within the medial-temporal and frontal lobes that may be compromised in schizophrenia. Temporal lobe dysfunction likely contributes to positive symptoms, consisting of delusions and hallucinations, and frontal lobe dysfunction likely contributes to negative symptoms, such as impoverished thought, lack of goal-directed activities, and social withdrawal.

The performance of schizophrenia patients on neuropsychological tasks has been used to elucidate cognitive deficits that may be secondary to brain abnormalities in these patients, as well as to develop hypotheses about the location of their neuropathology. Schizophrenia patients have been found to be impaired on a range of tasks, including ones purported to measure abstraction, sustained attention, language, and memory. Recently, Bilder et al. (2000) evaluated the performance of first-episode schizophrenia patients using a comprehensive neuropsychological test battery. They reported a large generalized deficit in schizophrenia patients with additional specific deficits in memory and executive functions. These results are not open to previous criticisms that cognitive deficits in schizophrenia merely reflect factors associated with chronic mental illness (e.g., long-term treatment) or depict global impairment. The findings are consistent with histological and neuroimaging findings that implicate temporal and frontal lobe involvement in schizophrenia.

Although it is now recognized that multiple neurotransmitters likely contribute to the etiology of schizophrenia, dopamine continues to be the primary neurotransmitter of interest.[3] The dopamine hypothesis, which originally asserted that schizophrenia results from a diffuse excess of dopamine in the brain, has been revised to suggest a dysregulation of dopamine resulting in an excess of dopamine in temporal areas and a depletion of dopamine in frontal areas. Further, it has now been proposed that the alteration in dopamine neurotransmission may not result from a primary deficit in dopamine neurons or receptors, but rather may result from abnormalities in the regulation of dopamine by limbic (medial-temporal lobe structures responsible for motivated and emotional behaviors) and frontal regions (More, West, & Grace, 1999). These are the same brain areas implicated by histological, neuroimaging, and neuropsychological studies. The dysregulation of dopamine neurotransmission that appears to occur in schizophrenia corresponds with behavioral and cognitive processes that are altered in this disorder. For example, within the frontal lobe, dopamine appears to specifically mediate aspects of working memory and motor planning that are impaired in schizophrenia (Goldman-Rakic, 1996). Dopamine and its interaction with other neurotransmitters, such as glutamate and gamma amino butyric acid (GABA), continue to be central to etiological models of schizophrenia.

Animal models[4] of schizophrenia hold promise for testing etiological theories, including neurodevelopmental models. Administration of neurotoxins in developing animals has been used to create disruptions in prenatal neuronal migration, perinatal oxygen deprivation has been used to imitate hypoxia associated with obstetric complications, and neonatal lesions to the hippocampus have been used to re-create structural brain abnormalities. To date, animal models have been able to reproduce a surprisingly broad range of neurobiological, behavioral, and cognitive aspects of schizophrenia. For example, some models have reproduced schizophrenia-like post mortem histological changes, impairment on working memory tasks, and withdrawn social behavior. In addition, animal models have demonstrated that some deficits are specific to neonatal rather than adult lesions, some symptoms show delayed emergence in adulthood, and some functions are returned to normal with the administration of drugs used to treat schizophrenia (neuroleptics). Behavioral outcomes can also vary with the genetic strain of an animal, suggesting an interaction between genes and environment. Although animal models integrate findings across research areas well, they have obvious limitations, including the fact that animal behaviors may be insufficient proxies for certain complex human behaviors.

PROSPECTIVE AND HIGH-RISK STUDIES

Neurodevelopmental models implicitly predict that signs of disorder predate the onset of florid psychosis. Indeed, research has demonstrated that individuals who later develop schizophrenia exhibit motor, cognitive, and behavioral abnormalities during childhood. In an innovative archival study, Walker and Lewine (1990) showed that preschizophrenic children could be reliably differentiated from their well siblings in home videos taken during early childhood, primarily on the basis of abnormal movements and reduced facial expression. Jones, Rodgers, Murray, and Marmot (1994) studied a British cohort of 4,746 children born in 1946, of which 30 later developed schizophrenia. The preschizophrenic individuals were more likely than control subjects to have exhibited delayed early motor development; obtained low educational test scores at ages 8, 11, and 15; preferred solitary play at ages 4 and 6; and been rated by teachers as anxious in social situations at age 15.

Researchers have also investigated abnormalities in the unaffected first-degree relatives of schizophrenia patients. These individuals are at genetic risk because they share on average half of their genes with schizophrenia patients. Healthy relatives have been observed to demonstrate both behavioral and neurobiological impairments that are similar to those seen in affected patients. For nearly a century, higher rates of schizophrenia-related disorders, such as schizotypal personality disorder,[5] have been seen in these relatives compared with the general population. The most consistent finding in relatives has been eye movement dysfunction, a finding consistent with frontal involvement in the genetic diathesis for schizophrenia. The impaired performance of relatives on certain neuropsychological measures, such as working memory tasks, provides further convergent evidence for frontal lobe dysfunction. Relatives who are deviant on more than one of these measures may be at the greatest risk for schizophrenia and may be most informative when included in genetic studies of this disorder. Associations among schizophrenia-related disorders, cognitive task performance, and the quality of eye movements in relatives of schizophrenia patients are being investigated (for discussion, see Iacono & Grove, 1993).

VELOCARDIOFACIAL SYNDROME (VCFS) AS AN INTEGRATIVE EXAMPLE

VCFS is a congenital syndrome that affects multiple body systems and is associated with a small deletion of genetic material in a specific area of chromosome 22. The symptom profile of individuals with VCFS is variable but commonly includes facial malformations, oral palatal anomalies, nasal voice, and cardiac abnormalities. Various studies have demonstrated that the rate of schizophrenia among individuals with VCFS is approximately 25 times the rate found in the population overall (i.e., 1%), leading investigators to suggest that VCFS is a genetic subtype of schizophrenia (Bassett et al., 1998). The inverse relationship also holds, with multiple studies demonstrating that the rate of this deletion on chromosome 22 in schizophrenia patients is approximately 80 times the general-population rate of 1 in 4,000. VCFS and preschizophrenic individuals show strikingly similar developmental characteristics. Specifically, children with VCFS exhibit delayed motor development, below-average IQ, a tendency toward concrete thinking, bland affect, and lowered levels of social interaction.

Research has begun to suggest potentially shared pathophysiology for VCFS and schizophrenia that may stem from the deletion on chromosome 22. One theory proposes that both VCFS and schizophrenia are neurodevelopmental disorders that affect midline body structures, an idea consistent with the physical abnormalities seen in VCFS. It may be that the pathology also includes migration of cells destined to be midline brain structures, including medial-temporal lobe structures. VCFS and schizophrenia have been associated with similar neuropathology (e.g., enlarged ventricles and an underdeveloped cerebellum), as revealed by magnetic resonance imaging; these structural changes may play a role in predisposing individuals to psychosis (Vataja & Elomaa, 1998). Another potential mechanism stems from the observation that the chromosomal area deleted in VCFS is close to the catechol-O-methyl transferase (COMT) gene (Dunham, Collins, Wadey, & Scambler, 1992). COMT is an enzyme that metabolizes certain neurotransmitters, including dopamine. It has been proposed that a predisposition to psychosis could arise through either a decrease in the metabolism of these neurotransmitters in the brain or an increase in exposure to them during neurodevelopment. Although there are limitations to the notion that VCFS is a schizophrenia subtype, the case of VCFS illustrates how research can be integrated to handle multiple aspects of schizophrenia, including genetic predisposition to illness, presence of signs of disorder that predate psychosis, neurochemical deviations, and developmental brain abnormalities.

FUTURE DIRECTIONS

As much as schizophrenia research is yielding provocative findings, there continue to be important unanswered questions regarding etiology. To date, investigators have not been able to reliably identify susceptibility genes for schizophrenia, precluding mapping the pathway from genetic vulnerability to brain abnormalities. A better understanding of the dormancy period between early brain lesions and adult onset of the disorder is needed. Animal models have failed to support the idea that hormonal changes in puberty may trigger the appearance of symptoms, and theories suggesting that the onset of diagnostic symptoms coincides with ongoing frontal lobe development need to be more adequately investigated. The identification of environmental stressors that contribute substantially to risk for schizophrenia is required. Perinatal complications, such as obstetric complications and viral exposure *in utero*, are some of the leading risk contenders; however, they are likely insufficient to account for the 50% of identical twins who have schizophrenia but whose co-twins do not. In addition, these environmental events make different theoretical predictions based on their timing, the stage of brain development implicated, and the mechanism of action.

Although the neurodevelopmental model is making great strides in integrating diverse research findings, it may be but one of several useful models that ultimately characterize schizophrenia's multiple etiologies. The lack of cohesion of some of the research evidence may be due to schizophrenia resulting from different etiologies in different individuals. Such etiological heterogeneity confounds research into the cause (or causes) of schizophrenia, as study samples likely include individuals for whom the underlying cause of the disorder is not the same. One way to obtain samples with greater etiological homogeneity would be to supplement traditional diagnostic systems with measurement of traits that are likely more direct manifestations of the biological predisposition. For example, an investigator could select study samples of individuals who not only meet current diagnostic criteria for schizophrenia, but also demonstrate signs of neurodevelopmental origin for this disorder, such as those reviewed in this article. Research using a selection procedure such as this, one that is theoretically driven and also supported by recent research findings, likely holds the greatest promise for yielding etiological insight.

Recommended Reading

Cannon, T.D., Rosso, I.M., Bearden, C.E., Sanchez, L.E., & Hadley, T. (1999). (See References)

Iacono, W.G. (1998). Identifying psychophysiological risk for psychopathology: Examples from substance abuse and schizophrenia research. *Psychophysiology*, 35, 621–637.

Lillrank, S.M., Lipska, B.K., & Weinberger, D.R. (1995). Neurodevelopmental animal models of schizophrenia. *Clinical Neuroscience,* 3, 98–104.

Raedler, T.J., Knable, M.B., & Weinberger, D.R. (1998). Schizophrenia as, a developmental disorder of the cerebral cortex. *Current Opinion in Neurobiology,* 8, 157–161.

Weinberger, D.R. (1987). (See References)

Notes

1. Address correspondence to William G. Iacono, Department of Psychology, University of Minnesota, N218 Elliott Hall, 75 East River Rd., Minneapolis, MN 55455; e-mail: wiacono@tfs.psych.umn.edu.

2. The temporal lobe is located laterally in the brain, near the temples. A primary ability supported by medial-temporal lobe structures (e.g., the hippocampus) is memory. In addition, individuals with damage to the temporal lobe may experience hallucinations. The frontal lobe is located in the most anterior part of the brain. Primary abilities supported by the frontal lobe include attention, as well as higher-level planning and organizing skills sometimes referred to as executive functions. Individuals with damage to the frontal lobe may demonstrate working memory impairment (i.e., an inability to temporarily store and manipulate information needed to execute a task) and eye movement dysfunction (i.e., an inability to produce certain kinds of eye movements in experimental paradigms).

3. Dopamine is one of many identified neurotransmitters, chemicals that allow for communication between nerve cells (neurons). Neurotransmitters are typically released into the space between neurons (a synapse), where they may exert their effect by binding to specific neuroanatomical sites (receptors) of adjacent neurons. In this manner, neurotransmitters may serve to propagate electrochemical signals throughout the nervous system.

4. Animal models attempt to imitate or re-create some aspect of human functioning in animals in order to study specific processes under greater experimental control. For example, animal models of schizophrenia may create any combination of signs and symptoms of the disorder in order to gain better understanding of its etiology or treatments.

5. Schizotypal personality disorder is characterized by disturbances in interpersonal relationships, distorted thoughts or perceptions, and odd speech or behavior. These symptoms are generally believed to be similar, but subthreshold, to schizophrenia symptoms.

References

Bassett, A.S., Hodgkinson, K., Chow, E.W.C., Correia, S., Scutt, L.E., & Weksberg, R. (1998). 22q11 deletion syndrome in adults with schizophrenia. *American Journal of Medical Genetics, 81,* 328–337.

Bilder, R.M., Goldman, R.S., Robinson, D., Reiter, G., Bell, L., Bates, J.A., Pappadopulos, E., Wilson, D.F., Alvir, J.M.J., Woerner, M.G., Geisler, S., Kane, J.M., & Lieberman, J.A. (2000). Neuropsychology of first-episode schizophrenia: Initial characterization and clinical correlates. *American Journal of Psychiatry, 157,* 549–559.

Brzustowicz, L.M., Hodgkinson, K.A., Chow, E.W.C., Honer, W.G., & Bassett, A.S. (2000). Location of a major susceptibility locus for familial schizophrenia on chromosome 1q21q22. *Science,* 288, 678–682.

Cannon, T.D., Rosso, I.M., Bearden, C.E., Sanchez, L.E., & Hadley, T. (1999). A prospective cohort study of neurodevelopmental processes in the genesis and epigenesis of schizophrenia. *Development and Psychopathology, 11,* 467–485.

Dunham, I., Collins, J., Wadey, R., & Scambler, P. (1992). Possible role for COMT in psychosis associated with velo-cardio-facial syndrome. *The Lancet, 340,* 1361–1362.

Goldman-Rakic, P.S. (1996). Regional and cellular fractionation of working memory. *Proceedings of the National Academy of Sciences, USA,* 93, 13473–13480.

Iacono, W.G., & Grove, W.M. (1993). Schizophrenia research: Toward an integrative genetic model. *Psychological Science, 4*, 273–276.

Jones, P., Rodgers, B., Murray, R., & Marmot, M. (1994). Child developmental risk factors for adult schizophrenia in the British 1946 birth cohort. *The Lancet, 344*, 1398–1402.

Mednick, S.A., Machon, R.A., Huttunen, M.O., & Bonett, D. (1988). Adult schizophrenia following prenatal exposure to an influenza epidemic. *Archives of General Psychiatry, 45*, 189–192.

Moore, H., West, A.R., & Grace, A.A. (1999). The regulation of forebrain dopamine transmission: Relevance to the pathophysiology and psychopathology of schizophrenia. *Biological Psychiatry, 46*, 40–55.

Vataja, R., & Elomaa, E. (1998). Midline brain anomalies and schizophrenia in people with CATCH 22 syndrome. *British Journal of Psychiatry, 172*, 518–520.

Walker, E., & Lewine, R.J. (1990). Prediction of adult-onset schizophrenia from childhood home movies of the patients. *American Journal of Psychiatry, 147*, 1052–1056.

Weinberger, D.R. (1987). Implications of normal brain development for the pathogenesis of schizophrenia. *Archives of General Psychiatry, 44*, 660–669.

Cognition in Schizophrenia: Does Working Memory Work?

Deanna M. Barch[1]
Department of Psychology, Washington University, St. Louis, Missouri

Abstract

Recent research suggests that disturbances in social and occupational functioning in individuals with schizophrenia may be more influenced by the severity of cognitive deficits than by the severity of symptoms such as hallucinations and delusions. In this article, I review evidence that one component of cognitive dysfunction in schizophrenia is a deficit in working memory, associated with disturbances in the dopamine system in dorsolateral prefrontal cortex. I suggest that although the cognitive deficits in schizoprenia include working memory dysfunction, because they arise from a disturbance in executive control processes (e.g., the representation and maintenance of context), extend to a range of cognitive domains. Finally, I discuss the need for further research on the ways in which contextual processing deficits may influence other aspects of this illness, including emotional processing.

Keywords

schizophrenia; working memory; prefrontal cortex; cognition

Lay conceptions of schizophrenia typically focus on readily observable symptoms such as hallucinations, delusions, and disorganized speech. However, individuals with schizophrenia also commonly have disturbances in memory and cognition. Interestingly, recent research suggests that disturbances in social and occupational functioning in individuals with schizophrenia may be more influenced by the severity of their cognitive deficits than by the severity of symptoms such as hallucinations and delusions (Green, Kern, Braff, & Mintz, 2000). Such findings have led to a resurgence of interest in understanding the kinds of cognitive deficits present in this illness. In particular, a large body of research has focused on the idea that one of the primary cognitive functions disturbed in schizophrenia is working memory (WM). Although individuals with schizophrenia likely have disturbances in a number of different cognitive functions, I focus on WM for the same reasons that have driven much of the research on WM in schizophrenia: First, research with humans suggests that WM is crucial for a wide range of real-world outcomes and abilities. Second, a wealth of animal data indicates that the dopamine system (one of the brain's neurotransmitter systems) and prefrontal cortex (PFC; a region of the brain), both of which are impaired in schizophrenia, play a role in WM.

WM is often defined as the ability to maintain and manipulate information over short periods of time. Although this is a relatively straightforward definition, research has shown that WM involves several different processes. For example, Baddeley's (1986) influential theory of WM distinguishes among three subcomponents, short-term holding areas (i.e., buffers) for visual information (the visual-spatial scratch pad) and verbal information (the phonological loop) and a central executive component that guides the manipulation and transformation of information held within the storage buffers. Here I briefly review the literature suggesting that individuals with schizophrenia have deficits in WM, and that these deficits are associated with disturbances in the function of the dopamine system in PFC. I argue that WM deficits in schizophrenia are more likely to reflect a problem with processes engaged by the central executive than a problem with the buffer systems. Further, I argue that such executive control deficits also influence many cognitive domains other than WM, including inhibition (the suppression of unwanted or irrelevant information), selective attention (the selection of task-relevant information), and episodic memory (learning and retrieval of new information), all of which may then contribute to disturbances in higher cognitive processes such as problem solving, reasoning, and language production.

WORKING MEMORY IMPAIRMENTS IN SCHIZOPHRENIA

Early research by Park demonstrated that individuals with schizophrenia are impaired on WM tasks that require remembering spatial locations over a delay period (Park & Holzman, 1992). Other studies have shown that individuals with schizophrenia are also impaired on tasks that require a relatively large amount of information to be maintained in WM, even when this information only needs to be maintained for a short time (Barch, Csernansky, Conturo, Snyder, & Ollinger, 2002). Even individuals who do not have schizophrenia but are at risk for the disorder for a variety of reasons have impaired WM function. For example, the first-degree relatives of individuals with schizophrenia demonstrate WM deficits (Park, Holzman, & Goldman-Rakic, 1995). In addition, individuals who score high on measures of proneness to psychosis and individuals diagnosed with schizotypal personality disorder (a personality disorder thought to share genetic liability with schizophrenia; Farmer et al., 2000) display WM deficits. These results suggest that deficits in WM may represent an aspect of vulnerability for the development of schizophrenia. Moreover, such studies with at-risk populations control for alternative interpretations of the cognitive dysfunction associated with schizophrenia, such as those having to do with medication, hospitalization, or social factors associated with being diagnosed with a psychiatric disorder.

THE NEUROBIOLOGY OF WORKING MEMORY IN SCHIZOPHRENIA

The cognitive neuroscience literature points to an important role for dopamine (a neurotransmitter) in the PFC in WM function (see Fig. 1). For example, nonhuman primate studies suggest that PFC neurons show sustained activity during delay periods when monkeys are remembering spatial locations and objects (Goldman-Rakic, 1987). The nonhuman primate literature also suggests that optimal dopamine function in PFC is important for good WM performance. Numerous human neuroimaging studies have shown activation of two different areas of the PFC in WM tasks. One of these areas is toward the top and toward the outer surface of the brain (see Fig. 1) and is referred to as dorsolateral prefrontal cortex. The other area is more toward the middle of the PFC (also toward the outer surface) and is referred to as inferior PFC (see Fig. 1).

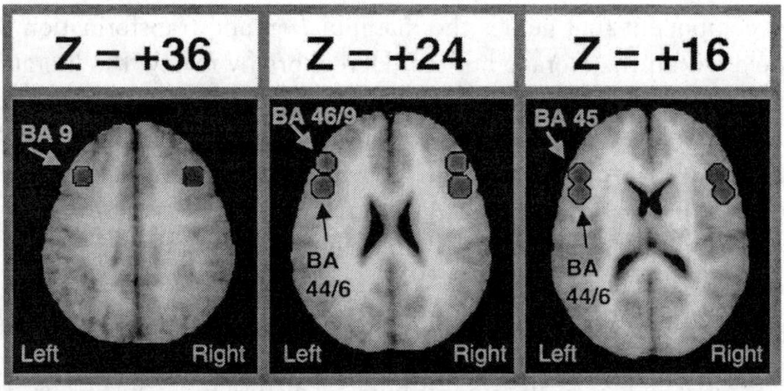

Fig. 1. Images of the brain highlighting regions of prefrontal cortex thought to be particularly important for working memory function. BA refers to Brodmann's areas, which are different areas of the brain defined by differences in the nature and organization of neurons in those areas. The regions labeled as BA 46 and BA 9 (on both the right and left sides of the brain) are often referred to as dorsolateral prefrontal cortex. The regions labeled as BA 44, 6, and 45 (on both the right and left sides of the brain) are often referred to as inferior or posterior prefrontal cortex. The Z numbers at the top of the figure refer to how many millimeters above a midpoint of the brain (the anterior and posterior commissures) each image is located.

Numerous studies of schizophrenia have shown abnormalities in PFC function during performance of WM tasks. Typically, these abnormalities involve reduced PFC activity in the individuals with schizophrenia, though a few studies have found increased PFC activity. There is also recent evidence that abnormal WM performance and PFC activity in schizophrenia reflect a disturbance in dopamine transmission (Abi-Dargham et al., 2002), which may be associated with mutations in genes governing dopamine metabolism (Egan et al., 2001).

WHAT ASPECT OF WORKING MEMORY IS IMPAIRED?

As I described earlier, Baddeley's (1986) model of WM distinguishes between buffer systems and a central executive that guides the manipulation of information held within the buffers. In this section, I discuss evidence indicating that schizophrenia is characterized by a disturbance in central executive processes, rather than in a particular buffer system.

A number of studies have shown that individuals with schizophrenia tend to perform well when required to remember only a few items over a short period of time, especially when there are no other tasks to be done at the same time that could interfere with maintaining the information (Cohen, Barch, Carter, & Servan-Schreiber, 1999; Park & Holzman, 1992). Such WM tasks may primarily depend on short-term storage buffers and require little manipulation of information. However, when individuals with schizophrenia need to remember a larger number of items (which may require them to use strategies such as grouping different items together to remember the information) or when distracting information is introduced during the task (e.g., they have to remember information while performing an intervening task), their performance declines (Goldberg, Patterson, Taqqu, & Wilder, 1998; Park & Holzman, 1992). WM theorists argue that central executive functions are particularly important when information in the buffers needs to be transformed in some way, or protected from interference. Thus, the conditions under which individuals with schizophrenia are particularly impaired suggest that they have a central executive deficit rather than a disturbance in the buffer systems.

Moreover, individuals with schizophrenia tend to show equal difficulty with WM tasks involving verbal (phonological loop), spatial (visual-spatial scratch pad), and object (visual-spatial scratch pad) information (Barch et al., 2002; Coleman et al., 2002). If WM deficits in schizophrenia were due to a disturbance in a specific buffer system, then one might expect to see greater problems for tasks that rely more on that system than the other. The fact that the data do not show this pattern suggests that the performance difficulties of individuals with schizophrenia result from poor central executive processes that are needed to support the manipulation of information or its protection from interference.

In addition, neurobiological evidence supports the hypothesis that the WM deficits in schizophrenia arise from the central executive. A number of theorists have argued that dorsolateral regions of PFC are critical for processes involved in the manipulation and transformation of information necessary to guide behavior (e.g., executive processes), whereas more inferior and posterior regions of PFC are more involved in the maintenance of information in WM through processes such as verbal rehearsal. In neuroimaging work, my colleagues and I have shown that schizophrenia is associated with deficits in dorsolateral PFC activity, but intact activity in more inferior and posterior regions of PFC (Barch et al., 2001, 2002). In addition, postmortem studies suggest that neuronal pathology in schizophrenia is selective to dorsolateral PFC and is not found in inferior PFC (Selemon, Mirzljak, Kleinman, Herman, & Goldman-Rakic, 2003). Such results indicate that the WM deficits associated with schizophrenia are due to a disturbance in central executive function supported by dorsolateral regions of PFC, rather than a disturbance in the kinds of rehearsal mechanisms that may be supported by more inferior PFC regions.

THE NATURE OF THE CENTRAL EXECUTIVE DEFICIT IN SCHIZOPHRENIA

Although I have argued that individuals with schizophrenia have a deficit in central executive function, it is informative to look more closely and consider what particular executive processes are disturbed. My colleagues and I have focused our work on a set of functions that we argue are critically important to executive control, namely, the ability to represent and maintain context information (Braver, Barch, & Cohen, 1999; Cohen et al., 1999). By context information, we mean information relevant to the task at hand that is represented in a form that can bias selection of the appropriate behavioral response. For example, suppose you were reading the sentence "In order for the farmer to keep chickens, she needed a pen." In this example, the first part of the sentence (referring to the farmer and chickens) serves as context that biases you toward interpreting "pen" as referring to a fenced enclosure, rather than a writing instrument (the more common interpretation of "pen"). We view context as a subset of representations within WM that govern how other representations are used. Further, we have argued that context processing is one of the specific components of executive control supported by dopamine function in dorsolateral PFC, and that it is impaired in schizophrenia. These hypotheses have been implemented in formal computational models that can simulate behavior in WM tasks, and the results indicate that a deficit in context processing can account for the performance of individuals with schizophrenia (Barch et al., 2001; Braver et al., 1999; Cohen et al., 1999).

ARE THE COGNITIVE IMPAIRMENTS IN SCHIZOPHRENIA UNIQUE TO WORKING MEMORY?

Another important question is whether cognitive deficits in schizophrenia are limited to the domain of WM. The answer to this question is clearly no, because individuals with schizophrenia show disturbances in a variety of domains, such as inhibition, selective attention, episodic memory, problem solving, language, and some sensory and perceptual processes. This pattern makes sense if executive processes such as the processing of context are important for a range of cognitive functions. In fact, my colleagues and I have found that deficits across a number of task domains (i.e., inhibition, WM, selective attention, episodic memory) are correlated in schizophrenia (Barch et al., 2002; Cohen et al., 1999). We have also found that individuals with schizophrenia show impaired activity in the same regions of dorsolateral PFC for both WM and episodic memory tasks. Taken together, such results suggest that a common underlying cognitive function (or set of functions) that is impaired in schizophrenia gives rise to performance deficits in a range of task domains.

FUTURE DIRECTIONS

Despite the growing evidence for WM deficits in schizophrenia and their relationship to the dopamine system in PFC, a number of critical questions remain unanswered. First, it is not yet clear what role WM deficits play in the development or maintenance of schizophrenia. For example, one possibility is that deficits in WM directly contribute to the development of specific symptoms in schizophrenia. In particular, a number of studies have focused on the role that WM may play in the disturbances of language production displayed by individuals with schizophrenia (often referred to as formal thought disorder). This research has suggested that formal thought disorder may reflect, at least in part, an inability to maintain prior discourse context in WM, and to use this information to constrain ongoing language production. Alternatively, however, WM deficits and symptoms in schizophrenia might have no direct causal relationship, and instead could be independent manifestations of one or more pathophysiological mechanisms.

A second major question is the extent to which deficits in WM (as well as other cognitive functions) are changeable and potentially amenable to treatment. Improving WM function in schizophrenia could have broad benefits given the data suggesting that functional outcome in schizophrenia is driven, at least in part, by the severity of cognitive dysfunction. Much of the existing longitudinal research on cognitive function in schizophrenia suggests that deficits in WM and other related cognitive functions tend to stay fairly stable, even when clinical symptoms change. In addition, initial research suggested that antipsychotic medications do not significantly alter WM function in schizophrenia. However, more recent research is more promising, with a number of studies demonstrating WM improvements following administration of the newer generation of antipsychotics. A growing area of research is focused on cognitive rehabilitation in schizophrenia. Results have been mixed, though some studies have found improvements in cognitive function after intervention, and one study showed improved PFC activity as well. Clearly, there is a need for more research on both psychological and pharmacological approaches to improving WM function in schizophrenia.

A third arena for future work on cognitive function in schizophrenia is the association between the impairment in WM and other aspects of this illness. Although researchers currently have little understanding of how deficits in emotion and cognition are related in schizophrenia, a growing literature suggests there are important links between the two kinds of impairment. For example, the language production of individuals with schizophrenia is more impaired when they discuss negative topics than when they discuss neutral or positive topics (a phenomena referred to as affective reactivity of language). Furthermore, the severity of affective reactivity of language in schizophrenia is related to the severity of specific kinds of cognitive deficits, such as context-processing disturbances. At the same time, the literature suggests that the PFC and another brain region, the hippocampus, play important roles in regulating emotional processing. There is evidence that individuals with schizophrenia have disturbances in the hippocampus, as well as the PFC. Thus, it is possible that at least a subset of the emotional disturbances in schizophrenia reflect deficits in the ability to use context information to regulate emotional processing.

Recommended Reading

Barch, D.M., Carter, C.S., & Cohen, J.D. (in press). Context processing deficit in schizophrenia: Diagnostic specificity, longitudinal course, and relationships to clinical symptoms. *Journal of Abnormal Psychology.*

Barch, D.M., Csernansky, J., Conturo, T., Snyder, A.Z., & Ollinger, J. (2002). (See References)

Braver, T.S., Barch, D.M., & Cohen, J.D. (1999). (See References)

Acknowledgments—This work was supported by Grants MH45156, MH47073, MH60887, and MH62130 from the U.S. National Institute of Mental Health and by a Young Investigators Award from the National Alliance for Research on Schizophrenia and Depression (NARSAD).

Note

1. Address correspondence to Deanna M. Barch, Department of Psychology, Washington University, Box 1125, One Brookings Dr., St. Louis, MO 63130; e-mail: dbarch@artsci.wustl.edu.

References

Abi-Dargham, A., Mawlawi, O., Lombardo, I., Gil, R., Martinez, D., Huang, Y., Hwang, D.K., Keilp, J., Kochan, L., Van Heertum, R., Gorman, J.M., & Laruelle, M. (2002). Prefrontal dopamine D1 receptors and working memory in schizophrenia. *Journal of Neuroscience, 22*, 3708–3719.

Baddeley, A.D. (1986). *Working memory.* New York: Oxford University Press.

Barch, D.M., Carter, C.S., Braver, T.S., McDonald, A., Sabb, F.W., Noll, D.C., & Cohen, J.D. (2001). Selective deficits in prefrontal cortex regions in medication naive schizophrenia patients. *Archives of General Psychiatry, 50*, 280–288.

Barch, D.M., Csernansky, J., Conturo, T., Snyder, A.Z., & Ollinger, J. (2002). Working and long-term memory deficits in schizophrenia: Is there a common underlying prefrontal mechanism? *Journal of Abnormal Psychology, 111*, 478–494.

Braver, T.S., Barch, D.M., & Cohen, J.D. (1999). Cognition and control in schizophrenia: A computational model of dopamine and prefrontal function. *Biological Psychiatry, 46*, 312–328.

Cohen, J.D., Barch, D.M., Carter, C., & Servan-Schreiber, D. (1999). Context-processing deficits in schizophrenia. *Journal of Abnormal Psychology, 108*, 120–133.

Coleman, M.J., Cook, S., Matthysse, S., Barnard, J., Lo, Y., Levy, D.L., Rubin, D.B., & Holzman, P.S. (2002). Spatial and object working memory impairments in schizophrenia patients. *Journal of Abnormal Psychology, 111*, 425–435.

Egan, M.F., Goldberg, T.E., Kolachana, B.S., Callicott, J.H., Mazzanti, C.M., Straub, R.E., Goldman, D., & Weinberger, D.R. (2001). Effect of COMT Val 108/158 Met genotype on frontal lobe function and risk for schizophrenia. *Proceedings of the National Academy of Sciences, USA, 98*, 6917–6922.

Farmer, C.M., O'Donnell, B.F., Niznikiewicz, M.A., Vaglmaier, M.M., McCarley, R.W., & Shenton, M.E. (2000). Visual perception and working memory in schizotypal personality disorder. *American Journal of Psychiatry, 157*, 781–786.

Goldberg, T.E., Patterson, K.J., Taqqu, Y., & Wilder, K. (1998). Capacity limitations in short-term memory in schizophrenia. *Psychological Medicine, 28*, 665–673.

Goldman-Rakic, P.S. (1987). Circuitry of primate prefrontal cortex and regulation of behavior by representational memory. In F. Plum & V. Mountcastle (Eds.), *Handbook of physiology: The nervous system* (Vol. 5, pp. 373–417). Bethesda, MD: American Physiological Society.

Green, M.F., Kern, R.S., Braff, D.L., & Mintz, J. (2000). Neurocognitive deficits and functional outcome in schizophrenia: Are we measuring the "right stuff"? *Schizophrenia Bulletin, 26*(1), 119–136.

Park, S., & Holzman, P.S. (1992). Schizophrenics show spatial working memory deficits. *Archives of General Psychiatry, 49*, 975–982.

Park, S., Holzman, P.S., & Goldman-Rakic, P.S. (1995). Spatial working memory deficits in the relatives of schizophrenic patients. *Archives of General Psychiatry,* 52, 821–828.

Selemon, L.D., Mirzljak, J., Kleinman, J.E., Herman, M.M., & Goldman-Rakic, P.S. (2003). Regional specificity in the neuropathologic substrates of schizophrenia. *Archives of General Psychiatry, 60*, 69–77.

Cognitive Activity and Risk of Alzheimer's Disease

Robert S. Wilson[1] and David A. Bennett

Rush Alzheimer's Disease Center (R.S.W., D.A.B.) and Departments of Neurological Sciences (R.S.W., D.A.B.) and Psychology (R.S.W.), Rush-Presbyterian-St. Luke's Medical Center, Chicago, Illinois

Abstract

Recent research suggests that frequent participation in cognitively stimulating activities may reduce risk of Alzheimer's disease in old age. We review epidemiological evidence of such an association. We then consider whether cognitive activity can account for the association between higher educational and occupational attainment and reduced risk of Alzheimer's disease. Finally, we discuss the behavioral and neurobiological mechanisms that may underlie the association between cognitive activity and risk of Alzheimer's disease.

Keywords

Alzheimer's disease; cognitive activity; longitudinal studies

Recent scientific data suggest that people with higher educational and occupational attainment tend to have a lower risk of developing Alzheimer's disease than do people with lower educational and occupational attainment (Stern et al., 1994). The mechanism underlying this pattern is unknown. One hypothesis is that the effects of education and occupation are due to their association with frequency of participation in cognitively stimulating activities (Evans et al., 1997). Although the idea that frequent intellectual activity might help one's mental faculties in old age predates the Roman empire, it has only recently become the subject of rigorous scientific investigation.

COGNITIVE ACTIVITY AND ALZHEIMER'S DISEASE

The first problem encountered in this line of research is defining the construct of cognitive activity. Most human activities involve some degree of cognitive function, but it is uncertain how best to quantify that degree, particularly when comparing persons from diverse cultural and socioeconomic backgrounds. Nonetheless, researchers have developed a number of scales to measure frequency of cognitive activity. For these measures, respondents rate their current or past frequency of participation in activities judged to primarily involve seeking or processing information. These activities range from pursuits that most people would agree are cognitively stimulating (e.g., reading a book or playing a game like chess or checkers), to pursuits that seem less cognitively demanding (e.g., listening to the radio or watching television), but that also involve information processing that may be important, especially in old age, when physical infirmities and social isolation may limit access to certain kinds of activities. Various summary measures of frequency of participation in cognitively stimulating activities have been shown to be related to educational level and performance on cognitive tests, so they appear to have some validity (Wilson, Barnes, & Bennett, in press; Wilson et al., 1999, 2000).

Several prospective studies have examined the association between summary measures of participation in cognitively stimulating activities and risk of developing Alzheimer's disease. In one of these studies (Wilson, Mendes de Leon, et al., 2002), older[2] Catholic clergy members who did not have dementia rated how frequently they participated in several cognitively stimulating activities at the beginning of the study. During an average of about 5 years of follow-up, persons reporting frequent participation in cognitively stimulating activities had only half the risk of developing Alzheimer's disease compared with those reporting infrequent cognitive activity. This association between cognitive activity and incidence of Alzheimer's disease has been confirmed in several studies of older persons from geographically defined communities (Scarmeas, Levy, Tang, Manly, & Stern, 2001; Wang, Karp, Winblad, & Fratiglioni, 2002; Wilson, Bennett, et al., 2002).

Because Alzheimer's disease is the leading cause of dementia in older persons and few potentially modifiable risk factors have been identified, understanding the basis of the association between cognitive activity and disease incidence is a matter of substantial public-health significance. In the remainder of this article, we examine three issues bearing on this association. We first consider whether cognitive activity accounts for the association between educational and occupational attainment and risk of Alzheimer's disease. We then discuss what is known about the behavioral and neurobiological mechanisms underlying the association between cognitive activity and Alzheimer's disease.

COGNITIVE ACTIVITY AND EDUCATION

Because cognitive activity is related to both risk of Alzheimer's disease and education, in a recent study we examined whether cognitive activity could explain the association between educational attainment and disease risk (Wilson, Bennett, et al., 2002). In this 4-year longitudinal study of older residents of a biracial community, those who had completed more years of schooling had a reduced risk of developing Alzheimer's disease compared with those who had less educational attainment. The prestige of a resident's main occupation had a similar association with disease risk. When frequency of participation in cognitive activity was added to the analysis, however, the associations of educational and occupational attainment with disease risk were substantially reduced and no longer statistically significant. By contrast, the association between frequency of cognitive activity and disease risk was not substantially affected by adding educational level, occupational prestige, or both to the statistical model. These findings suggest that the association between educational attainment and risk of Alzheimer's disease may in large part be due to the fact that persons with more education tend to be more cognitively active than persons with less education.

BEHAVIORAL MECHANISMS UNDERLYING THE ASSOCIATION

What might account for the association between cognitive activity and risk of Alzheimer's disease? It seems likely that the positive correlation between cognitive activity and cognitive function is one contributing factor. On average, cognitively active persons are apt to begin old age at a higher level of cognitive function than their less cognitively active counterparts. As a result, a cognitively active person would need to experience more cognitive decline than a less active person before reaching a level of cognitive impairment commensurate with dementia.

A more fundamental way in which cognitive activity might affect risk of Alzheimer's disease is through an association with the primary manifestation of the disease, progressive cognitive decline. That is, not only might cognitively active people begin old age with better cognitive skills than less cognitively active people, but those skills may also be less subject to decline. Two studies have demonstrated such an effect (Hultsch, Hertzog, Small, & Dixon, 1999; Wilson, Mendes de Leon, et al., 2002). In each, frequent cognitive activity was associated with reduced cognitive decline in analyses that controlled for initial level of cognitive function. Thus, the higher level of cognitive function and reduced rate of cognitive decline that are associated with frequent cognitive activity probably both contribute to the association between frequent cognitive activity and reduced risk of Alzheimer's disease.

Cognitive training programs that provide strategic instruction and practice have been shown to have substantial and long-lasting beneficial effects on cognitive function in older persons (Ball et al., 2002), further supporting the idea that level of cognitive activity may be causally linked with risk of Alzheimer's disease. The benefits of cognitive training appear quite specific, with improved performance restricted to the skill that was trained.

Evidence of this specificity can also be discerned in observational studies. Thus, some studies have found that frequency of cognitive activity, but not of physical activity, is related to risk of Alzheimer's disease (Wilson, Bennett, et al., 2002; Wilson, Mendes de Leon, et al., 2002). In addition, cognitive activity appears to be primarily associated with reduced decline in processing skills like perceptual speed and working memory (Hultsch et al., 1999; Wilson, Mendes de Leon, et al., 2002). These skills are notable for being involved in nearly all kinds of intellectual activity, so it makes sense that they would benefit most from the frequency of such activity. Further, among people who already have Alzheimer's disease, level of reading activity prior to the onset of dementia is related to decline in verbal abilities but not nonverbal abilities (Wilson et al., 2000), providing further evidence that a particular cognitive activity benefits mainly the skills involved in that activity.

NEUROBIOLOGICAL MECHANISMS UNDERLYING THE ASSOCIATION

The neurobiological mechanisms through which cognitive activity reduces the risk of Alzheimer's disease are unclear. One possibility is that cognitive activity actually reduces the accumulation of pathology associated with cognitive impairment, such as neuritic plaques and neurofibrillary tangles,[3] which are forms of Alzheimer's disease pathology, or cerebral infarction (i.e., stroke). Alternatively, cognitive activity may influence risk of Alzheimer's disease by affecting the development or maintenance of the interconnected neural systems that underlie different forms of cognitive processing.

Scientific interest has focused on the latter possibility for two main reasons. First, recent studies have found that the correlation of quantitative measures of Alzheimer's disease pathology with cognitive impairment or dementia are modest in size, which suggests that other neurobiological mechanisms are involved. Second, an extensive body of research has shown that environmental complexity is related to a variety of changes in the brains of adult animals, including formation of new neurons and connections between neurons, in brain regions that are critically involved in memory and thinking (Kempermann, Gast, & Gage, 2002; Shors et al., 2001). In humans, therefore, some researchers have hypothesized that cognitive activity contributes to structural and functional organization and reorganization that make selected neural systems more difficult to disrupt, so that more Alzheimer's disease pathology is needed to impair the skills mediated by those systems (Cummings, Vinters, Cole, & Khachaturian, 1998).

Support for this idea comes from a recent study (Bennett et al., in press) that examined the relation of education and a summary measure of Alzheimer's disease pathology to level of cognitive function near the time of death. Both years of education and amount of Alzheimer's disease pathology were related to level of cognitive function. Education was not related to measures of Alzheimer's disease pathology, but influenced the association between Alzheimer's disease pathology and cognitive function: A given amount of Alzheimer's disease pathology was associated with less cognitive impairment in a person with more education than in a person with less education. In other words, the deleterious impact of Alzheimer's disease pathology on cognitive function was reduced in persons with more education compared with those with less education. These data suggest that education—or variables related to education, such as cognitive activity—affects risk of cognitive impairment and dementia by somehow enhancing the brain's capacity to tolerate Alzheimer's disease pathology, rather than by altering the accumulation of the pathology itself.

Because Alzheimer's disease is thought to develop gradually over a period of years, another possibility is that a low level of cognitive activity is an early sign of the disease rather than an independent risk factor. The early-sign hypothesis is inconsistent with several observations, however. For example, excluding people with memory impairment, usually the first sign of Alzheimer's disease, or controlling for a well-established genetic risk factor for the disease (i.e., possession of an ε4 allele from a gene on chromosome 19 that codes apolipoprotein E, a plasma protein involved in cholesterol transport), does not appear to substantially affect the association between cognitive activity and Alzheimer's disease. In addition, the specificity of the association between frequency of participation in cognitive activity and level of function in different domains of cognition is not easily reconciled with the early-sign hypothesis. Thus, although early Alzheimer's disease may contribute to reduced cognitive activity, such an effect does not appear to be sufficient to explain the association between cognitive activity and disease incidence.

CONCLUSIONS

Several large prospective studies have found an association between frequency of cognitive activity and subsequent risk of developing dementia or Alzheimer's disease. Evidence from observational studies and cognitive intervention research suggests that the association of cognitive activity with disease incidence may be causal. Because few potentially modifiable risk factors for Alzheimer's disease have been identified, this area of research has important public-health implications. Much remains to be learned, however.

A central question is whether the protective effect of cognitive activity depends on when it occurs during the life span. In particular, it is uncertain to what extent cognitive stimulation in late life, as opposed to early life or adulthood, is critical. Answers to this question are likely to require advances in how researchers assess cognitive activity and features of the environment that support it (Wilson et al., in press). Such research could help determine the feasibility of large-scale trials of cognitive intervention.

Another challenge is to elucidate the structural, biochemical, and molecular mechanisms that underlie individual differences in the ability to tolerate Alzheimer's disease pathology. These mechanisms may differ for cognitive activity during development compared with cognitive activity in adulthood and old age. For example, in experimental animal studies, environmental experiences during development appear to affect mainly the number of neurons that survive into adulthood, whereas experiences late in life may affect cognition more by maintaining neural connections than by changing their number. Understanding these mechanisms may make it possible to develop new preventive strategies aimed at augmenting the ability of the brain to withstand the deleterious effects of Alzheimer's disease pathology and possibly other neurodegenerative conditions as well. To that end, we have recently begun a large epidemiological study of older persons who have a wide range of educational and occupational backgrounds and have agreed to annual clinical evaluation and brain donation at death.

Finally, short-term clinical trials are needed to identify efficient and practical ways to train and strengthen cognitive skills. In addition, clinical trials of several years' duration are needed to determine whether cognitive training can reduce cognitive decline in old age.

Recommended Reading

Ball, K., Berch, D.B., Helmers, K.F., Jobe, J.B., Leveck, M.D., Marsiske, M., Morris, J. N., Rebok, G.W., Smith, D.M., Tennstedt, S.L., Unverzagt, F.W., & Willis, S.L. (2002). (See References)

Kempermann, G., Gast, D., & Gage, F. H. (2002). (See References)

Wilson, R.S., Bennett, D.A., Bienias, J.L., Aggarwal, N.T., Mendes de Leon, C.F., Morris, M.C., Schneider, J.A., & Evans, D.A. (2002). (See References)

Wilson, R.S., Mendes de Leon, C.F., Barnes, L.L., Schneider, J.A., Bienias, J.L., Evans, D.A., & Bennett, D.A. (2002). (See References)

Acknowledgments—This research was supported by National Institute on Aging Grants P30 AG10161, R01 AG15819, and R01 AG17917.

Notes

1. Address correspondence to Robert S. Wilson, Rush Alzheimer's Disease Center, 1645 West Jackson Blvd., Suite 675, Chicago, IL 60612; e-mail: rwilson@rush.edu.

2. We use "older" to refer to persons who are 65 years of age or older.

3. Neuritic plaques accumulate outside neurons and consist mainly of an abnormal protein called beta-amyloid. Neurofibrillary tangles are found inside neurons and are composed primarily of an abnormal protein called tau that appears like a tangled mass of filaments under a microscope. If sufficient numbers of plaques and tangles are present, a pathological diagnosis of Alzheimer's disease can be made.

References

Ball, K., Berch, D.B., Helmers, K.F., Jobe, J.B., Leveck, M.D., Marsiske, M., Morris, J.N., Rebok, G.W., Smith, D.M., Tennstedt, S.L., Unverzagt, F.W., & Willis, S.L. (2002). Effects of cognitive training interventions with older adults: A randomized controlled trial. *Journal of the American Medical Association*, 288, 2271–2281.

Bennett, D.A., Wilson, R.S., Schneider, J.A., Evans, D.A., Mendes de Leon, C.F., Arnold, S.E., Barnes, L.L., & Bienias, J.L. (in press). Education modifies the relation of AD pathology to level of cognitive function in older persons. *Neurology.*

Cummings, J., Vinters, H., Cole, G., & Khachaturian, Z. (1998). Alzheimer's disease: Etiologies, pathophysiology, cognitive reserve, and treatment opportunities. *Neurology, 51*(Suppl. 1), S2–S17.

Evans, D.A., Hebert, L.E., Beckett, L.A., Scherr, P.A., Albert, M.A., Chown, M.J., Pilgrim, D.M., & Taylor, J.O. (1997). Education and other measures of socioeconomic status and risk of incident Alzheimer's disease in a defined population of older persons. *Archives of Neurology, 54*, 1399–1405.

Hultsch, D., Hertzog, C., Small, B., & Dixon, R. (1999). Use it or lose it: Engaged lifestyle as a buffer of cognitive decline in aging? *Psychology and Aging, 14*, 245–263.

Kempermann, G., Gast, D., & Gage, F.H. (2002). Neuroplasticity in old age: Sustained fivefold induction of hippocampal neurogenesis by long-term environmental enrichment. *Annals of Neurology,* 52, 135–143.

Scarmeas, N., Levy, G., Tang, M.-X., Manly, J., & Stem, Y. (2001). Influence of leisure activity on the incidence of Alzheimer's disease. *Neurology,* 57, 2236–2242.

Shors, T.J., Miesegaes, G., Beylin, A., Zhao, M., Rydel, T., & Gould, E. (2001). Neurogenesis in the adult is involved in the formation of trace memories. *Nature, 410*, 372–376.

Stern, Y., Gurland, B., Tatemichi, T.K., Tang, M.-X., Wilder, D., & Mayeux, R. (1994). Influence of education and occupation on the incidence of Alzheimer's disease. *Journal of the American Medical Association, 271*, 1004–1010.

Wang, H.-H., Karp, A., Winblad, B., & Fratiglioni, L. (2002). Late-life engagement in social and leisure activities is associated with a decreased risk of dementia: A longitudinal study from the Kungsholmen Project. *American Journal of Epidemiology,* 155, 1081–1087.

Wilson, R.S., Barnes, L.L., & Bennett, D.A. (in press). Assessment of lifetime participation in cognitively stimulating activities. *Journal of Clinical and Experimental Neuropsychology.*

Wilson, R.S., Bennett, D.A., Beckett, L.A., Morris, M.C., Gilley, D.W., Bienias, J.L., Scherr, P.A., & Evans, D.A. (1999). Cognitive activity in older persons from a geographically defined population. *Journal of Gerontology: Psychological Sciences, 54B*, P155–PI60.

Wilson, R.S., Bennett, D.A., Bienias, J.L., Aggarwal, N.T., Mendes de Leon, C.F., Morris, M.C., Schneider, J.A., & Evans, D.A. (2002). Cognitive activity and incident AD in a population-based sample of older persons. *Neurology,* 59, 1910–1915.

Wilson, R.S., Bennett, D.A., Gilley, D.W., Beckett, L.A., Barnes, L.L., & Evans, D.A. (2000). Premorbid reading activity and patterns of cognitive decline in Alzheimer's disease. *Archives of Neurology,* 56, 1718–1723.

Wilson, R.S., Mendes de Leon, C.F., Barnes, L.L., Schneider, J.A., Bienias, J.L., Evans, D.A., & Bennett, D.A. (2002). Participation in cognitively stimulating activities and risk of incident Alzheimer's disease. *Journal of the American Medical Association,* 287, 742–748.

Childhood Disorders, Life Cycle Transitions, and Mental Health and the Law

The topics in the final section of the textbook and reader continue to fascinate most students. The biggest problem often is finding the time to cover them in any depth. The supplementary readings from *Current Directions* can help by exposing students in more depth to specific and exciting topics, something that hopefully will motivate them to dig deeper into the psychological literature.

In *Attention Deficit Hyperactivity Disorder in Adults: Implications for Theories of Diagnosis*, Stephen Faraone examines current issues about the diagnosis of a childhood disorder that is increasingly being applied to adults, including college students who may find themselves struggling in the classroom. Faraone reviews some evidence supporting the validity of adult ADHD, but more importantly, he uses this important new diagnostic category as a point of departure for discussing reliability, validity, and how diagnoses are socially and scientifically constructed. His discussion is timely not only in relation to ADHD but the diagnosis of most mental disorders, especially psychological disorders of childhood where classification systems are still relatively undeveloped.

Three articles in the reader address difficult issues in normal life cycle transitions that often are associated with mental disorders or bring people into contact with a mental health professional for assistance in dealing with the life difficulty itself. These topics are of great interest to most students, and they often touch very personally on their own lives. In *Marital Conflict: Correlates, Structure, and Context*, noted researcher Frank Fincham reviews the extensive evidence linking marital troubles with a variety of psychological problems. Fincham notes the considerable importance of conflict to emotional well-being, but he challenges readers to think beyond conflict in close relationships and consider the importance of support, affection, and conflict within the personal and cultural context. Laura Carstensen and Susan Charles focus on the later but equally important life span concern of aging. In *Emotion in the Second Half of Life*, these leading researchers discuss their theory of socioemotional selectivity—how older people allocate their social time and emotional resources more carefully, but they also provide a very helpful and provocative overview of emotions among older adults. Among other things they conclude that, in comparison to their younger counterparts, older adults experience as much positive affect, less negative affect, reduced physiological arousal, and better emotion regulation. In the final article on life span transitions, Arthur Fisk and Wendy Rogers also discuss the very important contemporary issue of aging. Their article, *Psychology and Aging: Enhancing the Lives of an Aging Population*, addresses the pressing need to develop better programs and better research on improving the quality of life among older adults.

The last two articles in the reader address the always engaging and provocative topic of mental health and the law. Amy Holtzworth-Munroe addresses the important and timely issue of men's violence against women. Her thoughtful article, *A Typology of Men Who Are Violent Toward Their Female Partners: Making Sense of the Heterogeneity in Husband Violence*, reviews her theory that there is not one type of violent male partner but three: family only batterers, dysphoric-borderline batterers, and generally violent-antisocial batterers. Holtzworth-Munroe musters empirical support for this typology based on her impressive program of research. Finally, Martin Daly and Margo Wilson offer an evolutionary psychology account of one of our saddest and most troublesome social problems: violence against children. In *Violence Against Stepchildren*, an article that is sure to provoke reactions among students—and among many instructors too, Daly and Wilson marshal evidence that stepfathers are far more likely to abuse children than are biological fathers. They use this evidence as a point of departure for discussing the evolutionary psychology of family relationships, arguing, as one of their headings spells out, that parental love is more than just a role.

Attention Deficit Hyperactivity Disorder in Adults: Implications for Theories of Diagnosis

Stephen V. Faraone[1]

Pediatric Psychopharmacology Unit, Massachusetts General Hospital, Boston, Massachusetts; Department of Psychiatry, Massachusetts Mental Health Center, Boston, Massachusetts; and Harvard Medical School, Boston, Massachusetts

Abstract

The diagnosis of attention deficit hyperactivity disorder (ADHD) in adults has been a source of controversy, with some prominent researchers questioning its very existence and others suggesting it is an urgent clinical problem. This article reviews five domains of data addressing the validity of adult ADHD: clinical correlates, family history, treatment response, laboratory studies, and long-term outcome. If then shows how the debate over adult ADHD reflects a clash of theoretical paradigms and concludes by suggesting ways in which psychological science can collect the data needed to clarify the validity of adult ADHD.

Keywords

adult ADHD; diagnostic validity; nosology; psychometrics

Attention deficit hyperactivity disorder (ADHD) is a disorder of inattentiveness, impulsivity, and hyperactivity (Faraone & Biederman, 1998). Research implicates genes, pregnancy and delivery complications, marital distress, family dysfunction, and low social class as risk factors for ADHD or moderators of its course. That these risk factors affect specific brain regions is suggested by both neuropsychological and neuroimaging studies.

For children, the diagnosis of ADHD is straightforward. In contrast, leaders in the field have debated the validity of adult ADHD (Barkley, 1998; Shaffer, 1994; Spencer, Biederman, Wilens, & Faraone, 1994). For example, Shaffer (1994) noted that because the diagnosis requires onset prior to age 7, it requires accurate recall of distant events. Also, because the symptoms of other disorders could mimic ADHD, adults diagnosed with ADHD may have another disorder. Shaffer argued that the potential efficacy of stimulant treatment had drawn attention to adult ADHD, but the literature did not present overwhelming evidence of such treatment's efficacy. Finally, adult ADHD had become a darling of the media, leading many adults to diagnose themselves. Clinicians are skeptical about self-diagnoses because troubled individuals readily attribute problems to syndromes discussed on the talk-show circuit and in popular magazines.

These concerns have motivated researchers to examine the validity of adult ADHD. This article briefly reviews relevant research to show how the debate over adult ADHD raises questions about the theoretical underpinnings of diagnostic methods. It concludes by suggesting ways in which psychological science can clarify the validity of the disorder.

WHAT DO WE KNOW ABOUT ADULT ADHD?

The validity of a psychiatric disorder derives from a pattern of converging evidence: clinical correlates, family history, treatment response, laboratory studies, and long-term outcome. The evidence regarding clinical correlates includes the fact that adults with ADHD show ADHD's typical signs of inattentiveness, impulsivity, and hyperactivity. They also have high rates of antisocial, mood, and anxiety disorders. This psychiatric comorbidity provides ambiguous support for validity, however. Some clinicians view the comorbid disorders as mimicking ADHD and accounting for the poor functioning of these adults. Others note that because extensive comorbidity is seen among ADHD children, comorbidity in adults supports the idea that the adult and child syndromes are the same (Spencer et al., 1994).

Studies of children show that ADHD is familial (Faraone & Biederman, 1994). So, if adult ADHD is valid, parents of ADHD children should have ADHD, as should the relatives of ADHD adults. As a group, seven family studies have shown the parents of ADHD children to have a significantly increased risk for ADHD. For fathers, the mean prevalence is 24% for ADHD families and 7% for control families. For mothers, these prevalences are 15% and 3%, respectively. Two studies of families of adult ADHD patients found higher rates of ADHD among their relatives (mean = 49%) compared with control subjects (mean = 2.5%).

Many researchers have looked to psychopharmacologic studies in the hopes that a clear-cut response or nonresponse to stimulant medication, the mainstay of treatment for childhood ADHD, would reveal if ADHD adults truly have the disorder. Five early studies examined a total of 137 patients. They found an average response rate of 50%, much less than the average 70% rate seen in ADHD children. But the interpretation of these studies was clouded by their use of relatively low doses. When a study used higher doses, 87% of ADHD adults responded to stimulants, and only 13% responded to placebo (Spencer et al., 1995).

Because neuropsychological tests often show impairments in ADHD children, these tests have been used to validate the adult syndrome. If ADHD in adults is the same disorder as ADHD in children, we would expect to find similarities in the neuropsychological features seen in adults and children with the disorder. These similarities have been found for several neuropsychological abilities. Moreover, brain-imaging studies of adults with ADHD show abnormalities of brain regions that have been implicated in the etiology of ADHD in studies of children.

Molecular genetic studies of children have implicated several genes in the etiology of ADHD (Faraone & Biederman, 1998). Much attention has focused on the gene that controls the D4 dopamine receptor (DRD4). This receptor is a component of neurons that are activated by the neurochemical dopamine, which has been implicated in ADHD. Notably, the gene variant of DRD4 associated with ADHD mediates a blunted response to dopamine, and this is a reasonable candidate as a susceptibility gene for ADHD. The DRD4 data are relevant to adult ADHD because the gene variant implicated in children has also been implicated for adult ADHD (Faraone et al., 1999).

What percentage of children with ADHD grow up to be adults with ADHD? Despite the simplicity of the question, there is little agreement on the answer.

Barkley's (1998) review of follow-up studies showed a wide range of estimates: 11 to 70%. This variability suggests that the debate about adult ADHD's validity may be due to inconsistencies in how investigators formulate diagnoses.

IMPLICATIONS FOR THEORIES OF DIAGNOSIS

Although clinical, family, and treatment studies have provided much evidence for the validity of adult ADHD, some studies that have followed ADHD children over time have found low rates of ADHD in their adult years. This raises a serious question about the validity of ADHD in adults. If ADHD children do not grow up to be ADHD adults, how is it that clinical and family studies can identify ADHD in adults? This section discusses the underlying theoretical issues that have led to these conflicting data.

Psychiatric Comorbidity and the Hierarchical Diagnosis Paradigm

The third edition of the American Psychiatric Association's *Diagnostic and Statistical Manual* (DSM-III) marked a turning point for psychiatry. By discarding the theory-based diagnoses of the second edition of the manual, DSM-III improved reliability and created an empirical framework for nosological studies. But the authors of DSM-III faced a perplexing problem: There was much overlap in the symptoms expressed by different disorders.

To deal with symptom overlap, DSM-III described mental disorders as forming a hierarchy. Disorders higher in the hierarchy showed a wider range of symptoms than those lower in the hierarchy. For example, schizophrenic patients have psychotic symptoms, but they can also show anxiety. In contrast, patients with generalized anxiety disorder (GAD) rarely show the psychotic signs of schizophrenia. Thus, according to hierarchical diagnosis, a patient showing the symptoms of schizophrenia and GAD should be diagnosed with schizophrenia, not GAD, because schizophrenia is higher in the hierarchy.

Thus, clinicians were taught that careful diagnosis clarifies comorbidity. For example, DSM-IV, the fourth edition of the *Diagnostic and Statistical Manual*, describes three hierarchical guidelines for diagnosing ADHD: First, symptoms of depression such as sadness are called associated features of ADHD. Second, we are cautioned not to diagnose ADHD if its symptoms are better accounted for by another mental disorder. Third, we are told not to diagnose depression in ADHD children whose disturbance in mood is characterized by irritability. So, when a child meets criteria for both ADHD and depression, DSM-IV encourages clinicians to diagnose only ADHD.

The problem with hierarchical diagnosis is straightforward: It ignores epidemiological data showing comorbidity is pervasive for both child and adult disorders. Because of these data, many researchers use a comorbidity paradigm, which views diagnostic overlap as the rule, rather than the exception. The comorbidity paradigm encourages diagnosticians to assess all disorders without assuming that one accounts for another.

Reliance on hierarchical diagnoses impedes the identification of ADHD adults because some hierarchical rules encourage diagnosticians to diagnose comorbid conditions, not ADHD. For example, Mannuzza, Klein, Bessler, Malloy, and LaPadula (1993) found a very low rate of ADHD after age 20. Their study applied a hierarchical rule: It excluded children whose primary reason for referral had been aggressive behavior. But because aggressive children with ADHD are more likely to have a persistent disorder than nonaggressive children with ADHD, that study's low rate of ADHD at follow-up reflects its hierarchical method of diagnosis, not the natural history of ADHD.

Developmental Sensitivity and the Diagnosis of ADHD

Because developmental change is an irrefutable fact, it must be factored into diagnoses. For example, unlike depressed adults, depressed children are usually irritable but not sad. Such differences in symptom expression across the life cycle suggest that diagnostic criteria should be "developmentally sensitive"—that is, they should address the symptom changes that occur with development.

For ADHD, DSM-IV deals with development in several ways. It cautions diagnosticians that, with maturation, symptoms become less conspicuous. Older children may be restless and fidgety, but not overly hyperactive. With age, inattention predominates as tasks at school or work tax attentional capacity. Also, we rate symptoms as present only if inconsistent with developmental level. For example, consider the symptom "has difficulty sustaining attention." We expect a 17-year-old to study for 1 hr, but would not expect the same from a 6-year-old. Thus, although DSM-IV applies the same symptom to 6-year-olds and 17-year-olds, it urges clinicians to apply the symptom in different ways for the two age groups.

Given the different expectations we have of children and adults, you might expect the DSM-IV to have different diagnostic items for these groups. It does not. When diagnosing adults, clinicians must consider symptoms such as "often leaves seat in classroom or in other situations in which remaining seated is expected." This item is developmentally insensitive for two reasons. First, with development, children mature and conquer developmental challenges. Although remaining seated is difficult at age 5, it becomes easier as development improves the child's capacity for inhibiting impulses. Second, development also brings changes in the environment. For example, unlike schoolchildren, many adults are not required to sit for several hours each day.

As Barkley (1998) argued, development makes it difficult for children with ADHD to meet criteria for ADHD with age. This idea explains why follow-up studies have obtained such variable results. For example, Mannuzza et al. (1993) found that only 11% of formerly hyperactive children met full criteria for ADHD in adulthood. In contrast, Weiss and Hechtman (1986) found that 66% of formerly hyperactive children had at least one disabling ADHD symptom in adulthood. By lowering the symptom threshold, Weiss and Hechtman were able to improve the developmental sensitivity of their diagnoses.

Fischer (1997) showed how symptom data from the population could be used to define developmentally sensitive diagnoses. Her strategy was similar to that used to define deviance for tests of personality and intelligence. She collected ADHD symptom data from a large group of adults. For each adult, she computed a total symptom score. Then, she defined a deviant level of ADHD to be a score that was 1.5 standard deviations greater than the mean. When she applied this measure of ADHD to her follow-up study of ADHD children, she found that 68% had ADHD in adulthood. In contrast, when she applied criteria from the revised edition of DSM-III, only 3% had ADHD in adulthood.

NEW DIRECTIONS FOR PSYCHOLOGICAL SCIENCE: MEASUREMENT THEORIES OF DIAGNOSIS

The ability to create reliable and valid measures of psychological phenomena is, perhaps, the foundation of psychological science. Psychologists have operationalized definitions of psychological phenomena to clarify many issues. Although psychological measurement technologies have influenced the evolution of the DSM, the problems highlighted by the diagnosis of adult ADHD indicate the need for psychological science to play a greater role in formulating empirically valid approaches to comorbidity and developmental sensitivity.

We can address the problem of comorbidity with available measurement technologies. Using the models of Meehl and Golden (1982); Blashfield, McElroy, Pfohl, and Blum (1994); and other psychologists, we can create empirical diagnostic rules for comorbid conditions. But until the causes of comorbidity are fully understood, researchers should collect the comprehensive data needed to make comorbid diagnoses. If we assume that comorbid symptoms and diagnoses are "better accounted for" by another disorder, we may undermine our ability to fully describe psychopathological mechanisms.

Two traditions within psychological science are well suited to create developmentally sensitive diagnoses: psychometrics and developmental psychology. The application of psychometric principles has created developmentally sensitive tests of psychopathology, personality, adaptive behavior, and intellectual functioning. These tests define deviance in the context of age-specific norms. A psychometric perspective suggests we view the diagnosis of ADHD as we do the construct of intelligence. We would not have adults complete an intelligence test designed for children and then conclude that intelligence increases with age. Instead, we use different test batteries for different age groups, and within a single battery, we consider a score high or low in reference to people of the same age. Perhaps we should use a similar approach for ADHD.

But age is an imperfect proxy for development. Children of the same age can be at different developmental stages and can face different developmental challenges. Because little is known about how these variations affect symptom expression, the use of age-based norms might be premature. Perhaps we should view symptom expression in the context of the patient's developmental stage at the time of diagnosis.

SUMMARY AND CONCLUSIONS

Although some evidence suggests that adult ADHD is a valid disorder, debate over its validity continues. On the surface, this debate is a duel about data and its interpretation. But scrutiny shows it to be a clash of theoretical paradigms. Diagnosticians relying on hierarchical diagnosis find less adult ADHD than those who embrace the comorbidity paradigm. Clinicians using developmentally sensitive diagnoses find adult ADHD where others do not.

Solving the diagnostic dilemma posed by adult ADHD will put to rest the vexing questions about the disorder's validity and will free researchers to address two scientific questions: What are the mechanisms that explain the persistence of ADHD into adulthood in only some children? And how do these mechanisms provide insights into treatments that would alter the course of illness?

The debate over adult ADHD will not be solved by a new slew of conflicting studies. Research should focus not only on the validity of the disorder, but also on the validity of the theories that buttress the diagnosis. Therein lies a role for psychological science: to use the tools of psychometrics, measurement theory, and developmental psychology to create an empirical foundation for diagnostic theory.

Recommended Reading

Barkley, R.A. (1998). (See References)

Faraone, S.V., & Biederman, J. (1998). (See References)

Hechtman, L. (1992). Long-term outcome in attention-deficit hyperactivity disorder. *Psychiatric Clinics of North America, 1*, 553–565.

Shaffer, D. (1994). (See References)

Spencer, T., Biederman, J., Wilens, T., & Faraone, S.V. (1994). (See References)

Acknowledgments—This work was supported by National Institute of Mental Health Grant RO1MH57934-01 to S.V. Faraone and owes much to J. Biederman, T. Spencer, T. Wilens, and colleagues at the Massachusetts General Hospital's Pediatric Psychopharmacology Unit.

Note

1. Address correspondence to Stephen V. Faraone, Pediatric Psychopharmacology Unit, ACC 725, 15 Parkman St., Boston, MA 02114-3139; 941-395-0691 (voice); 941-395-1326 (fax); email: sfaraone@earthlink.net.

References

Barkley, R.A. (1998). *Attention deficit hyperactivity disorder: A handbook for diagnosis and treatment*. New York: Guilford Press.

Blashfield, R., McElroy, R., Pfohl, B., & Blum, N. (1994). Comorbidity and the prototype model. *Clinical Psychology: Science and Practice, 1*, 96–99.

Faraone, S.V., & Biederman, J. (1994). Genetics of attention-deficit hyperactivity disorder. *Child and Adolescent Psychiatric Clinics of North America*, 3, 285–302.

Faraone, S.V., & Biederman, J. (1998). Neurobiology of attention deficit hyperactivity disorder. *Biological Psychiatry, 44*, 951–958.

Faraone, S.V., Biederman, J., Weiffenbach, B., Keith, T., Chu, M.P., Weaver, A., Spencer, T.J., Wilens, T.E., Frazier, J., Cleves, M., & Sakai, J. (1999). Dopamine D4 gene 7-repeat allele and attention deficit hyperactivity disorder. *American Journal of Psychiatry, 156*, 768–770.

Fischer, M. (1997). The persistence of ADHD into adulthood: It depends on whom you ask. *ADHD Report*, 5, 8–10.

Mannuzza, S., Klein, R.G., Bessler, A., Malloy, P., & LaPadula, M. (1993). Adult outcome of hyperactive boys: Educational achievement, occupational rank and psychiatric status. *Archives of General Psychiatry,* 50, 565–576.

Meehl, P., & Golden, R. (1982). The three kinds of taxometric tasks. In P.C. Kendall & J.N. Butcher (Eds.), *Handbook of research methods in clinical psychology* (pp. 127–181). New York: John Wiley.

Shaffer, D. (1994). Attention deficit hyperactivity disorder in adults. *American Journal of Psychiatry, 152*, 633–638.

Spencer, T., Biederman, J., Wilens, T., & Faraone, S.V. (1994). Is attention deficit hyperactivity disorder in adults a valid disorder? *Harvard Review of Psychiatry, 1*, 326–335.

Spencer, T., Wilens, T., Biederman, J., Faraone, S.V., Ablon, J.S., & Lapey, K. (1995). A double-blind, crossover comparison of methylphenidate and placebo in adults with childhood-onset attention deficit hyperactivity. *Archives of General Psychiatry,* 52, 434–443.

Weiss, G., & Hechtman, L.T. (1986). *Hyperactive children grown up.* New York: Guilford Press.

Marital Conflict: Correlates, Structure, and Context

Frank D. Fincham[1]
Psychology Department, University at Buffalo, Buffalo, New York

Abstract

Marital conflict has deleterious effects on mental, physical, and family health, and three decades of research have yielded a detailed picture of the behaviors that differentiate distressed from nondistressed couples. Review of this work shows that the singular emphasis on conflict in generating marital outcomes has yielded an incomplete picture of its role in marriage. Recently, researchers have tried to paint a more textured picture of marital conflict by studying spouses' backgrounds and characteristics, investigating conflict in the contexts of support giving and affectional expression, and considering the ecological niche of couples in their broader environment.

Keywords

conflict patterns; marital distress; support

Systematic psychological research on marriage emerged largely among clinical psychologists who wanted to better assist couples experiencing marital distress. In the 30 years since this development, marital conflict has assumed a special status in the literature on marriage, as evidenced by three indices. First, many of the most influential theories of marriage tend to reflect the view that "distress results from couples' aversive and ineffectual response to conflict" (Koerner & Jacobson, 1994, p. 208). Second, research on marriage has focused on what spouses do when they disagree with each other, and reviews of marital interaction are dominated by studies of conflict and problem solving (see Weiss & Heyman, 1997). Third, psychological interventions for distressed couples often target conflict-resolution skills (see Baucom, Shoham, Mueser, Daiuto, & Stickle, 1998).

IS MARITAL CONFLICT IMPORTANT?

The attention given marital conflict is understandable when we consider its implications for mental, physical, and family health. Marital conflict has been linked to the onset of depressive symptoms, eating disorders, male alcoholism, episodic drinking, binge drinking, and out-of-home drinking. Although married individuals are healthier on average than the unmarried, marital conflict is associated with poorer health and with specific illnesses such as cancer, cardiac disease, and chronic pain, perhaps because hostile behaviors during conflict are related to alterations in immunological, endocrine, and cardiovascular functioning. Physical aggression occurs in about 30% of married couples in the United States, leading to significant physical injury in about 10% of couples. Marriage is also the most common interpersonal context for homicide, and more women are murdered by their partners than by anyone else. Finally, marital conflict is associated with important family outcomes, including poor parenting, poor adjustment of children, increased likelihood of parent-child conflict, and conflict between siblings. Marital conflicts that are frequent, intense, physical, unresolved, and child related have a particularly negative influence on children, as do marital conflicts that spouses attribute to their child's behavior (see Grych & Fincham, 2001).

WHAT ARE MARITAL CONFLICTS ABOUT?

Marital conflicts can be about virtually anything. Couples complain about sources of conflict ranging from verbal and physical abusiveness to personal characteristics and behaviors, Perceived inequity in a couple's division of labor is associated with marital conflict and with a tendency for the male to withdraw in response to conflict. Conflict over power is also strongly related to marital dissatisfaction. Spouses' reports of conflict over extramarital sex, problematic drinking, or drug use predict divorce, as do wives' reports of husbands being jealous and spending money foolishly. Greater problem severity increases the likelihood of divorce. Even though it is often not reported to be a problem by couples, violence among newlyweds is a predictor of divorce, as is psychological aggression (verbal aggression and nonverbal aggressive behaviors that are not directed at the partner's body).

HOW DO SPOUSES BEHAVE DURING CONFLICT?

Stimulated, in part, by the view that "studying what people say about themselves is no substitute for studying how they behave" (Raush, Barry, Hertel, & Swain, 1974, p. 5), psychologists have conducted observational studies, with the underlying hope of identifying dysfunctional behaviors that could be modified in couple therapy. This research has focused on problem-solving discussions in the laboratory and provides detailed information about how maritally distressed and nondistressed couples behave during conflict.

During conflict, distressed couples make more negative statements and fewer positive statements than nondistressed couples. They are also more likely to respond with negative behavior when their partner behaves negatively. Indeed, this negative reciprocity, as it is called, is more consistent across different types of situations than is the amount of negative behavior, making it the most reliable overt signature of marital distress. Negative behavior is both more frequent and more frequently reciprocated in couples that engage in physical aggression than in other couples. Nonverbal behavior, often used as an index of emotion, reflects marital satisfaction better than verbal behavior, and unlike verbal behavior does not change when spouses try to fake good and bad marriages.

Are There Typical Patterns of Conflict Behavior?

The sequences of behavior that occur during conflict are more predictable in distressed than in nondistressed marriages and are often dominated by chains of negative behavior that usually escalate and are difficult for the couple to stop. One of the greatest challenges for couples locked into negative exchanges is to find an adaptive way of exiting from such cycles. This is usually attempted through responses that are designed to repair the interaction (e.g., "You're not listening to me") but are delivered with negative affect (e.g., irritation, sadness). The partners tend to respond to the negative affect, thereby continuing the cycle. This makes their interactions structured and predictable. In contrast, nondistressed couples appear to be more responsive to attempts at repair and are thereby able to exit from negative exchanges early on. For example, a spouse may respond to "Wait, you're not letting me finish" with "Sorry . . . please finish what you were saying." Their interaction therefore appears more random and less predictable.

A second important behavior pattern exhibited by maritally distressed couples is the demand-withdraw pattern, in which one spouse pressures the other with demands, complaints, and criticisms, while the partner withdraws with defensiveness and passive inaction. Specifically, behavior sequences in which the husband withdraws and the wife responds with hostility are more common in distressed than in satisfied couples. This finding is consistent with several studies showing that wives display more negative affect and behavior than husbands, who tend to not respond or to make statements suggestive of withdrawal, such as irrelevant comments. Disengagement or withdrawal is, in turn, related to later decreases in marital satisfaction. However, inferring reliable gender differences in demand-withdraw patterns would be premature, as recent research shows that the partner who withdraws varies according to which partner desires change. So, for example, when a man desires change, the woman is the one who withdraws. Finally, conflict patterns seem to be relatively stable over time (see Karney & Bradbury, 1995).

Is There a Simple Way to Summarize Research Findings on Marital Conflict?

The findings of the extensive literature on marital conflict can be summarized in terms of a simple ratio: The ratio of agreements to disagreements is greater than 1 for happy couples and less than 1 for unhappy couples. Gottman (1993) utilized this ratio to identify couple types. He observed husbands and wives during conversation, recording each spouse's positive and negative behaviors while speaking, and then calculated the cumulative difference between positive and negative behaviors over time for each spouse. Using the patterns in these difference scores, he distinguished regulated couples (increase in positive speaker behaviors relative to negative behaviors for both spouses over the course of conversation) from nonregulated couples (all other patterns). The regulated couples were more satisfied in their marriage than the nonregulated couples, and also less likely to divorce. Regulated couples displayed positive problem-solving behaviors and positive affect approximately 5 times as often as negative problem-solving behaviors and negative affect, whereas the corresponding ratio was approximately 1:1 for nonregulated couples.

Interestingly, Gottman's perspective corresponds with the findings of two early, often overlooked studies on the reported frequency of sexual intercourse and of marital arguments (Howard & Dawes, 1976; Thornton, 1977). Both showed that the ratio of sexual intercourse to arguments, rather than their base rates, predicted marital satisfaction.

Don't Research Findings on Marital Conflict Just Reflect Common Sense?

The findings described in this article may seem like common sense. However, what we have learned about marital interaction contradicts the long-standing belief that satisfied couples are characterized by a *quid pro quo* principle according to which they exchange positive behavior and instead show that it is dissatisfied spouses who reciprocate one another's (negative) behavior. The astute reader may also be wondering whether couples' behavior in the artificial setting of the laboratory is a good reflection of their behavior in the real world outside the lab. It is therefore important to note that couples who participate in such studies themselves report that their interactions in the lab are reminiscent of their typical interactions. Research also shows that conflict behavior in the lab is similar to conflict behavior in the home; however, laboratory conflicts tend to be less severe, suggesting that research findings underestimate differences between distressed and nondistressed couples.

THE SEEDS OF DISCONTENT

By the early 1980s, researchers were attempting to address the limits of a purely behavioral account of marital conflict. Thus, they began to pay attention to subjective factors, such as thoughts and feelings, which might influence behavioral interactions or the relation between behavior and marital satisfaction. For example, it is now well documented that the tendency to explain a partner's negative behavior (e.g., coming home late from work) in a way that promotes conflict (e.g., "he thinks only about himself and his needs"), rather than in less conflictual ways (e.g., "he was probably caught in traffic"), is related to less effective problem solving, more negative communication in problem-solving discussions, more displays of specific negative affects (e.g., anger) during problem solving, and steeper declines in marital satisfaction over time (Fincham, 2001). Explanations that promote conflict are also related to the tendency to reciprocate a partner's negative behavior, regardless of a couple's marital satisfaction. Research on such subjective factors, like observational research on conflict, has continued to the present time. However, it represents an acceptance and expansion of the behavioral approach that accords conflict a central role in understanding marriage.

In contrast, very recently, some investigators have argued that the role of conflict in marriage should be reconsidered. Longitudinal research shows that conflict accounts for a relatively small portion of the variability in later marital outcomes, suggesting that other factors need to be considered in predicting these outcomes (see Karney & Bradbury, 1995). In addition, studies have demonstrated a troubling number of "reversal effects" (showing that greater conflict is a predictor of improved marriage; see Fincham & Beach, 1999). It is difficult to account for such findings in a field that, for much of its existence, has focused on providing descriptive data at the expense of building theory.

Rethinking the role of conflict also reflects recognition of the fact that most of what we know about conflict behavior comes from observation of problem-solving discussions and that couples experience verbal problem-solving situations infrequently; about 80% of couples report having overt disagreements once a month or less. As a result, cross-sectional studies of distressed versus nondistressed marriages and longitudinal studies of conflict are being increasingly complemented by research designs that focus on how happy marriages become unhappy.

Finally, there is evidence that marital conflict varies according to contextual factors. For example, diary studies illustrate that couples have more stressful marital interactions at home on days of high general life stress than on other days, and at times and places where they are experiencing multiple competing demands; arguments at work are related to marital arguments, and the occurrence of stressful life events is associated with more conflictual problem-solving discussions.

NEW BEGINNINGS: CONFLICT IN CONTEXT

Although domains of interaction other than conflict (e.g., support, companionship) have long been discussed in the marital literature, they are only now emerging from the secondary status accorded to them. This is somewhat ironic given the simple summary of research findings on marital conflict offered earlier, which points to the importance of the context in which conflict occurs.

Conflict in the Context of Support Giving and Affectional Expression

Observational laboratory methods have recently been developed to assess supportive behaviors in interactions in which one spouse talks about a personal issue he or she would like to change and the other is asked to respond as she or he normally would. Behaviors exhibited during such support tasks are only weakly related to the conflict behaviors observed during the problem-solving discussions used to study marital conflict. Supportive spouse behavior is associated with greater marital satisfaction and is more important than negative behavior in determining how supportive the partners perceive an interaction to be. In addition, the amount of supportive behavior partners exhibit is a predictor of later marital stress (i.e., more supportive behavior correlates with less future marital stress), independently of conflict behavior, and when support is poor, there is an increased risk that poor skills in dealing with conflict will lead to later marital deterioration. There is also evidence that support obtained by spouses outside the marriage can influence positively how the spouse behaves within the marriage.

In the context of high levels of affectional expression between spouses, the association between spouses' negative behavior and marital satisfaction decreases significantly. High levels of positive behavior in problem-solving discussions also mitigate the effect of withdrawal or disengagement on later marital satisfaction. Finally, when there are high levels of affectional expression between spouses, the demand-withdraw pattern is unrelated to marital satisfaction, but when affectional expression is average or low, the demand-withdraw pattern is associated with marital dissatisfaction.

Conflict in the Context of Spouses' Backgrounds and Characteristics

Focus on interpersonal behavior as the cause of marital outcomes led to the assumption that the characteristics of individual spouses play no role in those outcomes. However, increasing evidence that contradicts this assumption has generated recent interest in studying how spouses' backgrounds and characteristics might enrich our understanding of marital conflict.

The importance of spouses' characteristics is poignantly illustrated in the intergenerational transmission of divorce. Although there is a tendency for individuals whose parents divorced to get divorced themselves, this tendency varies depending on the offspring's behavior. Divorce rates are higher for offspring who behave in hostile, domineering, and critical ways, compared with offspring who do not behave in this manner.

An individual characteristic that is proving to be particularly informative for understanding marriage comes from recent research on attachment, which aims to address questions about how the experience of relationships early in life affects interpersonal functioning in adulthood. For example, spouses who tend to feel secure in relationships tend to compromise and to take into account both their own and their partner's interests during problem-solving interactions; those who tend to feel anxious or ambivalent in relationships show a greater tendency to oblige their partner, and focus on relationship maintenance, than do those who tend to avoid intimacy in relationships. And spouses who are preoccupied with being completely emotionally intimate in relationships show an elevated level of marital conflict after an involuntary, brief separation from the partner.

Of particular interest for understanding negative reciprocity are the findings that greater commitment is associated with more constructive, accommodative responses to a partner's negative behavior and that the dispositional tendency to forgive is a predictor of spouses' responses to their partners' transgressions; spouses having a greater tendency to forgive are less likely to avoid the partner or retaliate in kind following a transgression by the partner. Indeed, spouses themselves acknowledge that the capacity to seek and grant forgiveness is one of the most important factors contributing to marital longevity and satisfaction.

Conflict in the Context of the Broader Environment

The environments in which marriages are situated and the intersection between interior processes and external factors that impinge upon marriage are important to consider in painting a more textured picture of marital conflict. This is because problem-solving skills and conflict may have little impact on a marriage in the absence of external stressors. External stressors also may influence marriages directly. In particular, nonmarital stressors may lead to an increased number of negative interactions, as illustrated by the fact that economic stress is associated with marital conflict. There is a growing need to identify the stressors and life events that are and are not influential for different couples and for different stages of marriage, to investigate how these events influence conflict, and to clarify how individuals and marriages may inadvertently generate stressful events. In fact, Bradbury, Rogge, and Lawrence (2001), in considering the ecological niche of the couple (i.e., their life events, family constellation, socioeconomic standing, and stressful circumstances), have recently argued that it may be "at least as important to examine the struggle that exists between the couple . . . and the environment they inhabit as it is to examine the interpersonal struggles that are the focus of our work [observation of conflict]" (p. 76).

CONCLUSION

The assumption that conflict management is the key to successful marriage and that conflict skills can be modified in couple therapy has proved useful in propelling the study of marriage into the mainstream of psychology. However, it may have outlived its usefulness, and some researchers are now calling for greater attention to other mechanisms (e.g., spousal social support) that might be responsible for marital outcomes. Indeed, controversy over whether conflict has beneficial or detrimental effects on marriage over time is responsible, in part, for the recent upsurge in longitudinal research on marriage. Notwithstanding diverse opinions on just how central conflict is for understanding marriage, current efforts to study conflict in a broader marital context, which is itself seen as situated in a broader ecological niche, bode well for advancing understanding and leading to more powerful preventive and therapeutic interventions.

Recommended Reading

Bradbury, T.N., Fincham, F.D., & Beach, S.R.H. (2000). Research on the nature and determinants of marital satisfaction: A decade in review. *Journal of Marriage and the Family,* 62, 964–980.

Fincham, F.D., & Beach, S.R. (1999). (See References)

Grych, J.H., & Fincham, F.D. (Eds.), (2001). (See References)

Karney, B.R., & Bradbury, T.N. (1995). (See References)

Acknowledgments—This article was written while the author was supported by grants from the Templeton, Margaret L. Wendt, and J.M. McDonald Foundations.

Note

1. Address correspondence to Frank D. Fincham, Department of Psychology, University at Buffalo, Buffalo, NY 14260.

References

Baucom, D.H., Shoham, V., Mueser, K.T., Daiuto, A.D., & Stickle, T.R. (1998). Empirically supported couple and family interventions for marital distress and adult mental health problems. *Journal of Consulting and Clinical Psychology,* 66, 53–88.

Bradbury, T.N., Rogge, R., & Lawrence, E. (2001). Reconsidering the role of conflict in marriage. In A. Booth, A.C. Crouter, & M. Clements (Eds.), *Couples in conflict* (pp. 59–81). Mahwah, NJ: Erlbaum.

Fincham, F.D. (2001). Attributions and close relationships: From balkanization to integration. In G.J. Fletcher & M. Clark (Eds.), *Blackwell handbook of social psychology* (pp. 3–31). Oxford, England: Blackwell.

Fincham, F.D., & Beach, S.R. (1999). Marital conflict: Implications for working with couples. *Annual Review of Psychology,* 50, 47–77.

Gottman, J.M. (1993). The roles of conflict engagement, escalation, and avoidance in marital interaction: A longitudinal view of five types of couples. *Journal of Consulting and Clinical Psychology, 61*, 6–15.

Grych, J.H., & Fincham, F.D. (Eds.). (2001). *Interparental conflict and child development: Theory, research, and applications.* New York: Cambridge University Press.

Howard, J.W., & Dawes, R.M. (1976). Linear prediction of marital happiness. *Personality and Social Psychology Bulletin,* 2, 478–480.

Karney, B.R., & Bradbury, T.N. (1995). The longitudinal course of marital quality and stability: A review of theory, method, and research. *Psychological Bulletin, 118*, 3–34.

Koerner, K., & Jacobson, N.J. (1994). Emotion and behavior in couple therapy. In S.M. Johnson & L.S. Greenberg (Eds.), *The heart of the matter: Perspectives on emotion in marital therapy* (pp. 207–226). New York: Brunner/Mazel.

Raush, H.L., Barry, W.A., Hertel, R.K., & Swain, M.A. (1974). *Communication, conflict, and marriage*. San Francisco: Jossey-Bass.

Thornton, B. (1977). Toward a linear prediction of marital happiness. *Personality and Social Psychology Bulletin*, 3, 674–676.

Weiss, R.L., & Heyman, R.E. (1997). A clinical-research overview of couple interactions. In W.K. Halford & H. Markman (Eds.), *The clinical handbook of marriage and couples interventions* (pp. 13–41). Brisbane, Australia: Wiley.

Emotion in the Second Half of Life

Laura L. Carstensen and Susan Turk Charles[1]
Department of Psychology, Stanford University, Stanford, California

Research on aging has focused primarily on the functional decline people experience as they grow old. Empirical evidence from multiple subdomains of psychology, most notably cognition, perception, and biological psychology, documents reduced efficiency, slowing, and decreased elasticity of basic mental and physical processes with age. Though findings are far more mixed in social aging research, there remains widespread, if tacit, sentiment that the task of gerontological psychology is to assess the ways in which functional declines affect the life of the aging individual.

We assert that the focus on age-related declines in human aging may have steered researchers away from certain questions that, when answered, would paint a more positive picture of old age. Specifically, we argue that changes in the emotion domain challenge models of aging as pervasive loss and point to one central area that is better characterized by continued growth in the second half of life. We posit that old age is marked by greater saliency and improved regulation of emotions, and that emotional well-being, when it does suffer, declines only at the very end of life, when the cognitive and physical disabilities that often precede death in very old age overshadow previously vital areas of functioning (M.M. Baltes, 1998). These ideas are consistent with a curvilinear pattern of findings that document preserved or improved satisfaction with interpersonal relationships in older age groups (Diener & Suh, 1997), despite increased depressive symptoms and functional difficulties among the oldest old (e.g., Smith & Baltes, 1997).

The research we review here is rooted in socioemotional selectivity theory (Carstensen, 1993, 1995, 1998; Carstensen, Gross, & Fung, 1997; Carstensen, Isaacowitz, & Charles, 1999), a psychological model maintaining that limitations on perceived time lead to motivational shifts that direct attention to emotional goals. The theory posits that the resulting increased attention to emotion results in greater complexity of emotional experience and better regulation of emotions experienced in everyday life. One emotional goal that becomes paramount is interacting with individuals who provide emotionally fulfilling interactions. When people are relieved of concerns for the future, attention to current feeling states heightens. Appreciation for the fragility and value of human life increases, and long-term relationships with family and friends assume unmatched importance. Because of the inextricable association between age and time left in life, the theory maintains that aging is associated with preferences for and increased investment in emotionally close social relationships, as well as increased focus on other less interpersonal emotional goals. This age-related motivational shift leads to alterations in the dynamic interplay between individuals and their environments, so that optimization of socioemotional experience is prioritized in later life.

SELECTIVE SOCIAL INTERACTION ENHANCES EMOTIONAL ASPECTS OF LIFE

The program of research we have pursued over the years began with consideration of the highly reliable decline in social contact evidenced in later life and concern for the potential emotional consequences of this reduction. Because human emotions develop within social contexts, and throughout life the most intense emotional experiences, such as anger, sadness, jealousy, and joy, are intimately embedded within them, do fewer social contacts entail emotional costs?

Early theories in psychology and sociology most definitely presumed that reductions in social contact take a toll on emotional life. Although emotional quiescence was in some theories considered the cause and in others the consequence of reduced social contact, for many years no theories contested the idea that emotional experience suffers in old age. Jung (1933) proposed that emotions become progressively generated from internal sources and detached from external events when he wrote that the "very old person . . . has plunged again into the unconscious, and . . . progressively vanishes within it" (p. 131).

Our research on social networks, however, reveals that even though, overall, social networks are smaller in old age, they continue to include comparable numbers of very close relationships throughout later adulthood (Lang & Carstensen, 1994). The reliable age-related decrease in the size of social networks instead appears to result from circumscribed reductions in relatively peripheral relationships. These reductions are not accounted for by poor physical health or declining cognitive status and are not restricted to particular personality styles (Lang & Carstensen, 1994; Lang, Staudinger, & Carstensen, 1998). Moreover, longitudinal analysis suggests that reduction in contact with acquaintances and selective investment in fewer social relationships begins early in adulthood (Carstensen, 1992). It appears that social networks grow smaller across adulthood and are increasingly focused on fewer but emotionally significant social partners.

Socioemotional selectivity theory views the reduction in social contact as a proactive process associated with the growing desire to have meaningful experiences. We do not regard aging adults as "budding hedonists," directing social interactions solely to those relationships characterized by positive emotions; rather, we argue that the realization that time is limited directs social behavior to experiences that are emotionally meaningful. Moreover, the character of emotional responses changes. Awareness of constraints on time transforms once lighthearted and uniformly positive emotional responses into complex mixtures in which poignancy reigns. Spending time with a close friend, for example, with the awareness that it may be among the last of such occasions inevitably entails sadness along with joy. Our research, along with other findings concerning terminally ill patients, suggests that the prototypical emotional response to approaching endings is not morbid. On the contrary, people facing the end of life often say that life is better than ever before. We understand this evaluation to reflect experiences that are richer, more complex, and emotionally meaningful.

According to the theory, restricting the social world to longtime friends and loved ones in later life is adaptive, reflecting careful allocation of resources to the relationships that engender pleasure and meaning. Such a view helps to reconcile the findings that despite a myriad of well-documented losses and overall reductions in social contact, older people, on average, are even more satisfied with their lives than younger people (Diener & Suh, 1997) and, with the exception of the dementias and other organic brain syndromes, display lower prevalence rates of all psychiatric disorders, including depression (Lawton, Kleban, & Dean, 1993).

WHEN TIME IS LIMITED, EMOTIONALLY CLOSE SOCIAL PARTNERS ARE PREFERRED

If changes in social networks involve a proactive pruning process, explicit preferences for close over less close social partners should be evident in people faced with limited time. In a series of studies, we found age-related differences in social preferences and also demonstrated the notable malleability of these age differences as a function of perceived time.

In this series of studies, we presented research participants with three prospective social partners, instructed them to imagine that they had 30 min free and wished to spend it with another person, and asked them to choose a social partner from among the three options. Next, the research subjects were presented with experimental conditions in which future time was hypothetically constrained or expanded and were asked once again to indicate their preferred social partners.

The social partners subjects could choose from represented familiar and unfamiliar social partners who were more and less likely to satisfy different social goals: (a) a member of the immediate family, (b) the author of a book the subject just read, and (c) a recent acquaintance with whom the subject seemed to have much in common. Our previous work had shown that all three options promised enjoyable interactions and represented the conceptual categories we intended them to represent. A family member, for example, represents to most people an emotionally close social partner; the author represents a good source of new information; the acquaintance offers prospects in the future. We expected that approaching endings would be associated with preferences for the emotionally meaningful partner.

In our first study using this paradigm, we compared social choices of young and old research participants (Fredrickson & Carstensen, 1990). We hypothesized that older people, but not younger people, would display preferences for the familiar social partner. In a second condition, we imposed a hypothetical time constraint by asking subjects to imagine that they would soon be moving across the country (by themselves) but currently had 30 min free. We then had them choose again from among the same set of social partners. As predicted, older people chose the familiar social partner under both experimental conditions. In the open-ended condition, younger people did not display such a preference. In the time-limited condition, however, younger adults displayed the same degree of preference for the familiar social partner as the older subjects.

Recently, we replicated these findings in Hong Kong (Fung, Carstensen, & Lutz, in press), and even in this very different culture, older people, compared with their younger counterparts, showed a relative preference for familiar social partners. In the Hong Kong study, subjects were asked to imagine an impending emigration as the time-limiting condition. The findings replicated our previous ones. In the emigration condition, younger people also displayed a preference for familiar social partners.

In a third study, instead of limiting time, we presented American subjects with a hypothetical scenario that expanded time. Research subjects in that condition were asked to imagine that they had just received a telephone call from their physician telling them about a new medical advance that virtually ensured that they would live 20 years longer than they expected in relatively good health (Fung et al., in press). We also included the time-unspecified condition, which replicated previous findings. Older, but not younger, subjects expressed strong preferences for the familiar social partner. However, in the expanded-time condition, the preference observed among older subjects disappeared: Older and younger subjects' choices were indistinguishable. Thus, when the time constraint associated with age is removed, older individuals' preferences for familiar social partners disappear.

In another line of research, we used an experimental approach based on similarity judgments to examine age differences in the emphasis and use of emotion when forming mental representations of possible social partners. In these studies, research participants sorted descriptions of a variety of social partners according to how similarly they would feel interacting with them. A technique called multidimensional scaling was used to identify the dimensions along which these categorizations were based, and we also computed the weights various subgroups placed on particular dimensions.

In three different studies, we found evidence that place in the life cycle is associated with the salience of emotion in mental representations (Carstensen & Fredrickson, 1998; Fredrickson & Carstensen, 1990). Two of these studies examined age differences in the weights placed on the emotion dimension, and a third study compared how the dimensions were weighted by groups of men who were the same age but varied according to their HIV status. In this way, age was disentangled from place in the life cycle. Findings from all three studies suggest that when individuals are closer to the end of their lives, whether because of age or health status, emotion is more salient in their mental representations of other people.

In light of findings suggesting increased salience of emotion among people approaching the end of life, we hypothesized that age differences in memory for emotional versus nonemotional material might be evident as well. That is, if emotional information is more salient, it should be processed more deeply than nonemotional information and therefore remembered better subsequently. To test this hypothesis, we employed an incidental memory paradigm and examined age differences in the type of information recalled (Carstensen & Turk-Charles, 1994). Older and younger adults read a two-page narrative that described a social interaction and contained comparable amounts of neutral and emotionally relevant information. Roughly 45 min later, after completing a series of unrelated tasks, participants were asked to recall all that they could about the passage. Responses were transcribed, and the information in them was classified as either emotional or neutral. The proportion of emotional material correctly recalled from the original text was related to age; the proportion of recalled information that was emotional information was greater for older adults than younger adults. The differences in proportions were driven by a decrease in the amount of neutral information recalled by older adults, and not by an increase in their recall of emotional information. We speculate that the increased salience of emotion may have cognitive costs, in this case a focus on emotional information at the expense of nonemotional information, but these ideas are as yet untested (cf. Isaacowitz, Charles, & Carstensen, in press).

Thus, whether one asks people directly about the types of social partners they prefer, examines the ways in which people mentally represent social partners, or measures the proportion of emotional and informational material people remember, those people approaching the end of life appear to place more value on emotion, choosing social partners along affective lines and processing emotionally salient information more deeply.

THE INTEGRITY OF THE EMOTION SYSTEM IS WELL MAINTAINED IN OLD AGE

Do older adults experience emotions similarly to younger adults, or do age-related biological changes—from facial wrinkles to alterations in the central nervous system—degrade emotional experience? Despite numerous social reasons that could increase the likelihood of negative emotional experiences and biological reasons that might appear to decrease the ability to control them, research findings suggest the opposite.

A biological argument for the reduction of self-reported negative experiences lies in the notion of a reduced capacity to feel emotions. If emotions are not felt as strongly physiologically, they will not be subjectively perceived, and consequently, they will not be reported. However, findings from laboratory studies in which emotions are induced speak against a reduced-capacity argument. In a study measuring subjective experience, spontaneous facial expression, and psychophysiological responding (Levenson, Carstensen, Friesen, & Ekman, 1991), subjective intensity of emotional experience, outward facial expression, and the specific profiles of physiological activation were indistinguishable among older and younger adults. Interestingly, however, the overall level of physiological arousal was significantly reduced among the elderly. Similar reductions in levels of physiological arousal were observed in a study of married couples we describe later (Levenson, Carstensen, & Gottman, 1994).

AGE DIFFERENCES IN EMOTIONAL EXPERIENCE ARE POSITIVE

In addition to the findings concerning intact physiological mechanisms and greater emotional salience, there is evidence pointing to greater overall well-being—that is, less negative emotion and equivalent if not greater levels of positive emotions—among older adults compared with younger adults. Survey studies suggest that levels of positive affect are similar across successively older age cohorts, but a reliable reduction in negative affect is observed, and in studies finding reductions in positive affect, a closer analysis of the findings suggests that a circumscribed reduction in surgency (i.e., excitability) may account for this reduction. Excitement and sensation seeking, for example, are relatively reduced in old age. Other positive emotions, such as happiness and joy, are maintained (Lawton et al., 1993; Lawton, Kleban, Rajagopal, & Dean, 1992).

We recently completed a study in which emotions were sampled in everyday life (Carstensen, Pasupathi, & Mayr, 1998). Research participants spanning the ages 18 to 94 years carried electronic pagers and indicated on a response sheet the degree to which they were experiencing each of 19 positive and negative emotions at random times throughout the days and evenings for a week-long period. Findings revealed no age differences in the intensity of positive or negative experience. However, the frequency of negative emotional experience was lower among older than younger adults.

Data collected in this experience-sampling study also allowed us to explore the postulate that emotional experience is more mixed among older than younger people. In day-to-day life, people can experience multiple emotions in response to an event. Socioemotional selectivity theory predicts that emotional experience becomes more multifaceted with age because awareness of limited time elicits positive emotions and negative emotions, thus changing the very character of the experience. We tested this hypothesis in two ways. First, we computed the simple correlation between positive and negative emotional experience. Although, as expected, the correlation between positive and negative emotions was low, it was positively and significantly associated with age. That is, older adults tended to experience mixed positive and negative emotions more than younger adults. Second, with the use of factor analysis, we computed for each research participant the number of factors that best characterized his or her responses over the course of the study. More factors were required to account for older people's responses, suggesting that their emotional reactions were more complex or differentiated.

Thus, studies that measure subjective emotional experience, either in the laboratory or as they occur in everyday life, speak against an unqualified reduced-capacity argument. Once elicited, positive and negative emotions are experienced subjectively as intensely among the old as the young. Interestingly, the few studies that have measured autonomic nervous system activity have found that the strength of physiological arousal is reduced in the elderly. Whether the reduction is emotion-specific or due to more global age-related degradation of the autonomic nervous system remains unclear. Either way, to the extent that lessened physiological arousal is associated with less subjective discomfort, it may have serendipitously positive consequences. As P. Baltes (1991) argued cogently, deficits in circumscribed domains can sometimes prompt growth in other domains. Reduced physiological arousal associated with negative emotions may represent a case in point, a matter to which we turn in the next section.

OLDER PEOPLE REGULATE THEIR EMOTIONS BETTER THAN YOUNGER PEOPLE

Socioemotional selectivity theory maintains that an emphasis on emotional goals leads to active efforts on the part of individuals to emphasize and enhance emotional experience. Existing empirical evidence from cross-sectional studies about perceived control over emotions is clear: Compared with younger adults, older adults report greater control over emotions, greater stability of mood, less psychophysiological agitation, and greater faith in their ability to control the internal and external expression of emotions. Remarkably similar age-related patterns have been found across five diverse samples: Catholic nuns; African, European, and Chinese Americans; and Norwegians (Gross et al., 1997).

The consistency of findings across these diverse ethnic, religious, and regional groups reduces concern that the findings reflect stable differences among age groups (viz., cohort effects), as opposed to aging per se. In other words, although cohort effects cannot be ruled out entirely, the reliability of the profile across very different types of samples at least speaks against the alternative that emotional differences are unique to younger and older generations of white Americans.

Findings from three other recent studies also reduce the concern that older people's subjective sense that they have good control over their emotions is limited to their beliefs and fails to reflect age differences in actual control. First, Lawton, Parmelee, Katz, and Nesselroade (1996) examined reported negative affect sampled during the course of a 1-month period in a group of adults. Not only did older adults report relatively low levels of negative affect, but they varied little over time.

Second, in the experience-sampling study described earlier (Carstensen et al., 1998), we examined the probability that negative or positive emotions would occur given their occurrence at the immediately preceding time when subjects reported their emotions. Using the 35 emotion samples collected over a 1-week period for each subject, we examined the duration of positive and negative emotional experience. As did Lawton et al. (1996), we found that the duration of negative emotions was shorter for older than younger adults; interestingly, the natural duration of positive emotional experience was similar for old and young adults (Carstensen et al., 1998). Thus, even when emotions are sampled close to the time they occurred, so that global self-evaluations are avoided, similarly positive profiles of emotional experience are revealed.

Third, we conducted a study involving observations of married couples discussing emotionally charged conflicts in their relationships. Resolution of interpersonal conflict, especially in intimate relationships, provides an opportunity to examine a special case of emotion regulation. Effective resolution of marital conflict requires that spouses deal simultaneously with their own negative emotions and the negative emotions expressed by their partner. In this study, we hypothesized that older couples resolve conflicts better than their middle-aged counterparts. Middle-aged and older couples, all of whom had been married many years, were asked to identify a mutually-agreed-upon conflict area and then to discuss the conflict with one another toward its resolution (Carstensen, Gottman, & Levenson, 1995; Carstensen, Graff, Levenson, & Gottman, 1996; Levenson, Carstensen, & Gottman, 1993; Levenson et al., 1994). Discussions were videotaped and psychophysiological responses were measured throughout the interaction. As predicted, compared with middle-aged couples, older couples displayed lesser overall negative affect, expressing less anger, disgust, belligerence, and whining in their discussions. In addition, older couples were more likely to express affection to their spouses during the exchange, interspersing positive expressions with negative ones. The pattern appears to be highly effective in curbing the negative affect typically associated with emotionally charged discussions.

Thus, older adults are notably effective at managing negative emotions. This finding, in combination with findings that positive emotions are maintained in frequency and duration during old age, paints a picture that is quite positive. The findings are in keeping with socioemotional selectivity theory. In the studies reviewed, older individuals limited negative emotional experiences in day-to-day life more effectively than younger individuals. Similarly, older couples engaged in discussions of personally relevant topics in a way that limited their negativity. If, as the theory suggests, people become increasingly aware of endings toward the end of life, aging individuals are increasingly motivated to optimize the emotional climate of their lives. It is not that negative emotions do not occur or that felt emotions are less intense. Rather, negative emotions are better regulated.

CONCLUSION

The study of emotion in old age is relatively young, yet within a short period of time, empirical findings have suggested a reasonably cohesive profile of emotional experience and emotion regulation in the later years. Efforts on the part of multiple investigative teams have documented the ubiquitousness of emotion in cognitive processing, from mental representations to social preferences; stability in the frequency of positive affect; reductions in negative affect; reduced physiological arousability; and superior regulation of emotion.

Of course, a comprehensive understanding of emotion in later life is only beginning to take shape. Greater emphasis on emotional aspects of life probably entails benefits for some areas of functioning and costs to others. The manner in which emotions change and the conditions associated with such change remain elusive. The role of perceived time in emotional experience, suggested in socioemotional selectivity theory, requires further investigation to identify the precise conditions under which emotions grow mixed, are better regulated, and are less negative as people age. Implications of the reduction in the physiological arousal accompanying emotional experience also demand clarification.

The profile of empirical evidence reviewed here provides a far different picture of old age than the literatures on cognitive aging and physical health. Numerous problems are associated with old age. Health insults, loss of economic and political status, and deaths of friends and loved ones are but a few of the problems associated with old age, yet research on emotion and aging suggests that the emotion domain may be well preserved and perhaps selectively optimized (M.M. Baltes & Carstensen, 1996). The inherent paradox of aging refers to the fact that despite loss and physical decline, adults enjoy good mental health and positive life satisfaction well into old age. We suggest that the uniquely human ability to monitor the passage of time, coupled with the inevitable constraints of mortality, heightens the value placed on emotional aspects of life and deepens the complexity of emotional experience as people age.

Recommended Reading

Carstensen, L.L., & Fredrickson, B.L. (1998). (See References)

Carstensen, L.L., Isaacowitz, D.M., & Charles, S.T. (1999). (See References)

Magai, C., & McFadden, S.H. (1996). *Handbook of emotion, adult development, and aging.* San Diego: Academic Press.

Schaie, K.W., & Lawton, M.P. (Eds.). (1997). *Annual review of gerontology and geriatrics: Vol. 17. Focus on emotion and adult development.* New York: Springer.

Acknowledgments—We thank Ursula Staudinger for her comments about an earlier draft of this article.

Note

1. Address correspondence to Laura Carstensen, Department of Psychology, Bldg. 420, Jordan Hall, Stanford University, Stanford, CA 94305; e-mail: llc@psych.stanford.edu.

References

Baltes, M.M. (1998). The psychology of the oldest-old: The fourth age. *Current Opinion in Psychiatry, 11,* 411–418.

Baltes, M.M., & Carstensen, L.L. (1996). The process of successful ageing. *Ageing and Society, 16,* 397–422.

Baltes, P. (1991). The many faces of human aging: Toward a psychological culture of old age. *Psychological Medicine, 21,* 837–854.

Carstensen, L.L. (1992). Social and emotional patterns in adulthood: Support for socioemotional selectivity theory. *Psychology and Aging, 7,* 331–338.

Carstensen, L.L. (1993). Motivation for social contact across the life span: A theory of socioemotional selectivity. In J. Jacobs (Ed.), *Nebraska Symposium on Motivation: Vol. 40. Developmental perspectives on motivation* (pp. 209–254). Lincoln: University of Nebraska Press.

Carstensen, L.L. (1995), Evidence for a life-span theory of socioemotional selectivity. *Current Directions in Psychological Science, 4,* 151–156.

Carstensen, L.L. (1998). A life-span approach to social motivation. In J. Heckhausen & C. Dweck (Eds.), *Motivation and self-regulation across the life span* (pp. 341–364). New York: Cambridge University Press.

Carstensen, L.L., & Fredrickson, B.L. (1998). Socioemotional selectivity in healthy older people and younger people living with the Human Immunodeficiency Virus: The centrality of emotion when the future is constrained. *Health Psychology, 17,* 1–10.

Carstensen, L.L., Gottman, J.M., & Levenson, R.W. (1995). Emotional behavior in long-term marriage. *Psychology and Aging, 10,* 140–149.

Carstensen, L.L., Graff, J., Levenson, R.W., & Gottman, J.M. (1996). Affect in intimate relationships: The developmental course of marriage. In C. Magai & S.H. McFadden (Eds.), *Handbook of emotion, adult development, and aging* (pp. 227–247). San Diego: Academic Press.

Carstensen, L.L., Gross, J., & Fung, H. (1997). The social context of emotion. In K.W. Schaie & M.P. Lawton (Eds.), *Annual review of gerontology and geriatrics: Vol. 17. Focus on emotion and adult development* (pp. 325–352). New York: Springer.

Carstensen, L.L., Isaacowitz, D.M., & Charles, S.T. (1999). Taking time seriously: A life-span theory of social selectivity. *American Psychologist, 54,* 165–181.

Carstensen, L.L., Pasupathi, M., & Mayr, U. (1998). *Emotion experience in the daily lives of older and younger adults.* Manuscript submitted for publication.

Carstensen, L.L., & Turk-Charles, S. (1994). The salience of emotion across the adult life span. *Psychology and Aging, 9,* 259–264.

Diener, E., & Suh, M.E. (1997). Subjective well-being and age: An international analysis. In K.W. Schaie & M.P. Lawton (Eds.), *Annual review of gerontology and geriatrics: Vol. 17. Focus on emotion and adult development* (pp. 304–324). New York: Springer.

Fredrickson, B.F., & Carstensen, L.L. (1990). Choosing social partners: How old age and anticipated endings make us more selective. *Psychology and Aging, 5*, 335–347.

Fung, H., Carstensen, L.L., & Lutz, A. (in press). The influence of time on social preferences: Implications for life-span development. *Psychology and Aging.*

Gross, J., Carstensen, L.L., Pasupathi, M., Tsai, J., Götestam Skorpen, C., & Hsu, A. (1997). Emotion and aging: Experience, expression and control. *Psychology and Aging, 12*, 590–599.

Isaacowitz, D., Charles, S.T., & Carstensen, L.L. (in press). Emotion and cognition. In F.I.M. Craik & T.A. Salthouse (Eds.), *Handbook of aging and cognition* (2nd ed.). Mahwah, NJ: Erlbaum.

Jung, C.G. (1933). The stages of life. In *Modern man in search of a soul* (pp. 109–131). London: Kegan, Paul, Trench & Trubner.

Lang, F., Staudinger, U., & Carstensen, L.L. (1998). Socioemotional selectivity in late life: How personality and social context do (and do not) make a difference. *Journal of Gerontology: Psychological Sciences,* 53, P21–P30.

Lang, F.R., & Carstensen, L.L. (1994). Close emotional relationships in late life: Further support for proactive aging in the social domain. *Psychology and Aging, 9*, 315–324.

Lawton, M.P., Kleban, M.H., & Dean J. (1993). Affect and age: Cross-sectional comparisons of structure and prevalence. *Psychology and Aging, 8*, 165–175.

Lawton, M.P., Kleban, M.H., Rajagopal, D., & Dean, J. (1992). The dimensions of affective experience in three age groups. *Psychology and Aging*, 7, 171–184.

Lawton, M.P., Parmelee, P.A., Katz, I., & Nesselroade, J. (1996). Affective states in normal and depressed older people. *Journal of Gerontology: Psychological Sciences, 51*, P309–P316.

Levenson, R.W., Carstensen, L.L., Friesen, W.V., & Ekman, P. (1991). emotion, physiology, and expression in old age. *Psychology and Aging, 6*, 28–35.

Levenson, R.W., Carstensen, L.L., & Gottman, J.M. (1993). Long-term marriage: Age, gender and satisfaction. *Psychology and Aging,* 8, 301–313.

Levenson, R.W., Carstensen, L.L., & Gottman, J.M. (1994). Marital interaction in old and middle-aged long-term marriages: Physiology, affect and their interrelations. *Journal of Personality and Social Psychology,* 67, 56–68.

Smith, J., & Baltes, P.B. (1997). Profiles of psychological functioning in the old and oldest old. *Psychology and Aging, 12*, 458–472.

Psychology and Aging: Enhancing the Lives of an Aging Population

Arthur D. Fisk[1] and Wendy A. Rogers

School of Psychology, Georgia Institute of Technology, Atlanta, Georgia

Abstract

A pressing need for upcoming decades is ensuring that older adults, who constitute an increasing percentage of the population, are able to function independently and maintain an acceptable quality of life. One important concern is the usability of new technologies. Unfortunately, the science that could direct proper design and implementation of current and future technological advancement is underdeveloped and less mature than the engineering that supports technological advancement. We review data documenting age-related usability issues and how psychological science can remedy such problems. We also outline how training principles can be applied to older adults. We conclude that psychological science has much to contribute to the goal of enhancing the lives of older adults.

Keywords

cognitive aging; system design; training

From news reports or simple observation, it should be clear that within developed countries, the number of older adults is increasing faster than the number of their younger counterparts. Indeed, the life expectancy of the population in the United States and other countries is, collectively, increasing. Rowe and Kahn (1998) highlighted the dramatic nature of the increase in life expectancy when they estimated that of all humans who have ever lived to be 65 years or older, half of them are currently alive. This demographic shift brings with it certain challenges if society is to meet the needs of these older individuals. Psychological science is well positioned to help meet these challenges.

We use the term engineering Psychology to refer to the applied science with the goal of understanding how humans sense, process, and act on information. Engineering psychology also applies that knowledge to the design of and training for new and existing technologies to make them safe, efficient, and easy to use. To accommodate older populations, it is necessary to understand age-related differences in sensing, processing, and acting on information. It is also necessary to apply that knowledge base to ensure that products and systems are safe, efficient, and easy to use by older adults.

Psychologists have conducted considerable research on the fundamentals of cognitive aging (see Craik & Salthouse, 2000, for specific reviews). These data serve as the starting point for designing products and systems that older adults can use.

ARE EXISTING SYSTEMS AND PRODUCTS EASY TO USE?

Are existing systems and products easy to use? In a word, no. They are not easy to use by individuals of any age, and usability problems may be exacerbated for older adults. In his book *The Psychology of Everyday Things*, Norman (1988) illustrated how many products and systems are difficult to use. The typical response of users who encounter a problem is to assume that they made a mistake and the problem lies with them. Not so—typically the problem lies with either the design of the system or the instructions provided for using it.

In a study examining usability problems with everyday products such as cleaners, toiletries, over-the-counter medications, and health care products (Hancock, Fisk, & Rogers, 2001), we found that 72% of the respondents reported experiencing some usability problems. Reported problems included difficulty understanding written materials (29% of respondents), trouble interpreting symbolic information (21%), perceptual problems such as inability to see print clearly (47%), memory problems such as forgetting actions to perform or procedures to follow (45%), and motor control and manipulation difficulties (84%). The survey respondents' age range was 18 to 91, but people of all ages reported similar types and frequencies of usability problems; the only exception was that people over age 65 reported more perceptual and motor problems than people under 35.

Many of the difficulties reported in this survey might be classified as "annoyance problems" (e.g., difficulty reading text or opening a bottle). However, many usability problems are not just annoyances but have the potential to be dangerous or even life threatening. Studies of home health care technologies illustrate this point.

Blood glucose meters are devices used to self-monitor glucose levels in the blood. Often these devices are advertised as simple to use: "It's as easy to use as 1, 2, 3. Just set up the meter, check the system, and test your blood." Yet these devices are not so easy to use. A detailed task analysis of one presumably easy system revealed more than 50 substeps for the performance of the three basic steps (Rogers, Mykityshyn, Campbell, & Fisk, 2001). Further, in an observational study of 90 users of blood glucose meters, 62% were found to make at least one clinically significant error (Colagiuri, Colagiuri, Jones, & Moses, 1990). Unfortunately, Colagiuri et al. engaged in the common practice of "blaming the user," as evidenced by their statement that "the most commonly encountered . . . errors resulted from a *general lack of care on the part of the patient* [italics added] in complying with the manufacturer's instructions" (p. 803). Such blame does not lead to understanding human error or minimizing future errors, and it ignores errors caused by system design or inappropriate instructional materials.

Design can induce errors, and design problems are often coupled with poorly written diagnostic aids. This point can be illustrated by an anecdote. A news crew was filming a story on our research concerning the usability of home medical devices. A reporter, skeptical of the usability issues we were reporting, attempted to set up a blood glucose meter, and it displayed the message "ERROR 2." To correct the problem, he went to the manual section labeled "What to do if errors" and found "ERROR 2—Device may not be working properly." After he adhditted that there might be problems with the system design and the manual, we told him that he had the calibration strip in upside down. There were no markings on the strip to perceptually guide its insertion.

It is not only blood glucose meters that are difficult to use and to learn how to use. Home health care systems are often relatively complex, and existing instructions are not adequate (Gardner-Bonneau, 2001). Safe and effective uses of home health care technologies, especially those targeting older adult users, will require behavioral science-based design changes and development of adequate training materials.

CAN PSYCHOLOGICAL SCIENCE REMEDY THE USABILITY PROBLEMS?

In an effort to better understand how psychological science can improve the lives of older adults, we conducted a series of focus groups to document the usability problems older individuals encounter in their daily activities (Rogers, Meyer, Walker, & Fisk, 1998). Each reported problem was classified according to the activity the respondent was engaged in when he or she encountered the problem, the source of the problem (i.e., motor, visual, auditory, cognitive, external, or general health limitations), whether the problem was related to the inherent difficulty of the task or potential negative outcomes, and how the participant responded (e.g., stopped performing the task, compensated somehow).

Of the problems reported by the older adults in this study, 47% were due to financial limitations, health difficulties, or other general concerns not specific to the product's design. Each remaining problem was classified according to whether it could potentially be solved through redesign, training, or some combination of the two. Approximately 25% of the problems could potentially be remedied by improving the design of the systems involved to solve sensory or motor problems. For example, the possible remedies identified included lowering steps on buses, developing tools for grasping or scrubbing, improving chair design, and enlarging letter size on a label.

The remaining 28% of the reported problems had the potential to be solved through training, or through a combination of training and redesign. For example, an older person learning to drive for the first time would benefit from driver training tailored to his or her age-related needs. For other complex systems, such as personal computers or health care technologies, novices would need training; however, such systems clearly also have the potential for design changes that would improve their usability for users of all ages.

These data should not be interpreted as if the problems reported by older adults currently have solutions. Instead, the data imply that the potential exists to apply the science of psychology to enhance the lives of older adults. Design efforts must consider the capabilities and limitations of older adults, and the literature on cognitive aging provides a starting point for understanding more about this user population (e.g., Craik & Salthouse, 2000). In addition, the categories of usability problems we have reported in our studies (Hancock et al., 2001; Rogers et al., 1998) provide valuable information for design efforts. The application of task analysis and other tools used by engineering psychology to determine user requirements (see Salvendy, 1997, for a review of such tools) can be valuable for identifying both problems users have and how to minimize sources of design-induced errors (e.g., Rogers et al., 2001).

APPLICATION OF TRAINING PRINCIPLES

A goal of product design should be to minimize training requirements by designing systems that take into account the capabilities of users. However, even if products and systems are designed optimally, users often require training. Psychological science has much to contribute to efforts to optimize how younger and older adults are trained to use complex systems.

Training programs come in many forms and include materials ranging from written manuals to multimedia, experiential tutorials. What is the best way to develop such training programs? Theories of training abound in the research literature, but there has traditionally been a disconnect between developers of training theories and practitioners who could benefit most from the application of such theories (as discussed by Salas, Cannon-Bowers, & Blickensderfer, 1997). Applied psychology has the potential to serve as the bridge from the training principles in the literature to the development of training programs for practical applications. There must also be a link back to theory development to ensure that theories of training are refined on the basis of limitations that are discovered when the theories are applied to complex, real-world problems.

How, then, should trainers design programs for older adults to learn how to interact with technological systems? The background knowledge psychological science can bring to bear on such training is substantial. A review of the literature on skill acquisition and aging reveals basic principles: It is not the case that older adults cannot learn or that they always learn less or more slowly than younger adults; to understand age-related differences in learning, one must consider the task variables, the context, and the type and amount of training being provided (see Fisk & Rogers, 2000, for a review).

Older adults do exhibit declines in abilities important for learning and skill acquisition (Craik & Salthouse, 2000), such as working memory, perceptual speed, spatial ability, and fluid abilities in general (i.e., those abilities that are generally independent of processes that take advantage of the person's accumulated knowledge). Proper instructional design that capitalizes on intact abilities and compensates for declining abilities holds much promise for helping older adults obtain basic proficiency, as well as for improving their performance with additional training and helping them retain the levels of proficiency they achieve.

For example, we recently assessed the differential benefits of video-based versus user-manual-based training for younger and older adults learning to calibrate a blood glucose meter (Mykityshyn, Fisk, & Rogers, in press). The type of instruction was critical for determining older adults' performance. Older adults trained using the manual performed more poorly than all other groups. After only one calibration, older adults who received video training performed as accurately as the younger adults. Older adults' performance declined more than young adults' across a 2-week retention interval, but the benefit of the video training was maintained for the older adults. The video- based training provided environmental support for the learner by explicitly demonstrating the task sequence, and minimizing reliance on working memory (for visualizing) and reading comprehension (for drawing necessary inferences).

It is important to note that not just any video will result in superior performance. In one of our studies (Rogers at al., 2001), we demonstrated that the video provided by the manufacturer of a blood glucose meter was not sufficient for training users to operate the system. For a video to be effective, it must follow instructional principles.

Accurately assessing the expected benefits of a training approach is necessary for making informed selections among training options. Charness and Holley (2001) described one method for assessing the effectiveness of training using learning-curve data. A learning curve showing how many repetitions of an activity (i.e., trials) a particular group (e.g., older adults) needs to reach each of various levels of performance can provide the basis for making predictions. For example, by extrapolating from a learning curve, one can predict the number of trials that will be necessary to reach a higher level of performance than is shown in the curve itself. Rates of learning demonstrated after different kinds of training can be statistically compared to estimate their relative benefits. In addition, learning curves can be used to estimate how much training will be needed for a desired level of performance. Such predictions may be very useful in illustrating the effectiveness of training programs.

CONCLUSION

Through examples, we have highlighted opportunities for enhancing older adults' lives, particularly with respect to technology design and training. If research on training and system design is to be used to enhance performance of older adults, it can and should be driven by psychological theory. This view is shared by other scientists, as illustrated by a National Research Council (2000) report, *The Aging Mind*, which made recommendations for future cognitive research. One recommendation was to develop "knowledge needed to design effective technologies supporting adaptivity in older adults" (p. 35). The report also said that realizing such a goal "requires integrating behavioral science and engineering in a context of product design and development" (p. 36).

We agree and wish to extend this point. Certainly there still exists a gap between the knowledge base of the psychological scientist and the information needs of the nonscientist consumer of that knowledge. There is a crucial need for research programs aimed at clarifying how age-related changes in function affect older adults' ability to interact with technology successfully. To fulfill this need, researchers need to sample task environments, much as they sample participant populations (see Fisk & Kirlik, 1996, for examples). With such research, psychology will move toward fulfilling its promise of giving designers the science-based design principles they need for developing useful applications of current and future technologies.

Recommended Reading

Charness, N. (2001). Aging and communication: Human factors issues. In N. Charness, D.C., Park, & B.A. Sabel (Eds.), *Communication, technology, and aging: Opportunities and challenges for the future* (pp. 1–29). New York: Springer.

Czaja, S.J. (2001). Telecommunication technology as an aid to family caregivers. In W.A. Rogers & A.D. Fisk (Eds.), *Human factors interventions for the health care of older adults* (pp. 165–178). Mahwah, NJ: Erlbaum.

Mead, S.E., Batsakes, P., Fisk, A.D. & Mykityshyn, A. (1999). Application of cognitive theory to training and design solutions for age-related-computer use. *International Journal of Behavioral Development, 23*, 553–573.

Rogers, W.A., & Fisk, A.D. (2000). Human factors, Applied cognition, and aging. In F.I.M. Craik & T.A. Salthouse (Eds.), *The handbook of aging, and cognition* (2nd ed., pp, 559–591). Mahwah, NJ: Erlbaum.

Acknowledgments—Preparation of this manuscript was partially supported by Grants P01 AG17211, P50 AG11715, and R01 AGO7654 from the National Institutes of Health (National Institute on Aging).

Note

1. Address correspondence to Arthur D. Fisk, School of Psychology, Georgia Institute of Technology, Atlanta, GA 30332-0170; e-mail: af@prism.gatech.edu.

References

Charness, N., & Holley, P. (2001). Computer interface issues for health self-care: Cognitive and perceptual constraints. In W.A. Rogers & A.D. Fisk (Eds.), *Human factors interventions for the health care of older adults* (pp. 239–254). Mahwah, NJ: Erlbaum.

Colagiuri, R., Colagiuri, S., Jones, S., & Moses, R.G. (1990). The quality of self-monitoring of blood glucose. *Diabetic Medicine, 7*, 800–804.

Craik, F.I.M., & Salthouse, T.A. (Eds.). (2000). *The handbook of aging and cognition* (2nd ed.). Mahwah, NJ: Erlbaum.

Fisk, A.D., & Kirlik, A. (1996). Practical relevance and age-related research: Can theory advance without practice? In W.A. Rogers, A.D. Fisk, & N. Walker (Eds.), *Aging and skilled performance: Advances in theory and application* (pp. 1–15). Mahwah, NJ: Erlbaum.

Fisk, A.D., & Rogers, W.A. (2000). Influence of training and experience on skill acquisition and maintenance in older adults. *Journal of Aging and Physical Activity, 8*, 373–378.

Gardner-Bonneau, D. (2001). Designing medical devices for older adults. In W.A. Rogers & A.D. Fisk (Eds.), *Human factors interventions for the health care of older adults* (pp. 221–237). Mahwah, NJ: Erlbaum.

Hancock, H.E., Fisk, A.D., & Rogers, W.A. (2001). Everyday products: Easy to use . . . or not? *Ergonomics in Design, 9*, 12–18.

Mykityshyn, A.L., Fisk, A.D., & Rogers, W.A. (in press). Toward age-related training methodologies for sequence-based systems: An evaluation using a home medical device. *Human Factors.*

National Research Council. (2000). *The aging mind: Opportunities in cognitive research.* Washington, DC: National Academy Press.

Norman, D.A. (1988). *The psychology of everyday things.* New York: Harper Collins.

Rogers, W.A., Meyer, B., Walker, N., & Fisk, A.D. (1998). Functional limitations to daily living tasks in the aged: A focus group analysis. *Human Factors, 40*, 111–125.

Rogers, W.A., Mykityshyn, A.L., Campbell, R.H., & Fisk, A.D. (2001). Only 3 easy steps? User-centered analysis of a "simple" medical device. *Ergonomics in Design, 9*, 6–14.

Rowe, J.W., & Kahn, R.L. (1998). *Successful aging.* New York: Pantheon.

Salas, E., Cannon-Bowers, J., & Blickensderfer, E.L. (1997). Enhancing reciprocity between training theory and practice: Principles, guidelines, and specifications. In J.K. Ford, S.W.J. Kozlowski, K. Kraiger, E. Salas, & M.S. Teachout (Eds.), *Improving training effectiveness in work organizations* (pp. 291–322). Mahwah, NJ: Erlbaum.

Salvendy, G. (1997). *Handbook of human factors and ergonomics* (2nd ed.). New York: John Wiley and Sons.

A Typology of Men Who Are Violent Toward Their Female Partners: Making Sense of the Heterogeneity in Husband Violence

Amy Holtzworth-Munroe[1]
Department of Psychology, Indiana University, Bloomington, Indiana

Abstract

Although much research on men who are violent toward their wives has involved comparisons of groups of violent and nonviolent men, there is increasing evidence that maritally violent men are not a homogeneous group. Several recent studies support a batterer typology that distinguishes maritally violent subgroups. In an effort to identify different underlying processes resulting in husband violence, this article discusses how these subgroups differ along descriptive dimensions and in terms of their correlates in a developmental model of husband violence. The results suggest the importance of at least two continua (i.e., antisociality and borderline personality features) for understanding the heterogeneity in husband violence. The results also demonstrate the necessity of further studying low levels of husbands' physical aggression and of considering batterer subtypes when designing treatment interventions.

Keywords

batterer typology; husband violence

Violence of husbands toward their wives is a serious problem in this country. Data from nationally representative surveys suggest that, each year, one out of every eight married men will be physically aggressive toward his wife and up to 2 million women will be severely assaulted by their partners (Straus & Gelles, 1990). Although husbands and wives engage in aggression against their partners at very similar prevalence rates, a series of studies has demonstrated that husband violence has more negative consequences than wife violence; for example, husband violence is more likely to result in physical injury and depressive symptomatology (see the review in Holtzworth-Munroe, Smutzler, & Sandin, 1997). In attempting to understand the correlates and potential causes of husband violence, reviewers have noted that the most fruitful efforts have focused on characteristics of the violent man, as opposed to the female partner or the dyad (Hotaling & Sugarman, 1986). Indeed, much of the available data regarding husband violence has been gathered in studies comparing "violent" with "nonviolent" samples of men; in such studies, batterers are usually treated as a homogeneous group.

Recent research, however, has made it clear that maritally violent men are a heterogeneous group, varying along theoretically important dimensions. These findings suggest that the understanding of husband violence will be advanced by drawing attention to these differences. Comparing subtypes of violent men with each other, and pinpointing how each type differs from nonviolent men, may help researchers to identify different underlying processes resulting in violence.

PREDICTED SUBTYPES

After conducting a comprehensive review of 15 previous batterer typologies, Stuart and I observed that batterer subtypes can be classified along three descriptive dimensions: (a) severity and frequency of marital violence, (b) generality of violence (i.e., within the family only or outside the family as well), and (c) the batterer's psychopathology or personality disorders (Holtzworth-Munroe & Stuart, 1994). Using these dimensions, we proposed that three subtypes of batterers could be identified (i.e., family-only, dysphoric-borderline, and generally violent-antisocial).

Family-only batterers were predicted to be the least violent subgroup. We expected that they would engage in the least marital violence, the lowest levels of psychological and sexual abuse, and the least violence outside the home. We also predicted that men in this group would evidence little or no psychopathology. *Dysphoric-borderline* batterers were predicted to engage in moderate to severe wife abuse. Their violence would be primarily confined to the wife, although some extrafamilial violence might be evident. This group would be the most psychologically distressed (e.g., exhibiting depressed and anxious symptoms) and the most likely to evidence borderline personality characteristics (e.g., extreme emotional lability; intense, unstable interpersonal relationships; fear of rejection). Finally, *generally violent-antisocial* batterers were predicted to be the most violent subtype, engaging in high levels of marital violence and the highest levels of extrafamilial violence. They would be the most likely to evidence characteristics of antisocial personality disorder (e.g., criminal behavior and arrests, failure to conform to social norms, substance abuse).

We then integrated several intrapersonal models of aggression into a model outlining the developmental course of these differing types of husband violence (Holtzworth-Munroe & Stuart, 1994). The model highlighted the importance of correlates of male violence as risk factors for the differing batterer subtypes. Both historical correlates (i.e., genetic and prenatal factors, childhood home environment and violence in the family of origin, association with delinquent peers) and proximal correlates (correlates more current and directly related to battering; i.e., attachment and dependency; impulsivity; social skills, in both marital and nonmarital relationships; and attitudes, both hostile attitudes toward women and attitudes supportive of violence) were considered.

Based on this model, we predicted that, among the subtypes of batterers, family-only batterers would evidence the lowest levels of risk factors. We proposed that the violence of these men would result from a combination of stress (personal, marital, or both) and low-level risk factors (e.g., childhood exposure to marital violence, lack of relationship skills), so that on some occasions during escalating marital conflicts, these men would engage in physical aggression. Following such incidents, however, their low levels of psychopathology and related problems (e.g., impulsivity, attachment dysfunction), combined with their positive attitudes toward women and negative attitudes toward violence, would lead to remorse and help prevent their aggression from escalating.

In contrast, we hypothesized that dysphoric-borderline batterers come from a background involving parental abuse and rejection. As a result, these men would have difficulty forming a stable, trusting attachment with an intimate partner. Instead, they would be highly dependent on their wives, yet fearful of losing them and very jealous. They would be somewhat impulsive, lack marital skills, and have attitudes hostile toward women and supportive of violence. This group resembles batterers studied by Dutton (1995), who suggested that their early traumatic experiences lead to borderline personality characteristics, anger, and insecure attachment, which, in times of frustration, result in violence against the adult attachment figure (i.e., the wife).

Finally, we predicted that generally violent-antisocial batterers resemble other antisocial, aggressive groups. Relative to the other subtypes, they were expected to have experienced high levels of violence in their families of origin and association with deviant peers. They would be impulsive, lack relationship skills (marital and nonmarital), have hostile attitudes toward women, and view violence as acceptable. We conceptualized their marital violence as a part of their general use of aggression and engagement in antisocial behavior. In other words, their marital violence might not represent something unique about the dynamics of their intimate relationships, but rather might occur because wives are readily accessible victims for men who are often aggressive toward others.

TESTING THE MODEL

We recently completed a study testing this model (Holtzworth-Munroe, Meehan, Herron, Rehman, & Stuart, in press). From the community, we recruited 102 men who had been physically aggressive toward their wives in the past year; their wives also participated in the study. We included men who had engaged in a wide range of violence, in contrast to previous batterer typologies that were based on either clinical samples (i.e., men in treatment for domestic violence) or severely violent samples. In addition, we recruited two nonviolent comparison samples—couples who were experiencing marital distress and couples who were not.

Using measures of the descriptive dimensions (i.e., marital violence, general violence, personality disorder), we found that the three predicted subgroups of violent men emerged, along with one additional subgroup. There was general consistency in the subgroup placement of men across differing statistical solutions, although three men were placed into subgroups by the researchers, as they could fit into more than one subgroup.

The predicted subgroups generally differed as hypothesized along the descriptive dimensions and in terms of the developmental model's correlates of violence (i.e., childhood home environment, association with deviant peers, impulsivity, attachment, skills, attitudes). In addition, other recent batterer typologies have generally supported our predicted subgroups. Two studies of severely violent men (Jacobson & Gottman, 1998; Tweed & Dutton, 1998) identified subgroups that resembled our most violent subgroups (i.e., dysphoric-borderline and generally violent- antisocial). A third study, of more than 800 batterers entering domestic violence treatment, found three subgroups that closely resembled our proposed subtypes (Hamberger, Lohr, Bonge, & Tolin, 1996). Thus, our original three subgroup descriptions have generally been supported and describe the three main subtypes emerging in recent research.

The fourth, unpredicted cluster that emerged we labeled the *low-level anti-*

social group, given their moderate scores on measures of antisociality, marital violence, and general violence. On many measures, this group fell intermediate to the family-only and generally violent-antisocial groups (i.e., family-only men had lower scores; generally violent-antisocial men had higher scores). This new group probably corresponds to our originally proposed family-only group; the levels of violence and antisociality in this fourth group are similar to those predicted for the family-only group, which was derived from previous typologies of severely violent men. In contrast, in our study, in which the low-level antisocial group emerged, the sample was recruited from the community and included less violent men. Consequently, we believe that what was labeled the family-only group in our study had not been included in previous batterer typologies, but rather resembles the less violent men often found in studies of newlyweds, couples in marital therapy, and couples in the community who are not seeking therapy and have not been arrested for violence (i.e., community samples). We hope that our four-cluster typology will bridge a recognized gap in this research area—between research examining generally low levels of violence among community samples and research examining severe violence among clinical samples, that is, people who are seeking help in therapy or have been referred to therapy by the courts (e.g., "common couple violence" vs. "patriarchal terrorism"; Johnson, 1995).

Low levels of physical aggression (such as found among family-only batterers) are so prevalent as to be almost normative (statistically) in U.S. culture; one third of engaged and newly married men engage in low levels of physical aggression (e.g., O'Leary et al., 1989). Yet, we do not understand how these less violent men differ from men who are experiencing marital distress or conflict but who do not engage in physical aggression; for example, on our study measures (e.g., of psychopathology, attachment, impulsivity, skills, attitudes, family of origin, peer experiences, wives' depression, and marital satisfaction), family-only batterers did not differ from nonviolent, maritally distressed men. It is thus tempting to assume that low levels of aggression do not lead to particularly pernicious outcomes, at least not above and beyond effects attributable to marital distress. This, however, is not the case, as a recent longitudinal study of newlyweds demonstrated that even low levels of physical aggression predicted marital separation or divorce better than did marital distress or negative marital communication (Rogge & Bradbury, 1999). Thus, although previous batterer typologies have focused on severely violent samples, we believe that lower levels of male physical aggression also deserve attention.

It is possible to conceptualize three of our violent subtypes (i.e., family-only, low-level antisocial, and generally violent-antisocial) as falling along a continuum of antisociality (e.g., family-only batterers have the lowest levels of violence, antisocial behavior, and risk factors; generally violent-antisocial men have the highest; the new cluster has intermediate levels). However, the dysphoric-borderline group cannot be easily placed along this continuum, as these men had the highest scores on a different set of theoretically coherent variables (i.e., fear of abandonment, preoccupied or fearful attachment, dependency). This raises the possibility that two dimensions (i.e., antisociality and borderline personality characteristics) are needed to describe all of the subgroups.

No previous researchers have examined the stability of batterer typologies, but it has been suggested that the various subtypes could exemplify different developmental phases of violence rather than stable clusters. This point is particularly important when considering the family-only and low-level antisocial groups. We predict that some men will remain in these groups, whereas others will escalate their levels of abuse. Indeed, longitudinal research has demonstrated that although severe husband violence predicts the occurrence of future violence, violence is less stable among less severely violent men (e.g., Quigley & Leonard, 1996). The problem, at this point, is that researchers and clinicians cannot predict which men in the less severely violent groups will escalate their violence.

FUTURE DIRECTIONS

The batterer subtypes were found to have differing levels of marital violence. At this time, however, we need further theoretical development regarding whether the nature of aggression, and the motivation for it, differs across subtypes of maritally violent men. For example, it is possible to speculate that the violence of generally violent-antisocial men is instrumental (e.g., goal motivated, premeditated), whereas the violence of the other groups is more expressive (i.e., motivated by anger, frustration, and emotional dysregulation). The answers to such questions await future research.

At this time, it also is unclear if one unifying variable or theory will be able to explain the development of all subtypes of violent husbands (e.g., Dutton, 1995, has focused on an attachment model; our data suggest the importance of antisociality). Our own model is a multivariate one (e.g., attachment, impulsivity, skills, attitudes), based on our belief that more than one variable will be necessary to explain differing developmental pathways; however, this question is currently untested.

We also do not yet understand how differing types of husband violence emerge in the context of varying settings and environments. Our typology emphasizes characteristics of the individual; it is an intrapersonal model, focusing on individual differences. Yet, husband violence occurs in the context of interpersonal relationships, communities and subcultures, and society. Thus, future researchers may wish to consider the societal and interpersonal, as well as the intrapersonal, causes of violence and the interaction of factors at these differing levels of analysis.

Prospective studies are needed to identify the developmental pathways resulting in different subtypes of violent husbands. Future longitudinal studies should examine constructs assumed to predict the use of violence among adolescents or children and then observe the relationship between these variables and the emergence of relationship violence as study participants enter intimate relationships.

Future researchers also should examine how various subtypes of violent men respond to different treatment programs. At the present time, the overall effectiveness of batterers' treatment is not impressive (e.g., Rosenfeld, 1992). Along with others, we have suggested that this may be due to the fact that therapists do not match interventions to batterer subtypes. Initial supportive evidence comes from a study comparing two different treatments; batterers who scored high on an antisocial measure did better in a structured cognitive-behavioral-feminist intervention (e.g., focusing on skills and attitudes), and batterers scoring high on a measure of dependency did better in a new process-psychodynamic intervention (e.g., examining past traumas in the men's lives; Saunders, 1996).

In summary, research on batterer typologies makes it increasingly clear that violent husbands are not a homogeneous group, and that it is no longer adequate to conduct studies comparing violent and nonviolent men. Instead, researchers must systematically examine variability among violent men, along relevant theoretical dimensions of interest. Such research will help identify the different pathways to violence.

Recommended Reading

Dutton, D.G. (1995). (See References)
Holtzworth-Munroe, A., & Stuart, G.L., (1994). (See References)
Jacobson, N.S., & Gottman, J.M. (1998). (See References)

Note

1. Address correspondence to Amy Holtzworth-Munroe, Department of Psychology, 1101 East 10th St., Indiana University, Bloomington, IN 47405-7007.

References

Dutton, D.C. (1995). Intimate abusiveness. *Clinical Psychology: Science and Practice,* 2, 207–224.

Hamberger, L.K., Lohr, J.M., Bonge, D., & Tolin, D.F. (1996). A large sample empirical typology of male spouse abusers and its relationship to dimensions of abuse. *Violence and Victims, 11*, 277–292.

Holtzworth-Munroe, A., Meehan, J.C., Herron, K., Rehman, U., & Stuart, G.L. (in press). Testing the Holtzworth-Munroe and Stuart batterer typology. *Journal of Consulting and Clinical Psychology.*

Holtzworth-Munroe, A., Smutzler, N., & Sandin, E. (1997). A brief review of the research on husband violence: Part II. The psychological effects of husband violence on battered women and their children. *Aggression and Violent Behavior,* 2, 179–213.

Holtzworth-Munroe, A., & Stuart, G.L. (1994). Typologies of male batterers: Three subtypes and the differences among them. *Psychological Bulletin, 116*, 476–497.

Hotaling, G.T., & Sugarman, D.B. (1986). An analysis of risk markers in husband to wife violence. *Violence and Victims,* 7, 79–88.

Jacobson, N.S., & Gottman, J.M. (1998). *When men batter women.* New York: Simon & Schuster.

Johnson, M.P. (1995). Patriarchal terrorism and common couple violence: Two forms of violence against women. *Journal of Marriage and the Family,* 57, 283–294.

O'Leary, K.D., Barling, J., Arias, I., Rosenbaum, A., Malone, J., & Tyree, A. (1989). Prevalence and stability of physical aggression between spouses. *Journal of Consulting and Clinical Psychology,* 57, 263–268.

Quigley, B.M., & Leonard, K.E. (1996). Desistance of husband aggression in the early years of marriage. *Violence and Victims, 11*, 355–370.

Rogge, R.D., & Bradbury, T.N. (1999). Till violence does us part: The differing roles of communication and aggression in predicting adverse marital outcomes. *Journal of Consulting and Clinical Psychology,* 67, 340–351.

Rosenfeld, B.D. (1992). Court-ordered treatment of spouse abuse. *Clinical Psychology Review, 12*, 205–226.

Saunders, D.G. (1996). Feminist-cognitive-behavioral and process-psychodynamic treatments for men who batter. *Violence and Victims,* 4, 393–414.

Straus, M.A., & Gelles, R.J. (1990). *Physical violence in American families.* New Brunswick, NJ: Transactions.

Tweed, R., & Dutton, D.G. (1998). A comparison of impulsive and instrumental subgroups of batterers. *Violence and Victims,* 13, 217–230.

Violence Against Stepchildren

Martin Daly and Margo I. Wilson

On February 20th, 1992, 2-year-old Scott M. died in a Montreal hospital of massive internal injuries caused by one or more abdominal blows. At the manslaughter trial of his mother's 24-year-old live-in boyfriend, doctors testified that Scott's body displayed "all the symptoms of a battered child," mainly because of "numerous bruises of varying ages." The accused, who portrayed himself as Scott's primary caretaker, admitted assaulting the mother and other adults, but "I don't hurt kids." According to an acquaintance, however, the accused had admitted striking the child with his elbow because Scott was "bothering him while he was trying to watch television." The trial outcome was conviction.[1]

A reader of any major newspaper is likely to have encountered similar stories, and may even have noticed that the victims are often the progeny of their killers' predecessors. Is step-relationship really a significant risk factor for lethal assaults on children? (Persons who reside with a partner and the partner's child or children of prior unions are here deemed stepparents regardless of marital registration.)

This issue has been obscured by a scarcity of relevant information in official records. In the United States, for example, the census has not distinguished between genetic parenthood and stepparenthood, and the national archive of homicide cases (the Federal Bureau of Investigation's *Supplementary Homicide Reports*) is also incomplete in this regard. But local data sets can be more informative. We examined the Chicago police department's homicide records, for example, and found that 115 children under 5 years of age were killed by their putative fathers in 1965 through 1990, while 63 were killed by stepfathers or (more or less co-resident) mothers' boyfriends. Most of these children were less than 2 years old, and because very few babies reside with substitute fathers, the numbers imply greatly elevated risk to such children. Just how great that risk might be cannot be determined, however, without better information on the living arrangements of Chicago children.

Canadian data permit somewhat more precise comparisons. A national homicide archive maintained by Statistics Canada from 1974 to 1990 included the relevant distinctions among parental relationships, and recent national probability sample surveys provide estimates of the age-specific distribution of such relationships in the population at large. Estimated rates of homicide by stepfathers versus genetic fathers in Canada are portrayed in Figure 1.[2] Because step-relationships were in fact increasing from 1974 to 1990, the use of recent surveys for population-at-large estimation ensures a conservative comparison: It is virtually certain that estimated numbers of stepfathers in the population are higher than actually prevailed over the 17-year period, and that the estimated homicide rates by stepfathers are therefore low. Nevertheless, the differential is immense.

VIOLENCE IN STEPFAMILIES

Research on child abuse proliferated after Henry Kempe and colleagues' 1962 proclamation of a battered-child syndrome. However, no study addressed the inci-

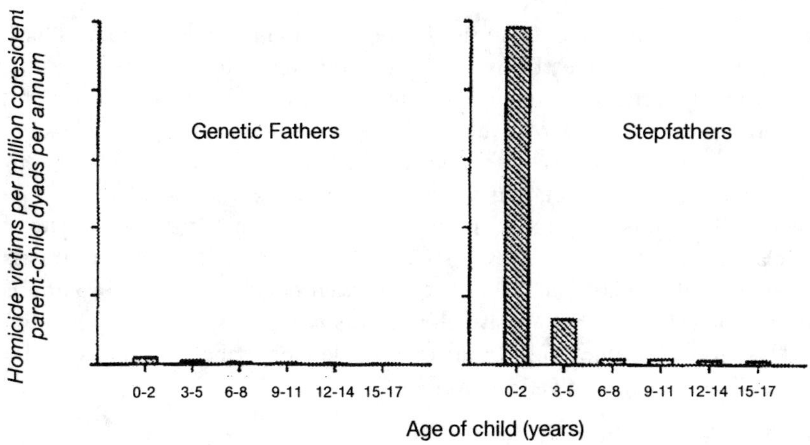

Fig. 1. Estimated rates of homicide by genetic fathers versus stepfathers in Canada, 1974–1990. Rate numerators are based on a Statistics Canada national archive of all homicides known to Canadian police. Denominators are age-specific estimates of the numbers of Canadian children residing with each type of father, based on census information on the numbers of Canadian children in each age class in each year and age-specific proportions living with genetic fathers versus stepfathers averaged across two national surveys, conducted in 1984 (Statistics Canada's *Family History Survey*) and 1990 (Statistics Canada's *General Social Survey*). Homicide rates for stepfathers are probably underestimates, for reasons explained in the text.

dence of child maltreatment in step- versus genetic-parent homes that until 1980, when we reported stepchildren constituted a much higher proportion of U.S. child abuse cases than their numbers in the population at large would warrant.[3] This excess could not be dismissed as an artifact of bias detection or reporting because it was most extreme in the fatal cases, for which such biases should be minimal: Whereas young children incurred about seven times higher rates of physical abuse in step-plus-genetic-parent homes than in two-genetic-parent homes, the differential in fatal abuse was on the order of 100-fold. Canadian and British data tell much the same story, with a large excess of stepchildren among reported child abuse victims[4,5] and an even larger excess among children fatally abused.[6,7]

Genetic parents kill children, too, but recent analyses indicate that the motives in these cases tend to be different. Whereas filicidal parents are often deeply depressed and may even construe murder-suicide as a humane act of rescue, homicidal stepparents are seldom suicidal and typically manifest their antipathy to their victims in the relative brutality of their lethal acts.[7] In Canada, 44 of 155 men (28%) who slew their preschool-age children during a 17-year period did so in the context of a completed suicide, compared with just 1 of 66 men who killed stepchildren, and whereas 82% of the victims of stepfathers were beaten to death, the majority of children slain by genetic fathers were killed by less assaultive means. These contrasts are replicated in British cases.

Given that the rate of abuse and murder is greatly elevated in step-families, one may still question whether step-relationship is itself germane. Might it not be an incidental correlate of other risk factors? Several possible confounds have been examined, but none seems to account for the differential risks among family types. Poverty, for example, is an important risk factor in its own right, but is virtually uncorrelated with the incidence of step-relationship in two-parent families in the United States or Canada and thus cannot explain away the family composition effects.[4,8] Large family size and maternal youth are additional factors with effects on abuse risk that are apparently distinct from the effects of step-relationship.[4,8] Finally, excess risk in stepfamilies might be due to excess numbers of violent personalities among remarried persons, but this hypothesis is refuted by evidence that abusive stepparents typically spare their own children.[4,9] Step-relationship itself remains the single most important risk factor for severe child maltreatment yet discovered.

DISCRIMINATIVE PARENTAL SOLICITUDE AND STEP-PARENTAL INVESTMENT

Elevated risk at the hands of stepparents has been abundantly confirmed, in a range of societies and with respect to the gamut of forms of child maltreatment.[3–11] But conflict in stepfamilies is not confined to these extremes. Research on nonviolent stepfamilies is a growth industry with a single focus: how people cope with the problems characteristic of step- relationships. It is important to emphasize that many people do indeed cope very well. Nevertheless, the research consistently indicates that step-relationships are, on average, less investing, more distant, more conflictual, and less satisfying than the corresponding genetic parent-child relationships.[8,12]

These results gibe with popular belief. Undergraduates impute unfair treatment and hostility to persons merely labeled stepfather or stepmother, negative attributions that are mitigated but not eliminated in people who have actually been stepchildren.[13] Folk tales of stepparental antipathy and mistreatment are cross-culturally ubiquitous and familiar to everyone.[14] Given these facts and the prominence of stepfamilies in a typical child protection worker's caseload, it is remarkable that almost two decades of intensive child abuse research elapsed before anyone asked whether step-parent households are really more dangerous than genetic-parent households, and, if so, to what degree.

It was neither folklore nor familiarity with case materials that inspired us to address these questions. We were stimulated by evolutionary logic and by the results of research on nonhuman animals. Current theory implies that natural selection shapes social motives and behavior to function nepotistically on behalf of blood kin, and animals have demonstrably evolved a variety of psychological mechanisms functioning to protect parents against parasitism by unrelated young.[15] Parental care is costly, and animals usually avoid expending it on behalf of young other than their own. But then why is the human animal so willing to enter into step-relationships that may entail prolonged, costly pseudoparental investments?

One hypothesis is that stepparenthood was simply not a recurring adaptive problem for ancestral humans, so people never evolved any psychological defenses against it. Nonnutritive saccharin, an evolutionarily unforeseen component of novel environments, tickles an evolved system for the recognition of nutritive sugars. Might substitute parenthood constitute a sort of social saccharin: an evolutionarily novel circumstance in which the evolved psychology of parenthood is activated in a context slightly different from that for which it evolved? We consider this hypothesis implausible because step-relationship is assuredly not a modern novelty. Mortality levels in contemporary tribal foragers suggest that remarriage and stepparenthood must have been common for as long as people have formed marital bonds with biparental care.[16] Moreover, the available evidence indicates that half-orphans who entered the perilous status of stepchild in a nonstate society faced a major diminution in the quality and quantity of parental care, and an elevated risk of death. In one study of a contemporary South American foraging people, for example, 43% of children raised by a mother and stepfather died before their 15th birthdays, compared with just 19% of those raised by two genetic parents.[11]

An alternative explanation for stepparental investment that is more plausible than the social-saccharin hypothesis derives from comparative studies. Although animals usually avoid caring for their mates' offspring of prior unions, exceptions have been observed in certain species of fish, birds, and mammals.[14] In each case, stepparental investment has been interpreted as *mating effort,* that is, as part of the cost of courting a single parent who, despite the burden of dependent young, remains an attractive prospective mate in a limited mating market. This explanation fits the human case, too. Stepparents assume their obligations in the context of a web of reciprocities with the genetic parent, who is likely to recognize more or less explicitly that stepparental tolerance and investment constitute benefits bestowed on the genetic parent and the child, entitling the stepparent to reciprocal considerations.

In this light, the existence of stepparental investment is not so surprising. But the fact of such investment cannot be taken to imply that stepparents ordinarily (or indeed ever) come to feel the sort of commitment commonly felt by genetic parents. Evolutionary thinking suggests that stepparental affection will tend to be restrained. Indulgence toward a mate's children may have had some social utility for many millennia, but it must rarely have been the case that a stepchild's welfare was as valuable to one's expected fitness as one's own child's welfare. We would therefore expect evolved mechanisms of parental feeling to be buffered against full activation when one merely assumes a parental role, and the empirical literature on stepfamily life confirms this expectation.[12]

PARENTAL LOVE IS MORE THAN JUST A ROLE

Even within the history of Western nations, step-relationships are no novelty. In fact, they were more prevalent in Europe in recent centuries than they are now, thanks to higher death rates of parents whose children were still dependent.[17] In premodern Germany, the age-specific mortality of children was elevated if one parent died and, more remarkably, was further elevated if the surviving parent remarried.[18] It seems that Cinderella was more than a fairy tale.

The cross-cultural ubiquity of Cinderella stories[14] reflects basic, recurring tensions in human society. Stepparental obligations are seldom attractive, and dependent children decrease a widowed or forsaken parent's value in the marriage market. In remarriages, preexisting children remain a focus and a source of marital conflict,[12] including marital violence.[19] People in all societies face these problems, and they deal with them in various ways. One solution is for remarrying parents to leave children in the care of postmenopausal female relatives. Another is for a widow to retain her children and marry her dead husband's brother, a practice widely perceived as reducing the likelihood or severity of exploitation and mistreatment, because the stepfather is an uncle who may be expected to have some benevolent interest in his brother's children. In the absence of such practices, children have been obliged to tag along as best they can, hoping that their welfare will remain a high priority of the surviving genetic parent. Sometimes the genetic parent has to choose between the new mate and the child, and may even become complicit in the exploitation and abuse of the latter.

American social scientists have interpreted stepparenthood as a role, only partly coincident with that of genetic parenthood. The role concept has usefully directed attention to the importance of socialization and scripts, but it is at best a limited metaphor that has diverted attention away from motivational and emotional aspects of the social psyche. There is more to social action than mere familiarity with the relevant roles. Why are people motivated to embrace certain roles and to shun others? Parents are profoundly concerned for their children's well-being and future prospects, but human concerns have no part in role theorists' explanations of human action.

As Donald Symons has argued, it is especially in the domain of social motives and feelings that psychology needs Darwinism.[20] Some aspects of human physiological and mental adaptations may be elucidated without consideration of how natural selection works, but the investigation of social motives and feelings gains crucial guidance from the recognition that it is genetic posterity, rather than happiness or life span or self-esteem, that has been the arbiter of their evolution. As any evolutionist might have anticipated, it appears that stepparents do not typically experience the same child-specific love and commitment, nor reap the same emotional rewards from unreciprocated parental investment, as genetic parents. Enormous differentials in the risk of violence are one particularly dramatic result of this predictable difference in feelings.

Martin Daly and Margo I. Wilson conduct research on the evolutionary psychology of violence. Address correspondence to Martin Daly, Department of Psychology, McMaster University, Hamilton, Ontario, Canada L8S 4K1; e-mail: daly@mcmaster.ca.

Acknowledgments—Our research on step-relations and violence has been supported by grants from the Harry Frank Guggenheim Foundation, Health & Welfare Canada, the Natural Sciences & Engineering Research Council of Canada, the Social Sciences & Humanities Research Council of Canada, and the North Atlantic Treaty Organization.

Notes

1. R. Laurent, Manslaughter trial ordered in death of 2-year-old boy, *Montreal Gazette* (March 14, 1992), p. A3; C. Buckie, Man accused in boy's death denies charge,

Montreal Gazette (April 3, 1993), p. A3; M. King, Man convicted of manslaughter in infant's death, *Montreal Gazette* (April 22, 1993), p. A3.

2. The great majority of stepparental homicides, in Canada and elsewhere, are perpetrated by men, but of course small children seldom live with stepmothers. Stepparents of both sexes are overrepresented as both abusers and killers, relative to same-sex genetic parents, but stepmother homes are too rare for reliable estimation of rates.

3. M.I. Wilson, M. Daly, and S.J. Weghorst, Household composition and the risk of child abuse and neglect, *Journal of Biosocial Science, 12*, 333–340 (1980).

4. M. Daly and M.I. Wilson, Child abuse and other risks of not living with both parents, *Ethology and Sociobiology, 6*, 197–210 (1985).

5. S.J. Creighton, An epidemiological study of abused children and their families in the United Kingdom between 1977 and 1982, *Child Abuse and Neglect, 9*, 441–448 (1985).

6. M. Daly and M.I. Wilson, Evolutionary social psychology and family homicide, *Science, 242*, 519–524 (1988).

7. M. Daly and M.I. Wilson, Some differential attributes of lethal assaults on small children by stepfathers versus genetic fathers, *Ethology and Sociobiology, 15*, 207–217 (1994).

8. M.I. Wilson and M. Daly, Risk of maltreatment of children living with stepparents, in *Child Abuse and Neglect: Biosocial Dimensions*, R.J. Gelles and J. B. Lancaster, Eds. (Aldine de Gruyter, New York, 1987).

9. J.L. Lightcap, J.A. Kurland, and R.L. Burgess, Child abuse: A test of some predictions from evolutionary theory, *Ethology and Sociobiology, 3*, 61–67 (1982).

10. M.V. Flinn, Step- and genetic parent/offspring relationships in a Caribbean village, *Ethology and Sociobiology, 9*, 335–369 (1988); K. Kim and B. Ko, An incidence survey of battered children in two elementary schools of Seoul, *Child Abuse and Neglect, 14*, 273–276 (1990); D.E.H. Russell, The prevalence and seriousness of incestuous abuse: Stepfathers vs. biological fathers, *Child Abuse and Neglect, 8*, 15–22 (1994).

11. K. Hill and H. Kaplan, Tradeoffs in male and female reproductive strategies among the Ache, part 2, *in Human Reproductive Behavior*, L. Betzig, M. Borgerhoff Mulder, and P. Turke, Eds. (Cambridge University Press, Cambridge, England, 1988).

12. C. Hobart, Conflict in remarriages, *Journal of Divorce and Remarriage, 15*, 69–86 (1991); J.W. Santrock and K.A. Sitterle, Parent-child relationships in stepmother families, in *Remarriage and Stepparenting: Current Research and Theory*, K. Pasley and M. Ihinger-Tallman, Eds. (Guilford Press, New York, 1987); L.K. White and A. Booth, The quality and stability of remarriages: The role of stepchildren, *American Sociological Review, 50*, 689–698 (1985).

13. L.R. Bryan, M. Coleman, L. Ganong, and S.H. Bryan, Person perception: Family structure as a cue for stereotyping, *Journal of Marriage and the Family, 48*, 169–174 (1986). Unfortunately, by calling these attributions stereotypes and myths, researchers have misleadingly implied that they are unfounded.

14. M. Daly and M.I. Wilson, Stepparenthood and the evolved psychology of discriminative parental solicitude, in *Infanticide and Parental Care*, S. Parmigiani and F. vom Saal, Eds. (Harwood Science Publishers, Chur, Switzerland, 1993).

15. M. Daly and M.I. Wilson, Discriminative parental solicitude and the relevance of evolutionary models to the analysis of motivational systems, in *The Cognitive Neurosciences*, M. Gazzaniga, Ed. (MIT Press, Cambridge, MA, 1995).

16. See, e.g., N. Howell, *Demography of the Dobe !Kung* (Academic Press, New York, 1979). This argument against the social-saccharin hypothesis specifically, applies only to stepparenthood, which has long been an incidental consequence of remarriage, and not to the apparently novel Western practice of adopting children unrelated to either parent.

17. J. Dupâquier, E. Hélin, P. Laslett, M. Livi-Bacci, and S. Segner, Eds., *Marriage and Remarriage in Populations of the Past* (Academic Press, London, 1981).

18. E. Voland, Differential infant and child mortality in evolutionary perspective: Data from late 17th to 19th century Ostfriesland, in *Human Reproductive Behavior*, L. Betzig, M. Borgerhoff Mulder, and P. Turke, Eds. (Cambridge University Press, Cambridge, England, 1988).

19. M. Daly and M.I. Wilson, Evolutionary psychology and marital conflict: The relevance of stepchildren, in *Sex, Power, Conflict: Feminist and Evolutionary Perspectives*, D.M. Buss and N. Malamuth, Eds. (Oxford University Press, New York, in press).

20. D. Symons, If we're all Darwinians, what's the fuss about? in *Sociobiology and Psychology*, C. Crawford, M. Smith, and D. Krebs, Eds. (Erlbaum, Hillsdale, NJ, 1987).